# IN THIS WAY WE CAME TO ROME

*With Paul on the Appian Way*

"*In This Way We Came to Rome* charts for us in great detail, Paul's journey to Rome as recorded at the end of the Acts of the Apostles. Unlike some of the recent commentaries on Acts (with the exception of Craig Keener's magisterial four-volume work) this 200-page monograph takes seriously that Luke's account reflects an actual historical journey in detail. The maps and charts and pictures provide us with a rich resource, not available in one source before now. I highly recommend this work as an invaluable contribution to our understanding of the work of our earliest Christian historian."

—BEN WITHERINGTON III, Amos Professor of NT for Doctoral Studies,
Asbury Theological Seminary

"Glen Thompson and Mark Wilson have written an extraordinary book. They trace in detail the seven-day journey of the prisoner transport which took Paul from Puteoli to the city of Rome— the 'detail' including geographical information (complete with GPS coordinates), archaeological information, and inscriptional and literary evidence for the roads on which Paul traveled and for the monuments Paul would have passed by. Maps and color photographs help readers to vividly experience the text. No ancient road or road-system has ever been described in such detail. The book will be invaluable for New Testament scholars and classical scholars alike, and not least for the average reader who intends to retrace Paul's steps on a visit to Italy: using this volume as guide will ensure that such readers are travelers and not mere tourists."

—ECKHARD J. SCHNABEL, Mary F. Rockefeller Distinguished Professor
of New Testament Gordon-Conwell Theological Seminary

"A model guide to the journey by road from Puteoli to Rome during the early Roman empire— clear, engaging, up-to-date, with excellent maps and photos. Let's go!"

—RICHARD TALBERT, Research Professor of History, University of North Carolina;
editor of *Barrington Atlas of the Greek and Roman World*

"In this richly-illustrated book, Thompson and Wilson—two first-rate scholars and trustworthy guides—escort us along the 150 miles of the Via Campana Consularis and the famous Via Appia that Paul, along with his companions, fellow-prisoners, and guards, traveled from the port of Puteoli to the city of Rome where he would await his trial before the imperial courts. Through their own painstaking—and physical—retracing of Paul's likeliest steps and their immersion in the archaeology of these ancient roads and their supporting infrastructure, they laid bare for us the lived realities of the wearying week-long journey that we otherwise pass over in second as a mere four verses in Acts 28:13–16. In so doing, they have also given students of the early Christian mission and the Roman world a valuable window into travel on Rome's famous system of roads."

—DAVID A. DESILVA, Trustees' Distinguished Professor of New Testament and Greek, Ashland Theological Seminary

# IN THIS WAY WE CAME TO ROME

*With Paul on the Appian Way*

Glen L. Thompson and Mark Wilson

*In This Way We Came to Rome: With Paul on the Appian Way*

Copyright 2023 Glen L. Thompson and Mark Wilson

Lexham Press, 1313 Commercial St., Bellingham, WA 98225 | LexhamPress.com

You may use brief quotations from this resource in presentations, articles, and books. For all other uses, please write Lexham Press for permission. Email us at permissions@lexhampress.com.

All figures and maps are owned by the authors unless stated below.

Fig. 1: Glass flasks of Puteoli, CMoG 62.1.31. Image licensed by The Corning Museum of Glass, Corning, NY (www.cmog.org), under CC BY-NC-SA 4.0. Used by permission.

Fig. 10: VCC under San Lorenzo ad Septimum. Graphic by Pasquale Argenziano (Melillo Faenza, Jacazzi, and Argenziano 2009, 213). Used by permission.

Fig. 11: Inscription on Appius Claudius Caecus. Image by Olga Lyubimova, licensed under CC BY-SA 4.0, http://ancientrome.ru/art/artworken/img.htm?id=6189.

Fig. 14: VA on the Peutinger Map. Images courtesy of the Österreichische Nationalbibliothek. Used by permission.

Fig. 30: Bridge at Forum Appii. Image courtesy of Associazione culturale GoTellGo / Maria Teresa Natale. Used by permission.

Fig. 31: Artistic reconstruction of Forum Appii. Art by Evelien Witmer, Groningen Institute of Archaeology, commissioned by Gijs Tol and Tymon de Haas for Tol, de Haas, and Anastasia 2019. Used by permission.

Fig. 32: Excavations at Tres Tabernae. Photo by Bárány László. Used by permission.

Fig. 45: Reconstruction of the Chelmsford *mansio*. Courtesy of the Chelmsford City Museum (Chelmsford, Essex, UK). Used by permission.

Unless otherwise noted, Scripture quotations are the author's own translation.

Print ISBN 9781683597247
Digital ISBN 9781683597254
Library of Congress Control Number 2023933079

Lexham Editorial: Barry J. Beitzel, Douglas Mangum, James Spinti, Katy Smith, Erin Mangum
Cover Design: Joshua Hunt
Typesetting: Abigail Stocker, Mandi Newell

# Contents

List of Maps and Key................................................ix
List of Figures....................................................xi
Abbreviations...................................................xiii
Preface..........................................................xv
Acts 28:11–31: Paul's Arrival in Rome............................. xx

Introduction: Voyage to Italy...................................... 1
Day 1: Puteoli to Capua.......................................... 29
Day 2: Capua (RM 132) to Sinuessa (RM 107)....................... 55
Day 3: Sinuessa (RM 107) to Itri (RM 83)......................... 75
Day 4: Itri (RM 83) to Tarracina (RM 63)......................... 91
Day 5: Tarracina (RM 63) to Forum Appii (RM 43)................. 109
Day 6: Forum Appii (RM 43) to Aricia (RM 16).................... 125
Day 7: Aricia (RM 16) to Rome................................... 143
Conclusion: Paul in Rome........................................ 179

Appendix 1: Paul's Land Journey in Bible Atlases.................189
Appendix 2: Bypass at Tarracina..................................191
Appendix 3: *Mansiones* and *Stationes*..........................195
Appendix 4: GPS Coordinates for Places Mentioned.................199
Bibliography.................................................... 209
Index of Bible Passages..........................................237
Index of Ancient Sources........................................ 239
Index of Modern Authors......................................... 245
About the Authors............................................... 249

# List of Maps

Map 1. Paul's Route to Rome . . . . . . . . . . . . . . . . . . . . . . . . . xiv
Map 2. Paul's Captivity Journey. . . . . . . . . . . . . . . . . . . . . . xxii
Map 3. Gulf of Naples. . . . . . . . . . . . . . . . . . . . . . . . . . . . . . . . 11
Map 4. Puteoli and Its Harbor. . . . . . . . . . . . . . . . . . . . . . . . 14
Map 5. Puteoli to Capua . . . . . . . . . . . . . . . . . . . . . . . . . . . . . 28
Map 6. Puteoli to *Ad Quartum*. . . . . . . . . . . . . . . . . . . . . . . 34
Map 7. Northward from *Ad Quartum* . . . . . . . . . . . . . . . . . 43
Map 8. *Ad Septimum* to Capua. . . . . . . . . . . . . . . . . . . . . . . 47
Map 9. Capua. . . . . . . . . . . . . . . . . . . . . . . . . . . . . . . . . . . . . . 50
Map 10. Capua to Sinuessa. . . . . . . . . . . . . . . . . . . . . . . . . . 54
Map 11. Capua to Urbana . . . . . . . . . . . . . . . . . . . . . . . . . . . 59
Map 12. Urbana to Sinuessa . . . . . . . . . . . . . . . . . . . . . . . . . 65
Map 13. Sinuessa . . . . . . . . . . . . . . . . . . . . . . . . . . . . . . . . . . . 71
Map 14. Sinuessa to Itri . . . . . . . . . . . . . . . . . . . . . . . . . . . . . 74
Map 15. Minturnae . . . . . . . . . . . . . . . . . . . . . . . . . . . . . . . . . 78
Map 16. Formiae . . . . . . . . . . . . . . . . . . . . . . . . . . . . . . . . . . . 82
Map 17. Itri . . . . . . . . . . . . . . . . . . . . . . . . . . . . . . . . . . . . . . . . 88
Map 18. Itri to Tarracina. . . . . . . . . . . . . . . . . . . . . . . . . . . . . 90
Map 19. Fundi . . . . . . . . . . . . . . . . . . . . . . . . . . . . . . . . . . . . . 95
Map 20. Tarracina . . . . . . . . . . . . . . . . . . . . . . . . . . . . . . . . . 100
Map 21. Tarracina to Forum Appii . . . . . . . . . . . . . . . . . . . 108
Map 22. Forum Appii . . . . . . . . . . . . . . . . . . . . . . . . . . . . . . 118

*In This Way We Came to Rome*

Map 23. Forum Appii to Aricia . . . . . . . . . . . . . . . . . . . . . . . 124
Map 24. Tres Tabernae . . . . . . . . . . . . . . . . . . . . . . . . . . . . . . . . . 127
Map 25. Northwest of Cisterna . . . . . . . . . . . . . . . . . . . . . . . . 130
Map 26. Deviation at Aricia . . . . . . . . . . . . . . . . . . . . . . . . . . . 135
Map 27. Aricia to Rome . . . . . . . . . . . . . . . . . . . . . . . . . . . . . 142
Map 28. Miles 1–3 . . . . . . . . . . . . . . . . . . . . . . . . . . . . . . . . . . . 162
Map 29. Paul in Rome . . . . . . . . . . . . . . . . . . . . . . . . . . . . . . . .178
Map 30. Tarracina . . . . . . . . . . . . . . . . . . . . . . . . . . . . . . . . . . .192

## Key for Maps

| | | | |
|---|---|---|---|
| ▫ | colony/city marker | = | aqueduct |
| — | main road | ⋯ | viaduct |
| ⨯ | bridge | xxxxx | reticulated wall |
| ▦ | road with Roman traces | ⌂ | mansio |
| ▤ | aerial traces of road | ▢ | colony/city walls |
| –·– | Via Latina | ▣ | colony wall extensions |
| –·– | alternate VA | ▫ | architectural structures |
| ––– | diverticulum/other roads | ⋮⋮ | centuriation |
| ····· | canal | | |

# List of Figures

Figure 1. Glass flask of Puteoli . . . . . . . . . . . . . . . . . . . . . . . . . .16

Figure 2. Grafitto of crucified woman . . . . . . . . . . . . . . . . . . . . 22

Figure 3. Paul's seven-day itinerary . . . . . . . . . . . . . . . . . . . . . .27

Figure 4. Via Celle tombs . . . . . . . . . . . . . . . . . . . . . . . . . . . . . 36

Figure 5. VCC paving . . . . . . . . . . . . . . . . . . . . . . . . . . . . . . . .37

Figure 6. Photograph and etching of tomb on Via S. Vito . . . 39

Figure 7. Montagna Spaccata . . . . . . . . . . . . . . . . . . . . . . . . . . 40

Figure 8. *Mansio* (?) at *Ad Quartum*. . . . . . . . . . . . . . . . . . . . . . 42

Figure 9. Cupa Orlando . . . . . . . . . . . . . . . . . . . . . . . . . . . . . . 44

Figure 10. VCC at S. Lorenzo ad Septimum. . . . . . . . . . . . . . . 46

Figure 11. Appius Claudius inscription . . . . . . . . . . . . . . . . . . 49

Figure 12. Hadrian's arch at Capua . . . . . . . . . . . . . . . . . . . . . 56

Figure 13. Bridge over Volturnum River at Casilinum
 (post-WWII) . . . . . . . . . . . . . . . . . . . . . . . . . . . . . . 56

Figure 14. VA on the Peutinger Map . . . . . . . . . . . . . . . . . . . . .61

Figure 15. Ancient itineraries: Capua to Rome . . . . . . . . . . . . 63

Figure 16. Paving near Mondragone cemetery. . . . . . . . . . . . . 68

Figure 17. Paving south of Sinuessa . . . . . . . . . . . . . . . . . . . . . 70

Figure 18. Paving in forum of Minturnae . . . . . . . . . . . . . . . . 77

Figure 19. Fountain of San Remigio in Formiae. . . . . . . . . . . . 84

Figure 20. Tomb of Cicero (?) near Formiae . . . . . . . . . . . . . . 85

Figure 21. MP 85 and 84 south of Itri . . . . . . . . . . . . . . . . . . . 86

Figure 22. Paving in Sant'Andrea Valley . . . . . . . . . . . . . . . . . . 93

Figure 23. *Opus reticulatum* wall outside Fundi . . . . . . . . . . . . 93

Figure 24. Exedra east of Tarracina. . . . . . . . . . . . . . . . . . . . . . 101

Figure 25. Paving on Via Piazza Palatina . . . . . . . . . . . . . . . . . 103

Figure 26. Pavement in forum of Tarracina . . . . . . . . . . . . . . 106

Figure 27. Spring of Feronia . . . . . . . . . . . . . . . . . . . . . . . . . . . 110

Figure 28. Canal along *decennovium*. . . . . . . . . . . . . . . . . . . . . 113

Figure 29. Milestones 48, 49, 43, and 71 . . . . . . . . . . . . . . . . . . 116

Figure 30. Bridge at Forum Appii . . . . . . . . . . . . . . . . . . . . . . 119

Figure 31. Artistic reconstruction of Forum Appii. . . . . . . . . .120

Figure 32. Excavations at Tres Tabernae. . . . . . . . . . . . . . . . . .126

Figure 33. MP 19 in situ. . . . . . . . . . . . . . . . . . . . . . . . . . . . . . .134

Figure 34. Viaduct at Aricia . . . . . . . . . . . . . . . . . . . . . . . . . . .136

Figure 35. Diverticulum at Bovillae . . . . . . . . . . . . . . . . . . . . . 149

Figure 36. Paving in outskirts of Rome . . . . . . . . . . . . . . . . . .154

Figure 37. Inscription of three Jewish (?) freedmen . . . . . . . .159

Figure 38. Votive offerings of travelers . . . . . . . . . . . . . . . . . .165

Figure 39. Replica of MP 1 and original on
    the Campidoglio . . . . . . . . . . . . . . . . . . . . . . . . . . . .170

Figure 40. View through Porta Sebastiana to
    "Arch of Drusus," site of MP 1 . . . . . . . . . . . . . . . . . 171

Figure 41. Southernmost Columbarium in Vigna Codini . . . .173

Figure 42. Castra Praetoria. . . . . . . . . . . . . . . . . . . . . . . . . . . . 181

Figure 43. Comparison of distances for the two routes
    of the VA at Tarracina. . . . . . . . . . . . . . . . . . . . . . . .193

Figure 44. Comparison of the elevation for the two routes
    of the VA at Tarracina . . . . . . . . . . . . . . . . . . . . . . . 194

Figure 45. Reconstruction of the Chelmsford *mansio* . . . . . . .197

# Abbreviations

| | |
|---|---|
| *AE* | *Année épigraphique* |
| *Ann.* | Tacitus, *Annales* |
| *CIL* | *Corpus Inscriptionum Latinarum.* Berlin, 1862– |
| d. | year of death |
| *Geogr.* | Strabo, *Geography* |
| Gk. | Greek |
| *Hist.* | Livy, *History of Rome* |
| *ILLRP* | *Inscriptiones latinae liberae rei publicae.* Attilio Degrassi. 2 vols. Firenze: La Nuova Italia, 1957–1963 |
| *ILS* | *Inscriptiones Latinae Selectae.* Hermann Desau. 3 vols. Berlin, 1892–1916. |
| km | kilometer (0.62 mi.) |
| Lat. | Latin |
| m | meter (3.28 ft. or 1.09 yd.) |
| *Nat.* | Pliny the Elder, *Natural History* |
| ft. | foot (0.30 m) |
| mi. | statute mile (5,280 ft. or 1.61 km) |
| MP | milestone (Latin *mille passuum* = 1000 paces), the distance between milestones erected on the VA and whose number is the distance in Roman miles from Rome |
| RM | Roman mile (0.92 mi. or 1.48 km) |
| r. | period of rule |
| SEG | *Supplementum Epigraphicum Graecum* |
| VA | Via Appia (ancient road and its route) |
| VAA | Via Appia Antica (modern name of some Italian roads thought to follow closely the ancient VA but do so only part of the time) |
| VCC | Via Campana Consolaris |

# Preface

William Short, in a letter to Thomas Jefferson dated February 11, 1789, wrote: "The Appian way is the most famous of the ancient roads. From Terracina to Naples is the most agreeable and best made road I ever saw in any country. The present Pope also has much merit for his exertions in this way. Within a few years he has again opened a road where was formerly the Appian through the Pontine marshes. You go in a right line along a large canal of eighteen miles that he has made for the draining of these marshes. The road is fine" (Short 1789).[1]

In 1927 the British archaeologist Thomas Ashby (1927, 174) lamented: "Despite the fame of the Via Appia, a monograph dealing with it fully has never been written." In the century since Ashby penned these words, many books have appeared about the Via Appia (abbreviated VA). They range from popular travelogues to academic treatises. The travelogues present fascinating accounts, often of personal experiences traveling along the VA. Although somewhat dated, these reminiscences preserve a historical memory of the road at the author's time. But as Italy has changed through the years, many sites and monuments once seen by travelers no longer remain or were moved to museums. Monographs on the VA have appeared in recent years along with a voluminous amount of secondary literature, mostly in Italian.[2] Many publications address sections of the road or the regions through which it passes. Yet no volume exists that specifically describes the most famous trip upon it—that taken by the apostle Paul on his way to trial in Rome. This volume addresses geographical, historical, archaeological, and hodological issues related to that

---

1. The canal can be seen in fig. 28 below.
2. Perhaps the most familiar volume on the VA in English is that of Della Portella (2004).

journey.³ It centers on the 21 Roman miles he traveled on the so-called Via Campana Consularis (abbreviated VCC) from Puteoli to Capua and then on the 132 Roman miles traversed on the VA, the "first planned Roman road" (van Tilburg 2007, 4).

Writing this volume was challenging. As soon as a section was completed, a new monograph or article would appear, requiring review and the incorporation of relevant new information. It was like drinking out of a fire hose of sources. There was also the constant decision about what to include given the constraints of the manuscript's length. Detailed histories of the cities visited by Paul cannot be given, since such information is now readily available online or in volumes such as the older *Princeton Encyclopedia of Classical Sites* or the newer *Oxford Classical Dictionary*.⁴ Additionally, there were many primary sources in Latin and Greek literature to review. The website www.topostext.org and its phone app provide ready access to what ancient authors like Horace wrote about each city. We have frequently cited Greek and Latin authors. Their writings can be read in the original language or in translation, albeit sometimes in dated English, on the Perseus website.⁵

While Paul's final land journey to Rome is our main subject, it is necessary to begin with a brief description of Paul's sea voyage. It started in Caesarea Maritima and was interrupted by a shipwreck and layover in Malta before ending in Puteoli. Its final leg from Puteoli to Rome is described in a mere three verses in Acts 28.⁶ Luke has provided sufficient information to deduce Paul's route, which we have attempted to reconstruct in the following pages. Although some segments are based on hypothetical reconstructions, these were done on the basis of the latest archaeological and historical research. While we are convinced that Paul actually made the journey described in chapters 27–28, those

---

3. Hodology refers to the study of roads and road-building, derived from the Greek word for road, ὁδός (*hodos*). For the hodological perspective of ancient travelers, see Cioffi (2016, 20–21).

4. The bibliographic essay of Vistoli (2013) is useful for sources on the VA.

5. http://www.perseus.tufts.edu/hopper/collection?collection=Perseus:collection:Greco-Roman.

6. Hereafter, when a text in Acts is referred to in this book, generally only the chapter and verse are given.

*Preface*

unconvinced as to its historicity can still use the volume profitably to understand the experiences of any ancient traveler on such a journey in the first century AD.

Two distinct new contributions are offered for English-language readers. First, no previous description exists for the consular road that connected the major Roman port of Puteoli to the capital of Campania—ancient Capua.[7] On the basis of the geographical and archaeological studies of contemporary Italian scholars, a detailed account of that route is provided for the first time. Second, much of the volume is given to providing the most detailed account in English of the first 132 RM of the VA—the famous *Regina Viarum* ("Queen of Roads").[8] While numerous guidebooks exist in Italian, these do not generally focus on the route itself but often wander into descriptions of nearby sites and monuments. However, this volume addresses almost entirely what a first-century traveler would see and experience along the way, since we wanted readers to travel the road and see it through Paul's eyes. We have therefore attempted to provide complete information on the road traces that still exist today as well as to describe the path of the sections now lost.

Modern GPS technology and satellite imagery allow us to detail the exact routes of these ancient roads. Such data will help to explain our decisions, especially when various opinions exist. Precise geographical locations with GPS coordinates are provided in appendix 4. An asterisk after a road position* or monument* mentioned in the text signals that GPS coordinates are provided in the appendix. Pilgrims and hikers should find this useful as they trace Paul's route in Italy. Readers can also use this feature to follow Paul's entire land journey virtually on Google Maps either in the Satellite View or the Street View. The appendix can be downloaded at www.lexhampress.com/appianway.

---

7. The area is known in Latin as *Campania*. "Campania" is also the normal English spelling today, but in older works it is often spelled "Campagna." "Campana" is the Italian spelling. Thus, the spelling is dependent on the context.

8. This appellation comes from the poet Statius (*Silvae* 2.2.12) who called it *Appia longarum teritur regina viarum*.

Most of the ancient cities mentioned have archaeology museums either on site or in a nearby city. Of particular interest are the milestones and inscriptions related to the VA. Hopefully readers will be inspired to visit Italy and see these archaeological sites, which usually have excellent signage both in Italian and English. The historical significance of the Via Appia is underscored by Italy's Ministry of Culture placing the road on the UNESCO tentative list of World Heritage sites.[9]

The maps show the ancient remains or road paths superimposed upon the modern topography as displayed in OpenStreetMap©.[10] Map 2 was produced by Tutku Educational Travel of Izmir, Turkey.[11] The other twenty-eight maps were the work of Glen Thompson and Jesse Cordes. The photographs are our own, unless otherwise attributed. Since readers across the English-reading world will be using the volume, distances are given both in the imperial system and the metric system.[12] The English translations of ancient sources are usually drawn, with minor updating, from the Loeb Classical Library unless otherwise noted. Translations from Italian or other modern languages into English are our own. Bible quotations are also our own translations unless otherwise noted.

Despite the hindrances to on-site visitation along with restricted library access caused by the Covid pandemic, we were able to complete our research through the help of many Italian scholars who have generously shared their work and answered many questions virtually. These include Giuseppe Camodeca on Puteoli and the VCC; Giacinto Libertini on the VCC and centuriation in Campania; Pasquale Argenziano on *ad Septimum*, Capua, and Casilinum; Mario Pagano on Sinuessa and Capua; Carlo Ceraldi and Ugo Zannini on the Falernian Plain; Sergio Cascella on Sinuessa; Gianmatteo Matullo on Minturnae and Formiae; Andrea

---

9. UNESCO World Heritage Convention (2006b, ref. 349).

10. We gratefully acknowledge OpenStreetMap© contributors; see https://www.openstreetmap.org/copyright.

11. The authors periodically lead tours of Paul's route in Italy through Tutku Educational Travel; for details see www.tutkutours.com.

12. Distances are usually given as rounded numbers, so they will not be exactly equivalent. For example, instead of 800 ft./243.84 m, the measurement given may be 800 ft./245 m.

Di Rosa on Fondi and Tarracina; and Francesco Petrucci and Valerio Spaccini on Aricia. We also extend special thanks to Jerry and Kay Fischer and the Fischer Family Foundation for funding us and a small group of students on a focused research trip to Italy in 2018. We are grateful to Nataliya Braila of Niki Tours in Rome for coordinating our travel arrangements. During this trip the need for this book first became clear.

In conclusion, we quote the colorful observation of Catherine Nixey (2020): "Today, Roman roads are famous. They were so strong, so straight, so brilliantly efficient, that they are regarded less as simply a mode of transport, more a metaphor for Roman rule. Their engineering is awe-inspiring, with drains, firm foundations and astonishing durability. These are not mere roads; they are sermons in stone."[13]

We have sought not only to elucidate this "sermon" in situ but also to illuminate Christianity's most famous writer of sermons who walked these stones almost two millennia ago. The story told in this volume was experienced by thousands of persons who traveled over many centuries in ancient Italy. Roman authors such as Horace have left us descriptions of their own travels. However, few persons today have read or even know about these journeys. Yet over two billion Christians worldwide have read or heard about Paul's captivity journey to Rome that concludes the book of Acts. In a sense then, Paul becomes the ideal ancient traveler through whom we all vicariously experience the wonders, challenges, even dangers of travel in antiquity.[14] And something of that wonder and adventure we hope to have captured in this book.

---

13. For a general discussion of Roman roads, see Staccioli (2003); Adams (2012, 229–31), and Wilson (2019b, 175–92).

14. See Wilson (2018b, 17–20, 28–32). Gambash (2015, 157) similarly calls Paul "one of the most famous travellers of antiquity."

ACTS 28:11–31

# Paul's Arrival in Rome

¹¹ After three months we set sail in an Alexandrian ship that had wintered on the island [Malta]. Its figurehead was the Dioscuri.¹ ¹² We landed at Syracuse and stayed there three days. ¹³ From there we set sail and arrived at Rhegium. After waiting a day, a south wind came up, and on the second day we reached Puteoli. ¹⁴ Finding some brothers and sisters there, we were urged by them to stay for seven days. And in this way we came to Rome. ¹⁵ When the believers there heard the news about us, some came out to meet us at Forum of Appius, others at Three Taverns. Seeing them, Paul thanked God and was encouraged. ¹⁶ When we arrived in Rome, Paul was allowed to live by himself, with a soldier to guard him.

¹⁷ Three days later he convened a meeting with the leading Jews. When they had assembled, Paul said to them: "Brothers, although I have done nothing against our people or against our ancestral customs, I was delivered as a prisoner from Jerusalem into the hands of the Romans. ¹⁸ After examining me, they wanted to release me, because there was no charge against me deserving death. ¹⁹ But when the Jews objected—not that my nation had any accusation to make—I was forced to appeal to Caesar. ²⁰ Because of this charge I have requested to see you and speak with you since I am wearing this chain for the sake of the hope of Israel."

²¹ They said to him, "We have neither received any letters from Judea concerning you nor have any of the brothers come to report or speak something negative about you. ²² However, we desire to hear your thoughts concerning this sect, which has become known to us because people everywhere are speaking against it."

²³ Arranging a day to meet him, an even larger group came to his lodging. He expounded to them from morning until evening from the Law of

---

1. The twin gods Castor and Pollux, the patron gods of sailors.

Moses and the Prophets, testifying about the kingdom of God and persuading them concerning Jesus. ²⁴ Some were persuaded by the things he said, while others did not believe them. ²⁵ So disagreeing among themselves, they departed after Paul spoke a final word: "The Holy Spirit truly declared to your ancestors through Isaiah the prophet: ²⁶ 'Go to this people and say, "You will indeed hear but never understand; you will indeed see but never perceive." ²⁷ For the heart of this people has become calloused; with their ears they hear with difficulty and they have shut their eyes, lest they might open their eyes, listen with their ears, understand with their hearts, turn to the Lord, and I would heal them.' ²⁸ Therefore I want you to know that this salvation from God has been sent to the gentiles, and they will listen!"²

³⁰ For two entire years Paul resided in his own rented lodging and welcomed all who came to see him. ³¹ He continued to proclaim the kingdom of God and to teach about the Lord Jesus with all boldness and without hindrance! [trans. Thompson and Wilson]

---

2. Verse 29 is omitted in modern critical editions because it is found only in the Byzantine textual tradition, and so thought to be secondary. It reads: "And when he had said these things, the Jews left, having significant arguments among themselves."

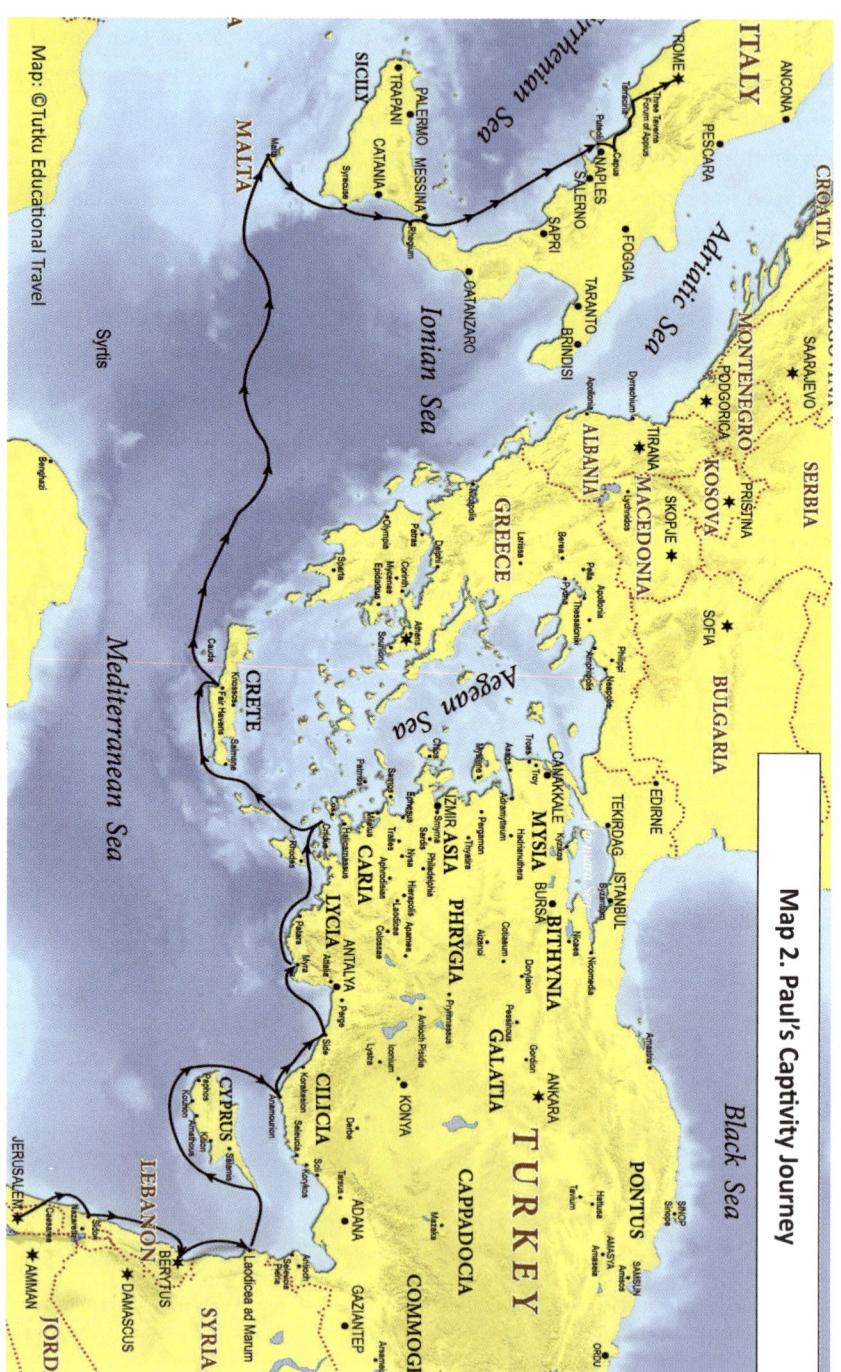
Map 2. Paul's Captivity Journey

Introduction

# Voyage to Italy

After two years of imprisonment in Caesarea Maritima, Paul must have been eager to begin his long-anticipated journey to Rome. This book is focused on the final 150-mile land portion of that trip—from Puteoli to Rome. But to understand fully that concluding leg, a brief overview of its background is necessary. This initial part comprises the sea voyage from Caesarea Maritima to Puteoli that began some four months earlier. Paul was at first incarcerated in the praetorium at Caesarea under the governor Felix (23:35).[1] Although Paul's initial hearing before the procurator ended inconclusively, his custodial arrangement was relaxed, for he was now allowed to receive visits from his friends (24:22–23). Later Paul was summoned to appear again before Felix, this time with his Jewish wife Drusilla (24:23–24).[2] The governor, as a favor to the Jews, continued to hold Paul in custody for two years.[3] Nevertheless, Felix frequently summoned Paul to converse about the Way, while at the same time hoping to receive a bribe from this prisoner, who was clearly a person of status with financial means (24:25–27). When Porcius

---

1. Herod's Palace in Caesarea served as a residence, headquarters, and praetorium for the Roman government in Paul's day; see Netzer (2008, 106–11). Paul's confinement was probably in quarters in the upper palace. Although unstated, Paul must have ultimately been delivered to the praetorium at Rome upon his arrival there (28:16). See the discussion below in day 7.

2. Felix became familiar with the Way from Drusilla, the daughter of King Herod Agrippa I and sister of Berenice, Mariamne, and Herod Agrippa II. Drusilla and her son Agrippa later died in the eruption of Mount Vesuvius in AD 79 (Josephus, *Antiquities* 20.7.2).

3. The Greek participle δεδεμένον (*dedemenon*; 24:27) only suggests confinement but not the place (e.g., "prison"; NRSV, ESV). Felix, after his initial examination, told Paul, "For now go. At a later opportune time I will summon you again" (24:25, trans. Wilson). This injunction makes sense only if Paul was held in quarters conveniently nearby.

Festus replaced Felix in AD 59, Paul was given another chance to plead his case.[4] He ended by publicly appealing to Caesar—the right of every Roman citizen (*provocatio ad imperatorem*).

Julius, a centurion belonging to the Augustan Cohort (Gk. σπείρης Σεβαστῆς [*speirēs Sebastēs*]; Lat. *cohors Augusta*), was assigned by Festus to take Paul to Rome (27:1). Michael Speidel (1982/1983) has argued on the basis of two other inscriptions that the Augustan Cohort included Roman troops assigned to serve Herod Agrippa II and that they were stationed in the Hauran Mountains in Transjordan to the east of Caesarea. He hypothesizes that Julius was among the troops who escorted Herod when he came to pay his respects to the new procurator, just a few days after Paul's hearing and appeal (25:13). After Festus asked Agrippa to help him compose the letter of charges that would accompany the prisoner (25:26–27), Agrippa listened attentively to Paul's spirited defense, concluding that he was innocent of any crime (26:32). According to Speidel (1982/1983, 237–40), Agrippa then volunteered Julius, one of his own centurions and a Roman citizen, to be Paul's guard on the way to Rome.[5] If Julius were among the officers present for Paul's defense (25:23) and heard the preliminary verdict of Festus and Agrippa (26:31–32), this may have disposed him favorably toward his future charge. Even at the outset of the trip there already appears to be a good relationship between them (27:3).[6]

Before his departure Julius would be given a diploma from Festus. Regarding such diplomas, Stephen Mitchell (1976, 125) notes that "governors with *imperium* in the provinces were entitled to issue them [diplomas] for official business, and that this was done without reference to any

---

4. Festus's succession to the procuratorship of Judea is dated variously in the late 50s; however, Festus issued coinage in the fifth year of Nero's reign—the year 59; see Jacobson (2019, 88, 95, fig. 14).

5. Speidel (1982/1983, 240) further suggests that Julius was selected because "he was still of a position and of a status that enabled him to deal with Roman officialdom in the capital" and that he had "the requisite knowledge in matters of 'superstition' to act as a witness in the forthcoming trial of Paul in Rome." Both are dubious assumptions since his task would have ended upon arrival in Rome when he handed over his prisoners with a letter containing their charges to local officials.

6. With his education, citizenship, and financial means, Paul must have appeared as a provincial of some social standing compared to the centurion (cf. 22:28). Paul, it seems, did not take advantage of this difference, and his humility when interacting with Julius must have contributed to the latter's good opinion and trust of Paul.

higher authority." This diploma would allow Julius to requisition goods and services for their journey.[7] Decrees were periodically issued by the emperors to prevent abuse of the system by restricting who could utilize such diplomas and the extent of their subvention of services from locals, particularly transport. In the case of Julius, this involved sea passage to the capital.

Luke implies that once Festus had decided to transfer his charge to Rome, Paul "and some other prisoners" (τινας ἑτέρους δεσμώτας [*tinas heterous desmōtas*]) were soon boarding a ship with Julius.[8] Were these other prisoners Roman citizens like Paul, who had also appealed to Caesar? Or was there some other reason for their transfer to Italy? Both their number and identity are unstated. Governors like Festus, according to John Richardson (1976, 35), "could punish anyone in his province with flogging or death, as well as large-scale confiscation of property." The exceptions were Roman citizens who had the right of appeal. Since Roman citizenship was rare in the Greek East in the middle of the first century, it is doubtful there were more than two or three other prisoners under the care of Julius.

Roman law allowed a prisoner to be attended by servants, so Paul brought along a Macedonian believer named Aristarchus.[9] The use of "we" throughout chapters 27–28 suggests that the narrator, traditionally Luke, also traveled with the group.[10] Julius would also be accompanied by a couple of lower-ranking soldiers and perhaps a personal servant.

---

7. Pliny the Younger (*Epistles* 10.120) informed Trajan that he never gave a diploma to anyone for personal convenience but only for those conducting official business for the emperor.

8. The number of other prisoners is impossible to determine from the Greek text. Luke uses the plural of the indefinite pronoun τίς, τί (*tis, ti*) several times in Acts to indicate an approximate number of persons or days. Usually this is translated "some" or "several." However, "some of the brothers" (10:23) are later said to number six (11:12). And "some disciples" that Paul met in Ephesus (19:1) actually numbered around twelve (19:7).

9. Several manuscripts in 27:2 add Secundus, Aristarchus's fellow Thessalonian, to Paul's party; see Metzger (1975, 497). This addition seemingly stems from his mention among those who accompanied Paul to Jerusalem two years earlier (20:4).

10. Hemer (1985, 108) rightly notes: "If the 'we-passages' reflect personal participation, they take us nearer to the historical Paul." He (94–102) details ten observations from these chapters that suggest Luke was a firsthand witness.

These soldiers later prevented the sailors from absconding (27:31–32) and tried to kill the prisoners to prevent their escape (27:42–43). Thus, between the Roman soldiers, Paul and his two friends, and several more prisoners and attendants, the party heading to Rome likely consisted of around ten, plus crew.

What was the practical nature of Paul's custody? Was he chained, and if so, on his wrists only or on his ankles as well? When Paul was first arrested in Jerusalem, the Roman commander Claudius Lysias had him bound with two chains, probably manacled to a soldier on either side (21:33). However, upon learning Paul was a Roman citizen, the tribune immediately removed his chains (22:29–30). Because Paul was uncharged, he remained unchained during his appearance before the Sanhedrin, his transfer to Caesarea, and his initial appearance before Felix (22:29–24:21). While under house arrest, he may again have been chained at times.[11] On the way to Rome, the prisoners could safely be granted more freedom aboard ship, but during harbor stops Julius would chain his prisoners to prevent their escape. Once the party reached Italy and began to travel by land, the prisoners' wrists would be shackled again. On the other hand, Paul's actions on the trip and during the shipwreck demonstrated to Julius that he felt divinely bound to stand before Caesar (27:24) and so did not pose a flight risk. Julius, however, did not have the same confidence about the other prisoners, thus they were likely bound with wrist shackles.[12]

## Caesarea Maritima to Myra

Julius secured passage for the party on a coasting vessel from Adramyttium, a port down the coast from Assos.[13] Fergus Millar (2004, 174) notes that "sea travel by official passengers or groups (like the escort which took a whole winter to bring Paul and other prisoners from Judaea to Rome)

---

11. Paul's reference to his chains in 26:29 may be a metonymy signifying imprisonment (cf. Phil 1:7), or he may have been shackled for his appearance before the dignitaries.

12. For a study of the conditions imposed on Roman prisoners, and Paul in particular, see Rapske (1994, passim). For the use of chains in Roman imprisonment see Wansink (1996, 46–49).

13. Pliny the Younger (*Epistles* 10.15) describes the use of such vessels for official travel: "Now I intend to go to my province partly by coasting vessels [*orariis navibus*], partly by land conveyances."

Introduction: Voyage to Italy                                                    5

depended on the availability of trading ships." Julius therefore took advantage of such a vessel, calculating that his party could reach Rome before the sailing season closed.[14] Luke's description of this final journey to Rome parallels that of Paul's return to Jerusalem (20:3–21:16).[15] Robert Tannehill (1990, 342) observes: "In both cases the stages of the journey are carefully noted, and there is special attention to Paul's contacts with local believers along the way." Just as Paul stayed with Christians in Troas, Tyre, and Caesarea (20:6; 21:4, 8–10), he visited Christians in Sidon (27:3) and resided with believers in Puteoli (28:14).

Julius and his party set sail around the middle of September.[16] Following an overnight stop in Sidon, the coasting vessel encountered strong winds as it sought to pass Cape Kleides at northeast Cyprus and so was forced to sail under the island's lee along the southern coast. Turning northward from Paphos, it then passed along the coasts of Cilicia and Pamphylia before arriving in Lycia.[17] Ships taking a coastal route typically docked at a convenient port each night to offload cargo as well as to secure food and shelter. The journey from Sidon to Myra was just under 400 nautical miles so Paul's ship "probably laid over a good many nights" (Casson 1951, 144 n. 35).[18] This slow progress, possibly taking fifteen days, brought them later than expected to Lycia and Andriake, the port of Myra.[19] Here they transferred to a massive Alexandrian grain ship (27:5–6). Generally, such grain ships would not be sailing in the autumn. But occasionally ship owners tried to deliver a second cargo of grain, "some making it as far as Italy under favorable conditions, others encountering autumnal weather and forced to

---

14. Papyrus Bingen 77 (http://aquila.zaw.uni-heidelberg.de/hgv/78045), dated to the mid-second century AD, contains entries regarding twelve ships that were sailing in the summer between Pamphylia, Cilicia, and Egypt. Most were small merchant galleys called *akatoi*, some with a capacity of ten to thirty-five tons while others held seventy-five to one hundred tons.

15. For the genre of periplus, see Wilson (2016, 233–39).

16. Hohlfelder (2000, 245 n. 17) dates the departure from Andriake/Myra to late September or early October. A mid-September departure from Caesarea is more probable, as discussed later.

17. For a discussion of the suggested routes for this part of the voyage, see Wilson (2022b, 343–66).

18. Johnson (1992, 445) also observes, "The planned itinerary gives the picture of a ship that moved in daily legs from one coastal port to another."

19. The Western text of 27:5 states that the journey took fifteen days; see Metzger (1975, 497).

winter somewhere enroute" (Davis 2009, 73). Because such late deliveries garnered high profits in Rome, owners and captains were willing to take the risk of sailing late in the year. This helps to explain the decision made in Crete to continue sailing despite potential problems with the weather.

Because Aristarchus was from Thessalonica (19:29; 20:4), John Chrysostom (*Homilies on Acts*, 53.1) suggested that he remained on the coasting vessel to bring news of Paul to the believers in Asia and then to those in Macedonia. If the letter to the Philippians was written from Caesarea via Epaphroditus (Phil 2:25; 4:18), Paul might now have dispatched Aristarchus to update the Macedonian churches about his current situation.[20]

## Crete, Shipwreck, and Malta

Prevailing winds limited progress for the huge grain ship, and by the time it arrived at Fair Havens, halfway along Crete's southern coast, it was "after the Fast" (27:9). The Fast probably refers not only to the Day of Atonement (Yom Kippur), which in AD 59 occurred on October 5, but also to the contiguous weeklong Feast of Tabernacles (Sukkoth). It was nearly mid-October then when the ship finally arrived in Fair Havens (27:8). Some days seemingly passed there before wind conditions allowed the ship to sail farther (27:12–13). Therefore, the ship's departure from Fair Havens occurred toward the end of October.[21]

Paul warned Julius about the dangers of continuing the journey, but the centurion listened instead to the helmsman and the captain/shipowner who were intent on wintering in a more favorable harbor (27:10–11). Soon after setting sail the ship was caught in a northeasterly typhoon-force wind

---

20. For a discussion of the pros and cons of a Caesarean provenance for Philippians, see Hawthorne (1983, xli–xliii). Paul mentions Aristarchus as his fellow prisoner (Phlm 24; Col 4:10). If Rome is accepted as the provenance of these prison letters, Aristarchus could either have continued aboard ship with Paul to Rome, or after visiting Philippi and Thessalonica continued on to Rome with news and aid from the Macedonian churches. If Aristarchus did leave at Myra (he is never mentioned again in Acts), Paul's group would now have one fewer person.

21. Although Vegetius (*On Military Matters* 4.39) observes that sailing from September 14 until November 8 was uncertain and more dangerous, a departure around November 1 was still possible. Schnabel (2012, 1037), however, suggests an earlier departure date between October 5 and 10.

called Euroclydon (27:14). Luke describes the fourteen-day storm and subsequent shipwreck in great detail using precise nautical terminology (27:13–44). At the height of the storm an angel appeared to Paul, assuring him that the lives of all 276 persons aboard would be saved (27:21–26, 33–37).[22] Despite this divine assurance, as the ship approached land the soldiers decided to kill their prisoners, lest they escape when the vessel ran aground. After everything these guards had experienced with Paul, why now did they want to kill him? Despite the extenuating circumstances of the storm, the guards realized that they would be held accountable if the prisoners escaped, possibly even receiving the death penalty. Since leaving Caesarea Maritima, the guards carried such a responsibility. Brian Rapske (1994, 30) writes, "Penalties were graduated on the basis of the degree of culpability of the guard and the importance or numbers of prisoners who had escaped." Once again showing favor to Paul, Julius intervened and ordered his guards to remove their shackles (if they were still chained at this point) so they could swim to land (27:42–44). Surviving the frigid mid-November water, Paul and his party washed ashore on Malta where they spent three months hosted by its chief official, Publius, and the residents (28:1–10).

When the spring sailing season was at hand, Julius secured passage for his prisoners on another Alexandrian grain ship bound for Italy that had wintered in Malta. Its figurehead depicted the Dioscuri—the twins Castor and Pollux—who were regarded as the patron gods of sailors. Lucian (*Navigium* 9, trans. Fowler and Fowler) provides an entertaining story of a grain ship that was helped out of danger: "a bright star—either Castor or Pollux—appeared at the masthead and guided the ship into the open sea on their left; just in time, for she was making straight for the cliff." Luke notes that their departure occurred after spending approximately three months on the island (28:11).

Ancient sources give dates ranging from February 8 (Pliny the Elder, *Nat.* 2.47) to March 10 (Vegetius, *On Military Matters* 4.39) for the beginning of the sailing season. At Corinth the annual ceremony of the Vessel

---

22. For a discussion of this example of divine guidance in Acts, see Wilson (2020b, 136–38).

of Isis (*Navigium Isidis*), held on March 5, marked its opening (Apuleius, *Metamorphoses* 11.16–17). A fresco of that event, found in the *sacrarium* of Pompeii's temple of Isis, suggests that a similar ceremony was also celebrated on the Bay of Naples.[23] While smaller coasting vessels continued to sail all winter if conditions permitted, Alexandrian grain ships adhered to a tight sailing program between April and October. Danny Davis (2009, 73) notes that their "centuries-long adherence to a strict and conservative sailing schedule appears to have been a mark of prudence and a strategy of minimizing financial risk; sailing during periods of unsettled weather with such large and valuable cargoes, along with a typically large complement of passengers, was simply too chancy." This is a fact for which Paul could vouch. The ship "Dioscuri" thus departed in early March as soon as sea travel was safe. It could then reach Puteoli in time to offload its cargo and join the fleet of grain ships departing for Alexandria around April 1.

## Sicily to Italy

A short sail brought Julius and his party to the southeastern coast of Sicily and the southern commercial harbor of Syracuse. Founded by colonists from Corinth around 734 BC, this city was one of the wealthiest of the numerous Greek cities collectively referred to as Magna Graecia by the Romans. These cities were founded in Sicily and in southern Italy by colonists from the Greek East. Paul would have felt right at home in such a Hellenic environment. Here his party had a three-day layover (28:12), possibly related to adverse winds (Barrett 1998, 1229) or perhaps to replace the prisoners' chains lost in the shipwreck. Jeremy Dummett (2010, 210 n. 3) rightly notes that while Paul met people on his travels in Athens, Corinth, and Sidon, "there is no mention of any contact being made in Syracuse."

As the grain ship sailed up Sicily's northeastern coast, it passed in the shadow of Mount Aetna and another Greek city named Tauromenium. To starboard, Paul soon saw the toe of Italy, ancient Bruttium, come into view.

---

23. This fresco is currently in the National Museum of Archaeology in Naples; https://commons.wikimedia.org/wiki/File:Fresco_Isis_N%C3%A1poles_02.JPG.

## Introduction: Voyage to Italy 9

A single day sufficed to sail the 78 mi. (125 km) to the port of Rhegium (Reggio Calabria). Greek colonists from Chalchis on the Black Sea had founded Rhegion around 720 BC, and it too became a prominent city in Magna Graecia.[24] Allying itself with Rome early in the third century BC, it eventually became a Roman *municipium* with the name Regium Iulium.[25] Its port was expanded by Caligula to better accommodate Alexandrian grain ships (Josephus, *Antiquities* 19.205). After capturing Jerusalem and destroying the Jewish temple in AD 70, Titus took much the same route to Rome as Paul's party. He sailed to Italy on a transport ship that stopped in Rhegium and Puteoli before continuing overland on the VA (Suetonius, *Titus* 5). After a one-day stopover (28:13), Paul's ship utilized a favorable south wind to continue its voyage.[26]

The first 12.4 mi. (20 km) took the ship through the Strait of Messina. On the Sicilian coast two famous lighthouses were visible—at Messana (Messina) and Pelorus (Punta del Faro). At this promontory the strait is a mere 1.9 mi. (3.1 km) wide. This dangerous passage is connected to the myth of Scylla and Charybdis. A coin minted by Sextus Pompey of Sicily (42–40 BC) shows the pharos at Messana on the obverse and Scylla on the reverse.[27] Scylla was the six-headed sea monster on mainland Italy while Charybdis was the whirlpool off Sicilian Pelorus. Since Paul would have studied Homer during his Greek education called παιδεία (*paideia*), the legend would be familiar to him (*Odyssey* 12.73–125). The ship then entered the Tyrrhenian Sea and continued northwest along the coast of Italy to Puteoli. Lionel Casson (1951, 140) has calculated the length of the

---

24. The National Archaeological Museum of Magna Graecia is located in Reggio Calabria; https://www.museoarcheologicoreggiocalabria.it/magna-grecia/?lang=en.

25. Land travel to Rome was also possible from Rhegium along the Via Popilia, which was constructed in the second century BC and ran 317 mi. (517 km) before connecting with the VA at Capua.

26. The NIV translation "the next day" fails to capture the time sequence. When Luke wishes to indicate "next day" in Acts, he uses ἐπαύριον (*epaurion*; ten times; e.g., 10:9, 23, 24; 25:6, 23). A day passed at Rhegium when the ship was becalmed (μετὰ μίαν ἡμέραν ἐπιγενομένου; *meta mian hēmeran epigenomenou*); the following day the ship sailed, arriving in Puteoli the following day, i.e., the second day (δευτεραῖοι [*deuteraioi*]).

27. For the example in the British Museum, see https://www.britishmuseum.org/collection/object/C_2002-0102-4797.

voyage between Rhegium and Puteoli to be 175 nautical miles (201 mi./324 km), taking approximately 1.5 days at an average speed of five knots.[28]

## Bay of Naples

On the second day, Capreae (modern Capri) came into view, where Augustus once had a residence (Strabo, *Geogr.* 5.4.9). Suetonius (*Augustus* 98.2) tells how in AD 14 the emperor saw an Alexandrian grain ship sailing past Capreae and how "the passengers and crew, clad in white, crowned with garlands, and burning incense, lavished upon him good wishes and the highest praise, saying that it was through him that they lived, through him that they sailed the seas, and through him that they enjoyed their liberty and their fortunes." His successor Tiberius built the Villa Jovis there, from which he ruled the empire from AD 27 to 37 (Tacitus, *Ann.* 4.67.5). Paul perhaps knew the story of how Herod Agrippa I, murderer of James the brother of John (12:1–2), had tried to visit Tiberius at Capri in AD 36. When the emperor learned that Agrippa still owed money to the imperial treasury, he barred him from the island. Upon repayment of the loan, their friendship was restored, and Agrippa was allowed to visit Capri (Josephus, *Antiquities* 18.6.4).

After Capreae, the ship entered the *Sinus Cumanus* (Gulf of Naples), a semicircular inlet of the Tyrrhenian Sea (map 3). This bay is 10 mi. (16 km) wide and extends southeastward for 20 mi. (32 km) from Cape Misenum on the west to Campanella Point on the southeast. It is easy to imagine Paul's wonder when viewing this majestic panorama for the first time. Perhaps Julius or one of the ship's officers played the role of tour guide, describing all the sights coming into view.

---

28. The estimate for this voyage on the Orbis geospatial modeling site (https://orbis.stanford.edu/) is 386 km taking 3.3 days, both of its calculations being too high.

## Introduction: Voyage to Italy

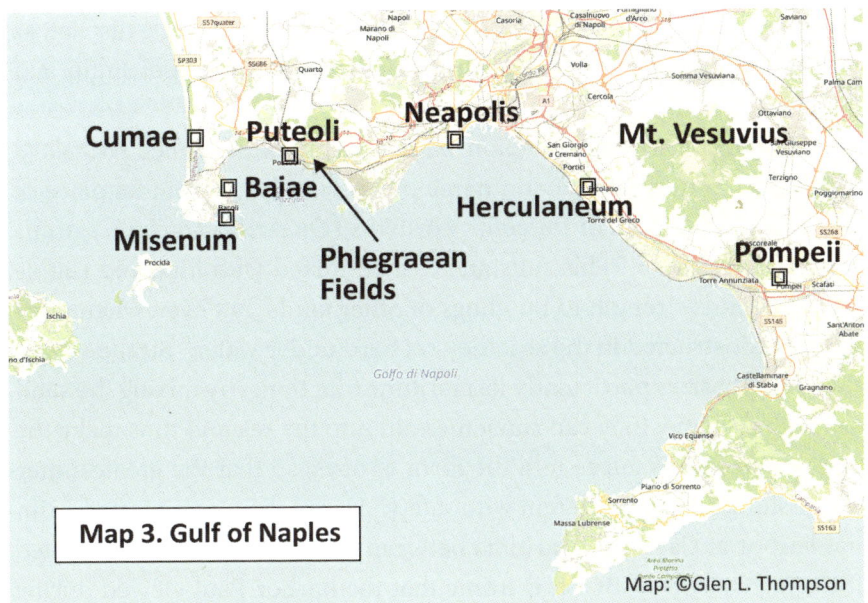

Map 3. Gulf of Naples
Map: ©Glen L. Thompson

To the northeast snowcapped Mount Vesuvius towered 4200 ft. (1280 m) above the coastal cities of Pompeii and Herculaneum, soon to be destroyed in the eruption of 79. Farther north along the coast was Neapolis (Naples), founded by Greek colonists in the sixth century BC. West of Neapolis were the famed Phlegraean Fields (*Campi Flegrei*). This steaming caldera consists of twenty-four craters and other geological formations where volcanoes have erupted and collapsed. At the west end of the bay this seismic activity has produced a phenomenon called bradyseism, wherein the coastline of the Roman age has collapsed to a depth of 33 ft. (10 m) below the present sea level. This bradyseismic effect is most visible at Baiae, the meat market (*macellum*) at Puteoli, and on Gaiola Island.[29] Strabo (*Geogr.* 5.4.6) suggests that Puteoli's name "was

---

29. A map showing the major archaeological sites of the Phlegrean Fields with descriptions in Italian is available at: https://www.google.com/maps/d/u/o/viewer?mid=11m0q-23GO8WNWfPjcAFCp0yS40Rc&ll=40.811818539139914%2C14.128926519316018&z=13; for a

from the foul smell [Lat. *puteo*] of the waters, since the whole district, as far as Baiae and Cumae, has a foul smell, because it is full of sulfur and fire and hot waters."

The volcanic ash of the region was rich with a silica called *pozzolana*. This material derives its Latin name *pulvis puteolanus* from its place of origin, thus the "dust of Puteoli." Vitruvius (*On Architecture* 2.6.1, trans. Morgan) observes: "This substance, when mixed with lime and rubble, not only lends strength to buildings of other kinds, but even when piers of it are constructed in the sea, they set hard under water." Strabo (*Geogr.* 5.4.6) emphasizes particularly its maritime function: "by mixing the sand-ash with the lime, they can run jetties out into the sea and thus make the wide-open shores curve into the form of bays, so that the greatest merchant-ships can moor therein with safety." Herod the Great created a similar harbor at Caesarea Maritima between 22–15 BC and later dedicated it to Augustus in 10 BC. It is ironic that the harbor Paul viewed during his two years of imprisonment in Judea was constructed of pozzolana imported from this area of Puteoli.

Sweeping his gaze now to the gulf's left side, Paul saw the two islands of Ischia and Procida. Next to appear was Cape Misenum, the home port for Rome's *classis Misenensis*, the military fleet that controlled the western Mediterranean Sea. Inside Misenum's double harbor, protected by moles, Paul saw all sizes and types of Roman warships and military vessels. Water was supplied to the eight cities on the gulf by the 60-mile-long (96 km) Serino aqueduct that Augustus had built between 30–20 BC. Carrying a large volume of water, the aqueduct terminated in Misenum in the massive cistern known as Piscina Mirabilis. Its capacity measures around 440,000 cu. ft. (12,459 m$^3$), and it is still admired by visitors today.

---

discussion of bradyseism in the Bay of Naples see UNESCO World Heritage Convention (2006a, ref. 2030).

Just north of Misenum was Baiae, the Riviera of ancient Rome, where the rich and famous enjoyed their hedonistic lifestyle in luxury villas.[30] The poet Horace (*Epistles* 1.1.83, trans. Kline), who himself enjoyed the thermal waters of its spa resorts, exclaimed: "No bay in the world outshines lovely Baiae." The sober Stoic philosopher Seneca the Younger (*Letters* 51.1–3) was less positive: "Baiae is a place to be avoided because, though it has certain natural advantages, luxury has claimed it for her own exclusive resort." According to him, a wise man would avoid its resorts because they were "foreign to good morals." Paul, who similarly criticized the profligate lifestyle of the rich (cf. 1 Thess 4:3–5; 1 Tim 6:9, 17), would have agreed.

Paul's informant was undoubtedly eager to tell how in AD 39 the emperor Gaius Caligula had constructed a pontoon bridge to connect Baiae with the mole of twenty-five arches at Puteoli (Molo Caligolano), a distance of 3.3 mi. (5.3 km). Caligula did this to refute the prediction that an astrologer had given Tiberius that his grandson Caligula had no more chance of becoming emperor than of riding over the Gulf of Baiae with horses. So he "brought together merchant ships from all sides, anchored them in a double line, and then heaped a mound of earth on top of them to create a likeness of the Appian Way" (Suetonius, *Gaius* 19). Gaius then rode across the bridge for two days, first on a horse and then in a chariot. According to Suetonius, the emperor further demonstrated his cruelty by inviting nobles to join him on the bridge and then throwing them overboard. When some tried to hang on to the rudders of the ships, he pushed them away with boathooks and oars (*Gaius* 32). The bridge was not only "a majestic propaganda exhibition" (Coulston 2001, 125), but it also exemplified the ingenuity of Roman engineering and indicated Puteoli's strategic link to Rome through the VA.

---

30. For an illustrated guide to Baiae, see Miniero (2006). The Aragonese Castle there houses the Archaeological Museum of the Phlegraean Fields and has many artifacts from Puteoli (Miniero 2006, 45–65).

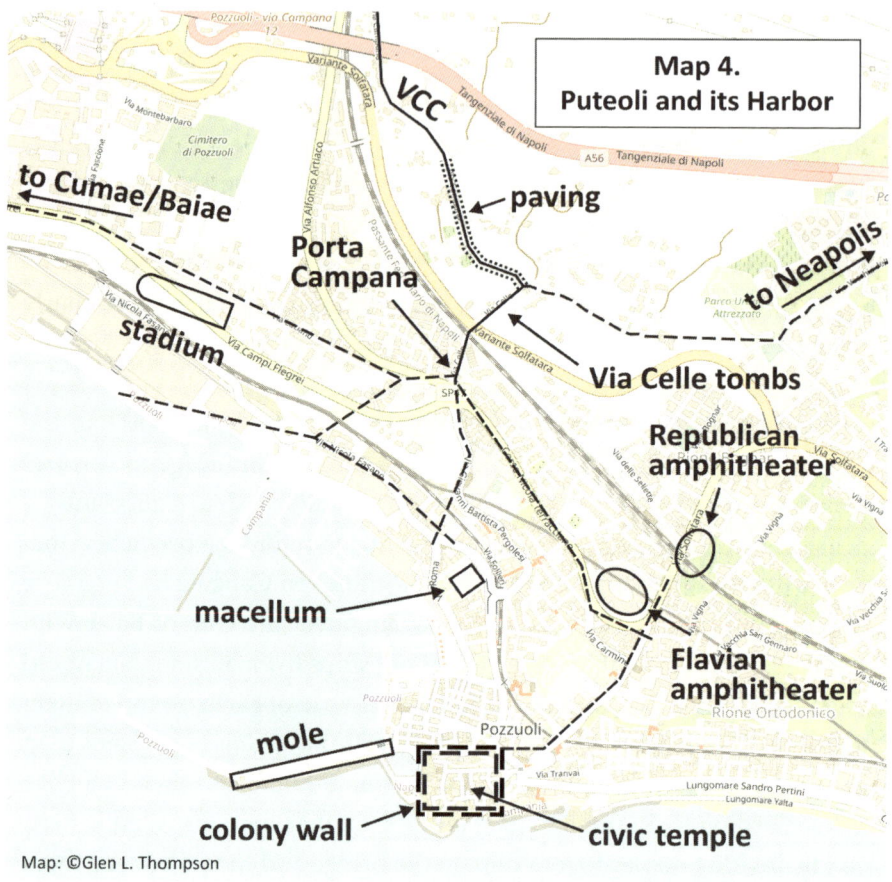

Map: ©Glen L. Thompson

## Puteoli as a Harbor City

At last Paul could see their port of debarkation—Puteoli (Pozzuoli)—the largest Roman city on the bay. The city was named Dikaiarchia when it was founded by Greeks fleeing from Samos in the sixth century BC.[31] In

---

31. Jerome (*Chronicon* B530) later dated this to the reign of Cambyses II (530–522 BC). He writes: "this Cambyses was called by the Hebrews Nebuchadnezzar II, in whose reign the story of

## Introduction: Voyage to Italy

194 BC the Romans brought in 300 Roman citizens and made it a Roman colony—*Colonia Iulia Augusta Puteoli* (Livy, *Hist*. 34.45). By Paul's day additional imperial favors had brought another name change—*Colonia Neronensis Claudia Augusta Puteoli* (Keppie 2009, 69–70, 73).[32]

Already about 125 BC Lucillius (3.118) referred to Puteoli as "little Delos," Delos being the preeminent Mediterranean emporium, slave market, and port of the time. For Polybius (*Histories* 3.91.2), Puteoli was one of "the most famous and beautiful cities of Italy." Strabo (*Geogr*. 5.4.6) noted that the city became a very great emporium because of its man-made harbors.

Its harbor was protected by a mole* 1220 ft. (372 m) long and 50 ft. (15 m) wide, which was still visible in the twentieth century.[33] Today it is encased in the modern concrete pier. Detailed depictions on souvenir glass flasks, produced in Puteoli in the third to fourth centuries AD, help us visualize the arcaded harbor mole (fig. 1). Two arches surmounted by hippocamps stand on the mole; between them are two columns (identified as *PILAE*), topped by statues, perhaps the Dioscuri. The mole's extremity is shaped like a ship's prow, and a flaming object that, on some flasks, rises above the mole, may represent the lighthouse. As Maggie Popkin (2018, 444) notes, "the flasks of the Puteoli group present the mole as a massive, richly ornamented structure—arguably, given the mole's dominance in the scenes' compositions, the most iconic and impressive of all the city's monuments." Another major waterfront site depicted on a flask is the station for weights and measures, the *sacomarium*. Here the office of the *praefectus annonae* ensured the use of standard measures, particularly for grain. Warehouses and other harbor installations lined the shore for 1.5 mi. (2.4 km) westward from the mole.[34] A fresco, discovered on the wall of a villa in nearby Stabiae and dating to the later first century AD,

---

Judith is composed" (trans. Pearse). This citation is erroneous since Nebuchadnezzar II, called "the Great" by the Jews, reigned earlier, from 605 to 562 BC.

32. The name would later be changed yet again to *Colonia Flavia Augusta Puteolana*.

33. When Morton (1936, 383) visited Pozzuoli, massive bronze rings to which the ancient galleys were tied could still be seen six feet underwater in the modern harbor.

34. Images of the ancient and modern pier can be seen in Stefanile (2015, 37, fig. 3).

likely provides another contemporary depiction of ancient Puteoli. This stylized depiction shows its mole and harbor along with the lighthouse at Cape Misenum.[35] In 39 BC, when Octavian, Antony, and Pompey agreed to discuss a ceasefire in the civil war, their famous meeting took place on Puteoli's mole "washed by the waves on both sides, and with ships moored around it as guards" (Appian, *Civil Wars* 5.8.72). Afterward Octavian and Antony returned to Rome by land on the VA (5.8.74).

**Figure 1.** Glass flask of Puteoli

---

35. For a brief discussion of the painting see Popkin (2018, 455). For a view of the fresco now in the National Museum of Archaeology in Naples, see https://en.wikipedia.org/wiki/Stabiae#/media/File:Wall_painting_from_Stabiae,_1st_century.jpg.

Puteoli's mole provided the berths required to unload the enormous Alexandrian grain ships. Pliny the Elder (*Nat.* 19.1.3) noted that a senator named Valerius Marianus once sailed from Alexandria to Puteoli in just nine days. These oversize freighters were the largest vessels sailing in the Mediterranean in the first century. Although exaggerating perhaps, the satirist Lucian (*Navigium* 5) described a ship called the Isis that measured 180 ft. (55 m) long, 45 ft. (14 m) wide, and 44 ft. (13 m) from deck to keel.[36] The ship, seen in the harbor of Piraeus, could carry approximately 1200 tons. Although most Alexandrian ships were smaller, they still carried at least 350 metric tons of grain (Casson 1995, 184–89; cf. Davis 2009, 59).[37] When Rome began to import obelisks from Egypt, giant ships were necessarily built for the task. After the first ship delivered its precious cargo of stone, Augustus had it placed in a permanent dock in Puteoli to celebrate the remarkable achievement. However, the ship was later destroyed by fire. Pliny the Elder (*Nat.* 36.14.2) mentions that the ship used by Caligula to bring a third obelisk from Egypt "was carefully preserved for several years by Claudius of revered memory, for it was the most amazing thing that had ever been seen at sea. Then caissons made of cement were erected in its hull at Puteoli; whereupon it was towed to Ostia and sunk there by order of the emperor, so to contribute to his harbor-works" (cf. Laurence 2020, 57).

Although a considerable distance from the capital, "Puteoli was Republican Rome's chief seaport. Here … vacation gaiety mingled with the daily bustle of export and import traffic," observed John D'Arms (1970, 52). The first luxury villa known to have been built in Puteoli dates to 165 BC so, like nearby Baiae, the city began to evidence ostentatious architecture.[38] Under Augustus Puteoli became "the single city in Italy most vital to the imperial economy" (D'Arms 1970, 81). Rome received about 135,000 tons

---

36. For exaggeration in Lucian, see Houston (1987, 446–50).

37. Since both Alexandrian ships on which Paul sailed carried around 300 passengers plus cargo, they were large indeed. Allowing 16 sq. ft. (c. 1.5 m²) for each person to sit or sleep, the minimum deck space required to accommodate everyone would be 4416 sq. ft. (410 m²). This suggests these ships measured at least 132 ft. (40 m) long with a width of 33 ft. (10 m), since the ratio of keel to beam is typically four to one in ancient vessels.

38. For a discussion of this architecture and the villas, see D'Arms (1970, 10, 12).

of grain annually from Egypt (Aurelius Victor, *On the Caesars* 1.6). Rome's grain needs, however, were 400,000 tons, so Egypt could only provide a four-month supply while North Africa supplied grain for the other eight months (Josephus, *Jewish War* 2.383, 386). In Paul's day over one thousand grain ships unloaded their cargo annually at Puteoli since it was the closest secure anchorage to Rome. Some of this cargo was offloaded and reloaded on one of the thousands of smaller coastal vessels transporting grain to Ostia and then up the Tiber River to Rome (Camodeca 1994, 110). Another large quantity was loaded into wagons for transport overland to Rome and the other cities of Latium and Campania. However, not all the Alexandrian grain arriving in Puteoli went to Rome. For as Casson (1980, 24) notes, "Sizable amounts stayed in Puteoli, not to relieve the local population of hunger, but to be warehoused for the greater profit of the local dealers." These grain merchants (*mercatores frumentarii*) formed a guild and had significant political and economic positions in the city (Camodeca 2018, 161–70). Claudius sent an urban cohort to protect the grain stored there against the danger from fire (Suetonius, *Claudius* 25.2).

Other kinds of cargo also arrived in Puteoli. The consul Mucianus once saw African elephants being offloaded at Puteoli: "Being terrified … at the length of the platform, which extended from the vessel to the shore, they walked backward, in order to deceive themselves by forming a false estimate of the distance" (Pliny the Elder, *Nat.* 8.3, trans. Bostock and Riley). These elephants were probably bound for Rome for use in wild animal hunts (*venationes*) held in an amphitheater. Perhaps Paul saw pachyderms for the first time while in Puteoli.

Latin authors heralded the port of Puteoli and its role in the Roman economy. Cicero mentions Puteoli some thirty-three times in his travel letters to Atticus. One of Statius's poems (*Silvae* 3.2.21–24) celebrated the arrival of the year's first grain ships from Alexandria.[39] And Seneca the

---

39. The celebrated Latin poet Vergil, author of the *Aeneid*, had a seaside villa at Pausilypon (Posillipo) between Puteoli and Neapolis, and his ashes were buried there after his death in 29 BC. A local tradition holds that while Paul was in Puteoli he visited Vergil's resting place and wept because Vergil's poems had been a key part of his literary education; see Leonard (1961, 28–29).

Younger, philosopher and advisor to Nero, colorfully described around AD 64 the arrival of the first convoy of Alexandrian grain ships.

> Suddenly there came into our view today the "Alexandrian" ships–I mean those which are usually sent ahead to announce the coming of the fleet; they are called "mailboats." The Campanians are glad to see them; all the rabble of Puteoli stand on the docks, and can recognize the "Alexandrian" boats, no matter how great the crowd of vessels, by the very trim of their sails. ... Accordingly, when they have made Capri and the headland whence 'Tall Pallas watches on the stormy peak,' all other vessels are bidden to be content with the mainsail, and the topsail stands out conspicuously on the "Alexandrian" boats. (*Letters* 77.1–2)

Who were the "rabble" that Paul met when he went ashore? Petronius set his *Satyricon* (6–8) in Puteoli where the narrator Trimalchio became lost and ended up in a brothel.[40] The apostle was no stranger to such a crowd, for he had spent five years evangelizing in the port cities of Corinth and Ephesus. When he wrote to the Corinthians, Paul reminded them of their past lives as fornicators, drunkards, liars, and con men (1 Cor 6:9–10). A later apocryphal work describes Peter as sailing from Caesarea to Puteoli where he was welcomed by a local innkeeper named Theon (Apocryphal Acts of Peter 6).[41]

Although Ostia is remembered today as Rome's chief port city, it was not so in Paul's day. Silt was regularly deposited at the mouth of the Tiber, preventing larger ships from sailing upriver from Ostia. Julius Caesar was the first to propose expanding the harbor at Ostia (Plutarch, *Caesar* 58.10),

---

40. Bodel (2017, 76–80) investigates the interesting commercial dimensions of Trimalchio's activity in Puteoli.

41. The fifth-century apocryphal work The Acts of Peter and Paul likewise provides an itinerary for Paul's journey to Rome. From the island of Malta he sailed to Syracuse, Rhegium, Messina, and Didymus (?) before arriving at Puteoli. From there he traveled by land to Baiae, Caieta, and Tarracina. From there he went by water, obviously the canal, to Tres Tabernae. The author clearly confuses this and Forum Appii because they are reversed geographically. Paul is said to meet some disciples sent by Peter from Rome to Tres Tabernae, a distance of 38 RM (actually 33 RM). On his final night he stayed in Aricia with the disciples, continuing into Rome the following day. There is sufficient verisimilitude in the itinerary with Acts 28 to make it plausible to later readers.

officially called *Portus Augusti Ostiensis* or simply *Portus Ostiensis* (Pliny the Elder, *Nat.* 16.76.3).[42] Claudius continued the project in AD 42 in order to forestall the famines that regularly threatened Rome (Suetonius, *Claudius* 20.1–3). Ostia was not intended to divert shipping from Puteoli; rather Claudius's "main concern was to provide security for the corn [grain] from Africa, Sicily, Sardinia, and the western provinces" (Meiggs 1973, 57). Ostia's development continued through Nero's reign. However, its vulnerability was again revealed by a storm in AD 62 when two hundred ships were destroyed while anchored in mid-harbor (Tacitus, *Ann.* 15.18.3). Although Ostia rose to new importance after the infrastructure improvements of Claudius and later Trajan, "Puteoli still remained a port of consequence" (McKay 1962, 154). A regular maritime service operated between Ostia and Puteoli, a journey of three days (D'Arms 1970, 134). For these reasons the Alexandrian grain ship upon which Paul sailed docked in Puteoli and not in Ostia.

## Sites of Puteoli

Overlooking the port was a promontory of tufa (Rione Terra) upon which stood a civic temple* remodeled from an earlier Republican temple, perhaps the Capitolium (Gialanella et al. 2022, 77–79).[43] Today it is the Cathedral of Pozzuoli (map 4). The columns, still visible, allow visitors to envision the original floorplan of the temple. It is a stunning architectural fusion of old and new. Although the Roman-era temple dates from sometime in the Augustan period (27 BC–AD 14), archaeologists have been unable to determine conclusively whether it was an Augusteum.[44] Paul had seen other examples of a Sebastion—the Greek version of the Augusteum—in cities like Pisidian Antioch, Corinth, and Caesarea Maritima. Seeing

---

42. A discussion of the later harbor at Portus, constructed near Ostia by Trajan starting in AD 103, lies beyond the scope of our study.

43. The thirteen volumes of the journal *Puteoli Studi di Storia Antica* published from 1977–1991 are a rich source of information about the ancient city. An index of the issues is available at: https://cittavulcano.wordpress.com/rivista-scientifica-pvteoli-studi-di-storia-antica-2/.

44. The study of De Gaetano (2013, 1:118–23) is extremely valuable for its summary and synthesis in English of research and publications about Puteoli. Volume 2 is a storehouse of maps, diagrams, photographs, and digital restorations of Puteoli and its harbor.

Introduction: Voyage to Italy

sanctuaries where the emperor and the imperial family were venerated was nothing new to Paul in the Greek East. If this were an Augusteum, Paul would have viewed it as a curiosity since in the Latin West Romans had not yet begun worshiping a living emperor as divine.

Facing the harbor was a *macellum*\* ("market"), although the complex has long been identified as a Temple of Serapis because a statue of this Egyptian god was discovered here. The surviving ruins with brick-faced concrete (*opus latericium*) date to the late first century AD, although surely an agora existed near the harbor since the city's founding.[45]

Stadiums for athletic games were common in the Greek East but rare in Italy. Only Puteoli, along with Neapolis and Rome, had a stadium\*. Already in the Republican period, Puteoli also had an amphitheater\* situated near a major road—the junction connecting Neapolis, Capua, and Cumae. When Tiridates I, king of Armenia, came to Italy in AD 66, Nero presented him with a costly gladiatorial exhibition there (Dio Cassius, *History* 63.3.1). A dozen arches from this smaller Republican amphitheater were found northeast of the later Flavian amphitheater\*, the third largest in the Roman world and one of the best preserved today. The glass flasks, mentioned earlier, portray both the stadium and the two amphitheaters, thus indicating that the Republican one continued in use (Ostrow 1979, 91–93, 113–19).[46] In the depiction, the Flavian amphitheater is marked with a palm to suggest its use for gladiatorial games; it is superimposed on the Republican structure whose emblem is a scourge used for animal fights.

Outside Pompeii's Porta Nocera, which led to Neapolis, Puteoli, and Cumae, a painted graffito (*CIL* 4.9983a) announced an upcoming show: "At Cumae, twenty gladiatorial pairs and their substitutes will fight on October 1, October 5, October 6, and October 7. There will be *cruciarii* [individuals to be crucified], a fight with wild beasts, and the *velarium* [awning] will be used [to shade the arena]" (Cook 2012, 71). Similar announcements

---

45. At the rear of the nearby Church of Santa Maria is a plaque commemorating Paul's visit inscribed with the Italian text of 28:13–14. For an illustrated guide in Italian to Puteoli and its surroundings, see Gentile (2011).

46. Since Ostrow did his doctoral studies on these flasks, at least four and possibly five more flasks have been found; see Popkin (2018, 430). Baiae and its coastal area are featured on the others.

advertised other shows in Herculaneum, Capua, and Puteoli. Dating probably to the year before Pompeii's destruction in AD 79, they are indicative of the public spectacles taking place in Puteoli when Paul arrived in the region.

The crucifixions mentioned in the Pompeii graffito were not exceptional. In 1959 excavations at Via Giambattista Pergolesi 146 uncovered eight *tabernae* (shops). In Taberna 5*, probably a guesthouse, numerous graffiti were found that date to the early second century AD, although the floor dates to the Neronian period. One graffito depicts the crucifixion of a person, probably a female because the name Alkimila is inscribed above the left shoulder (fig. 2). The placement of the ankles on either side of the upright stake is similar to that of the crucified man named Jehohanan ben Hagqol found in Jerusalem.[47] The numerous stripes across her back and left leg suggest she was scourged before her crucifixion. This graffito is believed to be the earliest surviving portrayal of Roman crucifixion. Paul may well have walked by this taberna while in Puteoli.

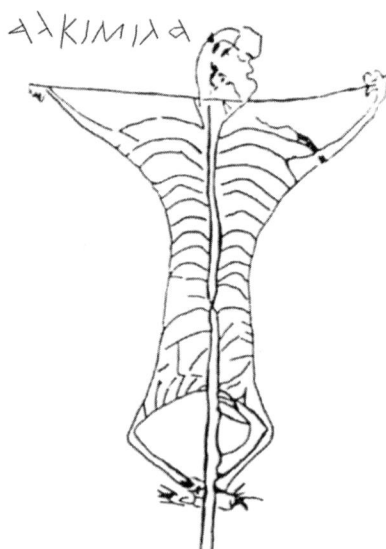

**Figure 2.** Grafitto of crucified woman

---

47. Located in the middle of the west wall, the cross measures 15.7 in. (40 cm) high and the crossbar 10.2 in. (26 cm) wide. The woman who sits on a peg (*sedile* or *cornu*) is 13.8 in. (35 cm) tall; see Cook (2012, 93–94).

A corpse inscription from Puteoli mentions that it was an Augustan colony in which "local enforcement of law and order required special provision, harbor towns being prone to unrest and vulnerable to crime" (Aubert 2005, 141).[48] The civic decree deals specifically with morticians who could be tasked by slave owners with the torture or execution of slaves either by crucifixion or by hanging on a fork. The colony also punished criminals of free status with execution. It was the responsibility of the executioner to provide nails free of charge for the crucifixion. Since a woman was rarely crucified, who was this person with the Semitic name Alkimila? Perhaps she was a slave who committed crimes against her master. Or was she an early Christian martyred in a local amphitheater? We can only speculate about her actual identity.

## Paul's Stay in Puteoli

After their arrival in Puteoli, the party took a weeklong break (28:14), unusual since they could have arrived in Rome within that time. If a Jewish community existed in a city, Paul would customarily visit the synagogue first (cf. 13:14; 14:1; 17:4; 18:1; 19:8). Such a community is known to have existed in Puteoli because of a strange tale told by Josephus (*Jewish War* 2.101–104). A young Jewish man in Sidon pretended to be Alexander, the slain son of Herod the Great. Resembling Alexander, the imposter claimed to have been kidnapped instead. In 4 BC he traveled to Rome seeking official recognition and deceiving Jewish communities at ports along the way. When he landed at Puteoli, the Jews there welcomed him and lavished him with presents. A report went out that he was going to Rome, undoubtedly on the VA, and "the whole multitude of the Jews that were there went out to meet him, ascribing it to divine providence that he had so unexpectedly escaped, and being very joyful on account of his mother's family. And when he was come, he was carried in a royal litter through the streets" (Josephus, *Antiquities* 17.330, trans. Whiston).[49]

---

48. Our discussion is drawn from column II, lines 3–14 of the inscription given in Aubert (2005, 144).

49. When Augustus heard about the arrival of "Alexander" in Rome, he was immediately suspicious. Interrogating the young man, he uncovered the deception. Sparing the life of the spurious

Paul was similarly greeted outside Rome by a delegation of Christians but under very different circumstances.

The Christian "brothers and sisters" (ἀδελφοί, *adelphoi*) that Paul found in Puteoli were undoubtedly both Jewish and gentile. These believers "implored" Paul and his party to stay with them. Most translations say "invite," but the Greek word παρακαλέω (*parakaleō*) suggests a strong entreaty.[50] Having the renowned apostle with them, they did not want to let him get away so soon. But why did Julius allow Paul to stay seven days in Puteoli? Various reasons have been advanced. James Dunn (1996, 377) has suggested that Julius left a guard with Paul while he himself took the other prisoners to Rome. Since the party had traveled this far together, it is unlikely that Julius would now leave his noteworthy charge behind. C. K. Barrett (1998, 1230) proposed that this period was needed to unload and load the ship again. However, since Paul's party had now disembarked, why would they have any further dealings with the ship? William M. Ramsay (1910, 315) suggested that the travelers needed to rest before undertaking the land journey to Rome since "the voyage on an ancient ship was rather trying at the best of times ... people slept hard and fared poorly." Yet the group had only spent a week on board ship after enjoying three months of rest in Malta. F. F. Bruce (1990, 535) postulated that Julius needed this time to secure supplies and transportation to Rome or perhaps to conduct business in the city in his capacity as *frumentarius*.

Julius had undoubtedly received a diploma from Festus before he left Caesarea so needed no further authorizations (cf. Pliny the Younger, *Epistles* 10.64). Is it possible that his diploma had been lost in the shipwreck and that this week was spent in obtaining a new one from Rome? Such a diploma would also have entitled him to receive the requisite transport, accommodations, and services needed throughout the journey. While the organized system of official travel, usually called the *cursus publicus*, is unmentioned

---

Alexander, Caesar instead conscripted him to a galley to work as a rower (Josephus, *Antiquities* 17.332–338).

50. Metzger (1975, 501) notes that later scribes, perhaps uncomfortable with the implication that the prisoners had been invited as if free to choose, modified the text to "replace the infinitive with a participle (ἐπιμείναντες [*epimeinantes*] or μείναντες [*meinantes*])." This permitted a meaning, "we were comforted (or consoled, or encouraged), staying with them for seven days." But again, "comforted" or "consoled" fails to convey the urgency of the invitation.

Introduction: Voyage to Italy

in sources until the late third century AD, Anne Kolb (2016, 4) observes: "Augustus created a system of state transport primarily to facilitate communication between the emperor and the administrative and military officials over the Empire, as well as for travel and transport on government business." This system was called *vehiculatio* in Latin and ἀγγᾰρεία (*angareia*) in Greek (cf. Millar 2004, 25). During the Imperial period official travelers did have the right to requisition vehicles, animals, and guides from local communities in Italy and the provinces (Mitchell 1976, 106). Since the journey to Rome was short, it is likely that Julius walked there with his party. Nevertheless, he probably requisitioned a pack animal or two to be led by his servant, which would carry their clothing, water, and supplies.

Part of the answer might also be that Julius did it as a favor to Paul who wished to spend time teaching and encouraging the local Christians. While a free man, Paul had made similar seven-day visits to Christians at the port cities of Troas and Tyre (20:6; 21:4). We (Thompson and Wilson 2016, 273) have argued that Paul on an earlier visit to Troas missed the weekly Christian assembly so decided to stay an additional seven days to meet with them the following Sunday evening. No matter what day the ship had arrived, a seven-day stay in Puteoli would have allowed Paul to attend the Sunday gathering of Christians. It is possible that Julius did require a few days to make arrangements but then agreed to stay a few days longer out of kindness toward the apostle. It has been suggested that such kindness indicated that Julius had either become a believer or at least an inquirer during his time with Paul. It is also possible that Julius, seeing Paul's reception by the believers, was merely showing deference to a man of perceived superior social status. Paul would soon be standing in front of important officials in Rome, and Julius did not wish any complaints about his treatment of the prisoners or reminders of the misjudgment that led to the shipwreck.[51]

Paul certainly used his time in Puteoli productively. A message was sent to Rome to inform the church there of his arrival in Italy. This becomes evident later when two groups of Roman Christians meet Paul outside of Rome (28:15). Paul's stay concludes with a surprising announcement: "In

---

51. For a discussion of these and other possible reasons for the delay, see Keener (2015, 3704–6).

this way we came to Rome" (28:14). Of course, Paul and his friends had not yet arrived in the imperial city. Two verses later Luke adds, "And when we arrived in Rome, Paul was allowed to live by himself." Thus Ramsay (1895, 346) observes: "The double expression of arrival at Rome in vv. 14 and 16 is remarkable."[52] Several explanations have been offered for this seeming duplication. Ramsay (1895, 347) suggested that the first mention refers to Rome's entire territory, the *Ager Romanus*, while the second refers to the walls of Rome itself. Kirsopp Lake and Henry Cadbury noted, however, that this is unlikely since verse 15 says that the believers came "from there" (κἀκεῖθεν [*kakeithen*]) to meet Paul, and thus verse 14 "must refer to τὴν Ῥώμην [*tēn Rōmēn*]" (Lake and Cadbury 1933, 345). Ray Laurence (1999, 26) seeks to catch Luke's sense by suggesting that by disembarking in Puteoli, a visitor like Paul "arrived at a version of Rome in setting foot in Italy. ... Rome and Italy became synonymous. After all, *tota Italia* by the mid-first century (BC) was populated by Roman citizens and in effect was Rome as much as the capital city itself." Also, around 7 BC Augustus divided Italy into eleven *regiones* (Pliny the Elder, *Nat.* 3.6). *Regio I* comprised Rome itself and all of Latium and Campania including Puteoli.[53] Thus, to arrive at Puteoli could already be considered arriving at Rome, his divinely appointed destination (19:21; 23:11).

However, a literary explanation for this declaration in verse 14 may also be advanced. Here Luke uses an arrival formula similar to other departure-arrival announcements in Acts.[54] The οὕτως (*houtōs*) is anticipatory, as in 27:44. Having just described the journey from Malta to Puteoli, Luke now ends with this announcement that fulfills the prophetic word given to Paul in 23:11: "you must also testify in Rome." The sense of the verse then is: "The following were the circumstances of our arriving in Rome, the goal of our journey" (Mecham 1973, 173).

---

52. Barrett (1998, 1230) also notes that verse 14 seems "at first sight to constitute the climax of the book; but in fact the travelers did not reach their destination till v. 16." Similarly, Witherington (1998, 786) writes: 'The second half of v. 14 has puzzled many scholars, especially in view of the fact that v. 16 seems to repeat the same information."

53. For a discussion of Latium within the ecology of the Mediterranean region, see Holden and Purcell (2000, 59–64). Map no. 4 on page 62 shows the physical structure of Latium.

54. For a discussion of this departure-arrival formula, see Wilson (2022a, 1–7).

Introduction: Voyage to Italy 27

| Day | Itinerary | Overnight | Distance | Est. Time |
|---|---|---|---|---|
| 1 | Puteoli to Capua | Capua | 20 mi. (32 km) | 8+ hours |
| 2 | Capua to Sinuessa | Sinuessa | 23 mi. (37 km) | 9+ hours |
| 3 | Sinuessa to Itri | Itri | 22 mi. (35 km) | 9+ hours |
| 4 | Itri to Tarracina | Tarracina | 18 mi. (30 km) | 7.5+ hours |
| 5 | Tarracina to Forum Appii | Forum Appii | 18 mi. (30 km) | 7.5+ hours |
| 6 | Forum Appii to Aricia | Aricia | 25 mi. (40 km) | 10+ hours |
| 7 | Aricia to Rome | Rome | 15 mi. (24 km) | 6+ hours |

**Figure 3.** Paul's seven-day itinerary

How many days did it take for Paul and his group to reach Rome? Procopius (*Wars* 5.14.6) observed that an unencumbered person could travel from Capua to Rome in five days. But Paul and his fellow prisoners were certainly encumbered, so the journey would take some additional time. Adding a day from Puteoli, the journey would total six days long. Others have suggested up to ten days.[55] After much thought, we propose that Paul's journey took seven days and thus have organized the following chapters around that hypothesis. This projection is based on previous research, which included walking from Troas to Assos along Paul's probable route (Thompson and Wilson 2016, 280). An ancient source discussing travel times is Gaius (*On the Provincial Edict* 1) quoted in Justinian (*Digest* 2.11.1). He states that the time allowed for a party to travel to a court appearance was based on a travel day of 20,000 paces, or 20 Roman miles (henceforth RM), the equivalent of 18.3 mi. (29.6 km).[56] A reasonable walking speed, depending on terrain, would be 2–2.5 mph (3–4 kph). Pack animals would not slow movement since they traveled at the same speed as humans. A week after arriving in Puteoli, Paul and his party were ready to begin their seven-day journey of 153 RM (141 mi./226 km) to Rome where the apostle would present himself for trial before the imperial court of Nero.

---

55. For five days see Barrett (1998, 1230); and Bock (2007, 747); for ten days see Schnabel (2012, 1055).

56. This distance is similar to that projected for travel on the Royal Road during the Persian period: 150 stadia a day (Herodotus, *Histories* 5.53). Since a stadion equals 609 ft. (185.6 m), the daily distance would be 17.3 mi. (27.8 km).

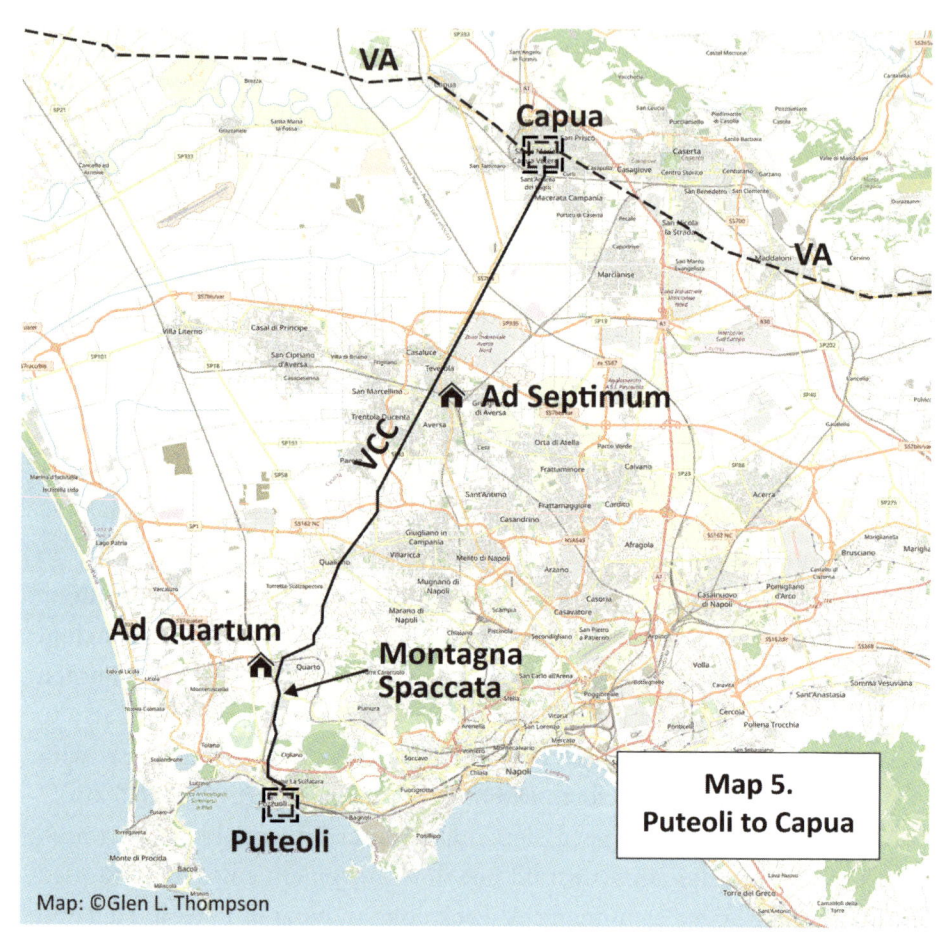

DAY 1

# Puteoli to Capua

Paul made the final part of his journey into Rome along the VA, for Luke in 28:15 specifically mentions two stations along the route—Forum Appii (Forum of Appius) and Tres Tabernae (Three Taverns).[1] But the VA passed some 21.5 RM (20 mi./32 km) north of Puteoli on its way from Rome to the southeastern coast of Italy. So how did Paul and his party get from Puteoli to the VA? First-century travelers could have continued by sea. It was feasible to sail farther up the coast to a harbor along the VA—either 35 mi. (55 km) to Sinuessa, 40 mi. (65 km) to Minturnae, or even 70 mi. (110 km) to Tarracina. The other option was to travel by land. Here they had two choices—a direct coastal road 26 mi. (42 km) long via Cumae that joined the VA at Sinuessa or an inland road that ran 20 mi. (32 km) northeast from Puteoli to join the VA at Capua. Since Capua was 22 mi. (35 km) east of Sinuessa, the total distance traveled on the inland route was 42 mi. (68 km). So 16 mi. (26 km) could be saved by taking the coastal route to Sinuessa. As there is no indication that Paul's party boarded a ship again, we are left with the two options by road.[2]

---

1. Meijer (2000, 188) likewise observes that Paul's company chose to travel overland on the VA. However, his map of the journey on page 54 fails to trace the route of the VA and omits Forum Appii and Tres Tabernae.

2. Luke normally lists the ports for Paul's sea voyages in detail, as in Acts 27, so the argument from silence here carries some weight.

## The Coastal Route in the First Century

As mentioned in the preceding chapter, the western end of the Bay of Naples was the site not only of Puteoli but also of the famous resort towns of Baiae and Misenum. Nearby was the ancient Greek city of Cumae, a mere 4.3 mi. (7 km) northwest of Puteoli and home of the famous Sibyl.[3] As a result, one would expect a well-traveled road directly up the coast through the cities of Liternum and Volturnum to the VA at Sinuessa. Such a journey might be covered on foot in a single long day—if the road had been good. Beyond Cumae, however, the road northward presented major problems. This section of coastline contained both extensive marshes and sandy soil, and the crossing of numerous streams and inlets was required. The result was a meandering, treacherous road that caused travelers to move at a snail's pace.[4] This made the journey take even longer than the distance listed in the late–third- or early–fourth-century Antonine Itinerary.[5]

According to Plutarch (*Caesar* 58.8–10), Julius Caesar had already planned to confront this problem—not by building a better road but by constructing a canal big enough for freighters. It would run just inland from the coast and extend not just to Sinuessa but all the way to the Tiber River west of Rome. The canal would not only make for quicker and safer travel but would also drain the swamps that plagued the area, thus creating new agricultural land for grain production. At the same time, it would encourage the repopulating of a large rural area (Suetonius, *Julius Caesar* 44.3).[6]

---

3. In the early Christian document, the Shepherd of Hermas, Hermas has visions while traveling to Cumae from Rome (1.3; 5.1). In a night vision he sees an elderly woman whom he thinks is the Sibyl but whom the interpreter explains is the church instead (8.1). The Campanian Road (τῇ ὁδῷ τῇ Καμπανῇ [tē hodō tē Kampanē]), called a public road (ἀπὸ τῆς ὁδοῦ τῆς δημοσίας [apo tēs hodou tēs dēmosias]; 22.2), was undoubtedly the coastal road—the Via Domitiana (Lookadoo 2021, 62).

4. On roads in this area before the construction of the Via Domitiana, see especially Cascella (2017, 45–48).

5. The Antonine Itinerary gives the following distances for the Via Domitiana: 24 RM from Sinuessa to Liternum, 6 RM farther to Cumae, then 3 RM into Puteoli. The 24, however, must be a mistake for 19 (most likely XXIIII for XVIIII), and therefore the correct total distance would be 28 RM (26 mi./41.8 km).

6. Arata (2014, §37) further notes that the imperial government was trying to reinvigorate grain production in Italy at a time when viticulture had become dominant.

Although never brought to fruition due to Caesar's assassination, the idea was revived and expanded nearly a century later by Nero. Suetonius (*Nero* 31.3–4) says that Nero's plan was to build a canal to connect Ostia with Lake Avernus west of Puteoli, one "wide enough to allow two *quinqueremes* to pass each other" (i.e., about 200 ft./60 m wide). The two main sections would be at each end—in the north from Ostia across the Pontine Marshes to Cape Circeo (c. 60 mi./95 km) and in the south from Minturnae or Sinuessa to Lake Avernus (c. 22 mi./35 km). The project was to be a smaller version of the Intracoastal Waterway that runs inland along the Atlantic and Gulf coasts of the United States.

Many scholars have seen this as just another of Nero's imaginative, megalomaniac, and impractical pipedreams. Beginning in the 1990s, however, aerial and surface surveys in the two areas just mentioned detected evidence that the project had apparently been started, although never completed, in antiquity (Arata 2014, §1).[7] While it has been difficult to give precise dates (causing the names of Augustus, Nero, and Trajan to be associated with these remains), evidence of ancient construction has been found between Lake Complice and the Torre Paola (at Cape Circeo, west of Tarracina), between Volturno and Cumae, and between Cumae and Baiae's Lago al Fusaro.[8] The project, begun about AD 65, ended with the emperor's death in 68.

Only in the time of Domitian (AD 81–96) were sufficient funds and effort expended to construct a well-paved road along the coast (Dio Cassius 67.14.1). A poem of 163 lines by the Roman poet Statius praised the new Via Domitiana, named for its builder. At least in places, the route seems to have run atop the eastern bank of the uncompleted *fossa* of Nero, using the earth excavated for the canal as its own foundation. A modern highway, following much of the ancient route, still bears the same name.

---

7. Pliny the Elder (*Nat.* 14.8) says that the famous Caecubum wine was grown in the plain of Fondi but had disappeared due to the destruction of the vineyard during the construction work on Nero's canal between Ostia and the Gulf of Naples. This is ancient evidence that considerable construction did take place before the project was abandoned.

8. The so-called Fossa del Castagno (40.830275, 14.062824).

Statius (*Silvae* 4.3) presents a wealth of detail not only about Domitian's new road, but also about the road it replaced.[9] He says it was constructed because the emperor sympathized with "the people's weary travels and the plains that held up every journey," and so he was "removing the long detours and stabilizing the heavy sand with a new dumping of earth" (lines 20–23). Before Domitian's improvements, travel was "sluggish" at best; travelers rode precariously on two-wheeled carts "while the spiteful earth sucked down its wheels" making riders seasick (lines 27–31). At other times the vehicles spun their wheels in the sandy roadbed, while the horses wore themselves out as they crept along (lines 32–35). However, the new road facilitated travel in two hours what had previously taken an entire day (lines 36–37).

While Statius's panegyric to the emperor is rife with hyperbole—he even claims that one can get from Rome to the Bay of Naples in a single day on the new road (lines 112–113)[10]—the reputation of the previous road emerges loud and clear. If Julius had decided to follow the coast, the track would have been this slow and swampy secondary road. As a result, the centurion almost certainly did not choose the shorter coastal route but took his prisoners along the well-paved, inland route through Capua.[11]

## Via Consularis Capuam Puteolis

The oldest map depicting the Roman road system, known as the Peutinger Map or Peutinger Table (see fig. 14), does not show a road connecting Puteoli and Capua. However, the number XXI appears between the

---

9. Bekker-Nielsen (2013, 5853) notes its importance: "No Roman technical treatises on road construction have been preserved, and the only extant literary description of Roman roadbuilding is found in Statius' *Silvae*."

10. The new road from Sinuessa to Puteoli allowed the journey to be comfortably traveled in a day. The journey from Rome, however, was about 125 mi. (200 km), possible only for a mounted imperial messenger.

11. An inscription (*CIL* 10.6824 = *ILS* 280) that mentions a renovation by Nerva causes Kolb (2015, 651) to speculate that "the Via Appia seems to have been only partially paved on the first stretch of 220 km from Rome to Capua." If the Via Domitiana was already paved by the end of the first century AD, surely the more traveled VA between Capua and Rome would also have been.

Day 1: Puteoli to Capua

two cities to indicate the distance in RM.[12] We will follow the custom of referring to the road connecting these two cities as the Via Campana Consularis (abbreviated VCC), although more properly it is the Via Consularis Capuam Puteolis—the "consular road from Capua to Puteoli." While there is no evidence that this name was used in antiquity, it does accurately suggest that its construction in the Republican period was overseen by an unnamed man of consular rank.[13] The size and construction techniques of the ancient road are known from remains excavated at *ad Septimum*. This confirms that it was the main road and therefore certainly built and maintained under consular supervision.[14]

By studying old maps, aerial photographs revealing ancient centuriation (land divisions resulting from Roman survey work), archaeological finds, and some road remains, much of the path of the VCC can be reconstructed confidently. Calculating the distance from Puteoli's Porta Campana to the southern gate of Capua, the reconstructed route was almost 21 RM (19.3 mi./31 km), the exact length given on the Peutinger Map.[15] As the crow flies, the distance was 1 mi. (1.6 km) shorter, and normally Roman roads took the shortest path. However, in the area immediately north of Puteoli as well as in several other places, the VCC followed an unusually circuitous route as it was forced to thread its way between protuberances caused by the extensive volcanic activity around the Bay of Naples. Since the route is over quite level terrain, the trip could be made in a single day.[16]

---

12. See Talbert (2010, 86–122) for the Peutinger Map; the section between Puteoli and Capua is shown in fig. 14.

13. Ashby (1927, 35–36) notes that while censors such as Appius Claudius were in charge of early road-building projects, they often delegated the work in more distant parts of Italy to men of consular rank.

14. However, neither Wiseman (1970, 132, fig. 2) nor Owens (2012, 5858, fig. 1) shows any Republican roads running south from Capua to the Bay of Naples, either to Puteoli or to Neapolis.

15. Ashby (1927, 38) also notes that mileage for the major roads was calculated from the gate where the road left Rome. The mileage for other main roads may also have been measured from city gate to city gate.

16. The first section of the ancient route was preserved quite nicely as late as the early nineteenth century, as can be seen in the 1793 map of Giovanni Rizzi-Zannoni, *Topografia dell'Agro Napoletano con le sue adjacenze* (online at: https://davidrumsey.georeferencer.com/maps/odca96ab-cbd7-4569-bbcd-d96f9556d44c/view).

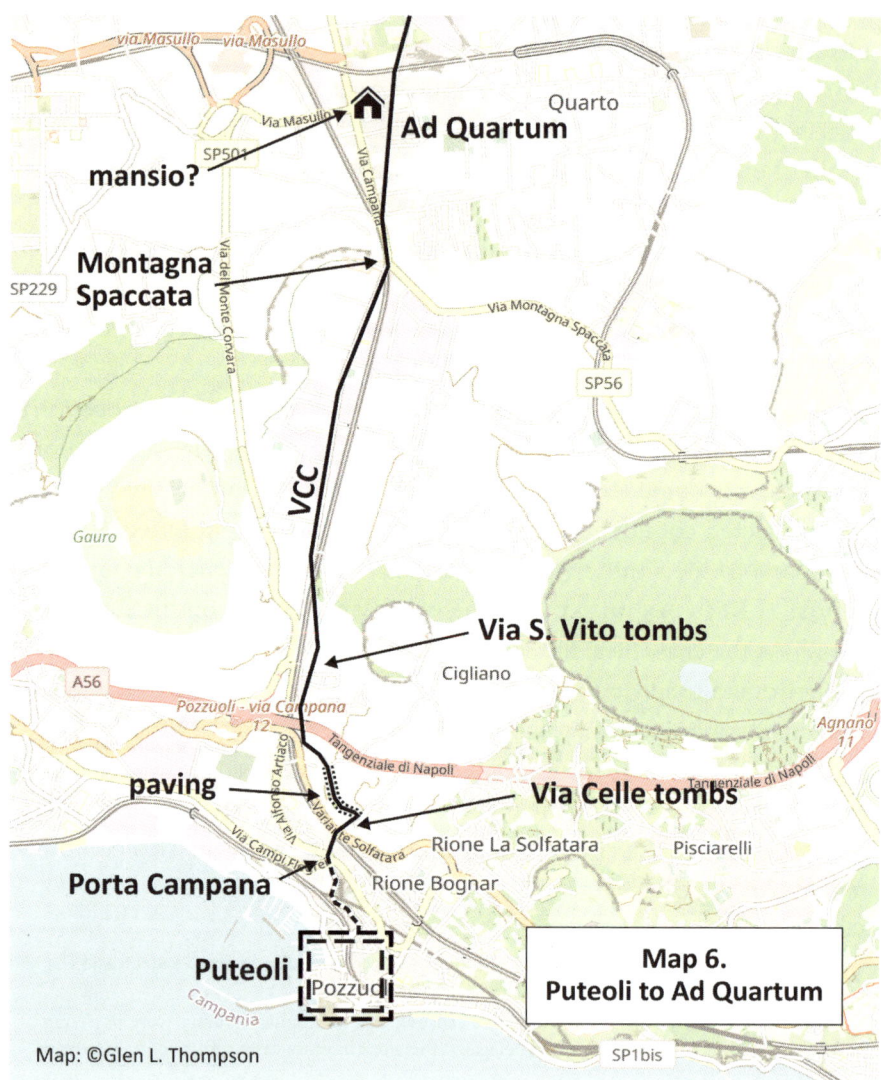

Map 6. Puteoli to Ad Quartum

## Porta Campana through the Via Celle

After a week in Puteoli, Julius and his soldiers readied Paul and his companions along with the other prisoners for travel overland to Rome. Early in the morning the group moved toward the northwestern city gate—the Porta Campana. There, just inside the gate, two roads converged, one

Day 1: Puteoli to Capua

coming directly from the harbor area (under Via Giovanni Pergolesi) and the other from the ancient amphitheaters (beneath Corso Nicola Terracciano). A few stones from the gate complex* have been preserved on the north side of Piazza Francesco Capomazza.

Porta Campana was one of the busiest gates in Italy since it served not only travelers going north to Capua but also those heading west to Cumae and south to Baiae and Misenum (Emmerson 2020, 155). Once outside the gate, Paul's group approached this second intersection. Just 330 ft. (100 m) along the Cumae/Baiae road, on the left side of the modern Via Luciano, archaeologists have uncovered a structure from the Augustan age about 58 ft. (18 m) long. Its portico and rooms, all aligned with the road, may have been part of a lodging for travelers (*statio*).[17] Tsao Cevoli and Nicola Melluzis (2015, 36–37) have further hypothesized that this complex was associated with some inscriptions discovered nearby that mention visitors from the Syrian city of Tyre. Thus, the remains have been referred to as the *statio* of the Tyrians*. If this was indeed a haunt for Syrians, perhaps Paul's party initially lodged here upon arriving in Puteoli, and it was from here that Paul made connections with the Christian community.

The second road turned to the northeast toward Capua, following the route of the current Via Celle. Paul's group took this road after leaving the city. Like other Roman cities, the major roads outside the walls of Puteoli were lined with rows of tombs along both sides. Since Roman law did not permit burials within a city's walls, the elite vied to obtain prime land close to the city for their family tombs and then constructed elaborate structures to honor their dead and display their wealth and status. Attesting to the prosperity of their inhabitants, the massive tombs outside Puteoli not only "stood along some of the busiest thoroughfares in the Roman world" but were "rivaled in size and grandeur only by the most outstanding funerary monuments of Rome itself" (Emmerson 2020, 153, 152). Today two surviving rows of tombs still assist us in reconstructing the path of the VCC north of Puteoli.

---

17. A later edict of Hadrian (SEG 55, 744 = AE 2005, 1348) may reflect why such a *statio* existed. Kolb (2016, 5) notes that "travellers were not supposed to rest in the inns inside the city, since they were not actually situated on the via publica. Instead, they were to use the way stations outside the city which were specially intended for use by travellers on official business. Having them stay in the city seems to have offered more opportunities for abuse."

**Figure 4.** Via Celle tombs

Every tomb has disappeared along the first section of the Via Celle. But where it emerges from the underpass beneath the railway and the expressway, travelers today can still see an unbroken row of fourteen tombs* along the right side for almost 500 ft. (150 m; fig. 4). Only one tomb, slightly hidden by modern buildings, remains of a similar row that once lined the left side. Although the remaining tombs have long since been stripped of their decorated exteriors of marble or painted stucco, the remains are still impressive. They date from the mid-first century BC to the mid-second century AD, so Paul passed many of them as he left Puteoli.[18]

At the northern end of these tombs, a hill rises directly ahead. The road split at this point. The road to the east—the Via Antiniana—took ancient travelers toward Neapolis. It passed through the Campi Flegrei, the volcanic area with its sulfurous fumes that the ancients thought to be the entrance to the underworld. This road and the one to Cumae featured

---

18. A detailed description of each of the Via Celle tombs is found in Amalfitano, Camodeca, and Medri (1990, 132–47). A plan of the Via Celle necropolis is found in Emmerson (2020, 157, fig. 5.21).

*Day 1: Puteoli to Capua*　　　　　　　　　　　　　　　　　　　37

tunnels engineered through the volcanic ridges with tracks wide enough for teams to pass and lit by window shafts cut into the rock (Seneca, *Letters* 57:1–2; Strabo, *Geogr.* 5.4.7).[19] Paul, however, took the turn to the west.

**Figure 5.** VCC paving

---

19. The tunnel between Puteoli and Neapolis (modern Crypta Neapolitana) was about 2297 ft. (700 m) long while that to Cumae (modern Grotta di Cocceio) was 3281 ft. (1000 m) long. Sherwood et al. (2020, 516) note that Seneca and Strabo present conflicting accounts. But "the archaeological evidence suggests that Strabo has confused his tunnels and is actually describing the tunnel at Cumae rather than the one at Puteoli [Neapolis]."

## Via Celle to Ad Quartum

Here the VCC traversed steep embankments on both sides as it wound in an arc northward over the next mile (1.6 km), avoiding the higher ground around the Cigliano crater. That this is the correct path is confirmed by the ancient paving* still visible for the first 1300 ft. (400 m; fig. 5)! After this section, the modern Via Celle becomes Via Vecchia Campana; shortly after, its arc straightens to parallel the railway line running just to its west. During railroad construction in the early twentieth century, the ancient VCC roadbed became visible at this point, confirming it lay beneath the modern road. Its route then veered slightly northeast under Via San Vito. About 800 ft. (250 m) farther, the second row of surviving tombs*, 575 ft. (175 m) long, line the right side of the road. This group is now protected by modern canopies. Although farther from the city, several of the San Vito tombs are still very elaborate. Some existed when Paul passed, although others were built slightly later. At least one of these tombs later became the resting place for early Christians. Dated to the third century, this tomb* is located on the left side behind the small seventeenth-century church of San Vito. It is now preserved beneath a glass floor in the Villa Elvira restaurant.[20]

The VCC veered left where the road of surviving tombs ends and passed west of a final circular monumental tomb*. This tomb has served as a landmark across the centuries. An etching from 1775 by Domenico Cunego shows workers excavating one of the San Vito tombs with the circular tomb in the background (fig. 6). The Norwegian painter Johan Christian Dahl has also left us a wonderfully impressionistic image of the tomb's appearance in 1820.[21] After continuing straight another 1600 ft. (485 m) and passing over the railroad tracks, the VCC veered northeasterly under today's Via Campana. The numerous ruins dotting both sides of the road confirm that this is still the path of the ancient road.[22] About 1000 ft. (300 m) after

---

20. Little has been published on the San Vito tombs, but the British Museum has several decorative elements from the most elaborate tomb; see Ling (1970, 153–82).

21. Now in New York's Metropolitan Museum (https://www.metmuseum.org/art/collection/search/440331).

22. That the ancient road joined Via Campana at approximately 40.85100, 14.11905 is shown by the fact that no Roman remains exist farther south along the modern road. The ruins remaining* begin about 330 ft. (100 m) to the north and stretch to Montagna Spaccata.

Day 1: Puteoli to Capua

joining the modern road, the remains of an ancient suburban villa*, probably belonging to a member of the *gens Bovi*, was excavated on the right and is now preserved under a protective roof (Cevoli and Meluziis 2015, 35–40).

**Figure 6.** Photograph and etching of tomb on Via S. Vito. A 1775 etching by Domenic Cunego of a tomb excavation shows this tomb in the background.

For almost 1 mi. (1.55 km) the party continued across the plain, actually the bottom of one of the many craters in the area. Upon reaching the northern crater wall, the road bends slightly to the left at a place known today as Montagna Spaccata* ("Split Mountain"). Here, over a length of 950 ft. (290 m), the Roman engineers made a vertical cut 23 ft. (7 m) wide and 164 ft. (50 m) down through the crater wall to allow the road to pass on a level path (fig. 7). To prevent rockslides, they then reinforced the walls with the diamond-patterned brickwork known as opus reticulatum. This type of construction was popular from the first century BC through much of the first century AD, especially during the Julio-Claudian era. It is visible on many tombs and structures mentioned in this chapter, making its presence likely in Paul's day. Today the VCC remains the only road through the crater toward the north. Though it may seem narrow to modern motorists, the cut was an impressive engineering feat of adequate width when Paul passed through it.

**Figure 7.** Montagna Spaccata

# Day 1: Puteoli to Capua

After emerging into the plain again, the VCC veered northwest, eventually following the path of the modern Via Consolare Campana through modern Quarto. The path of the VCC for the first 1150 ft. (350 m) after the mountain cut is uncertain. It may have followed the modern road for up to 820 ft. (250 m) where the modern VCC turns to the right. Or it may have immediately veered to the right and run beneath the modern Via Viticella. It appears, however, that the modern VCC indicates the ancient route from the point where it straightens in an almost due northerly direction until it reaches Corso Italia.

Near that point there was also an ancient intersection. Here the party found one of the rest stops where government couriers could change horses or travelers might get food and lodging. Quarto, the modern name for the town, preserves the name of the ancient rest stop—*Ad Quartum* ("at the fourth mile[stone]").[23] Remarkably, an ancient building with walls of *opus reticulatum* still survives which may well be part of that *mansio*\* (fig. 8). It is situated about 165 ft. (50 m) southwest of the road junction and has been incorporated into a modern structure. A side street (*diverticulum*) with ancient paving crosses a small bridge\* and leads from the road to the ancient edifice. Paul's party may well have made a brief stop here before continuing on their way.

---

23. The area's archaeological remains are numerous and have been helpfully catalogued in De Carlo (2009, 48–90).

**Figure 8.** *Mansio* (?) at *Ad Quartum*

## Ad Quartum to Ad Septimum

Just as *ad Quartum* marked 4 mi. (6.4 km) along the road from Puteoli, *ad Septimum* marked 7 mi. (11.3 km) from Capua. There were 10 RM between these two stopping places, and much of this stretch of the VCC is difficult to detect today (map 6). From the *mansio* at *ad Quartum*, the road continued northeast another 3.1 mi. (5 km) to pass through modern Qualiano. Only 0.62 mi. (1 km) of this stretch can be distinguished with some certainty today. From Corso Italiano the ancient VCC seems to lie roughly beneath the modern Via Scarlatti, then below the Via Casalanno until it curves eastward. At that point[24] the VCC probably continued northeast under the current farm road for another 2133 ft. (650 m), then straight across the current field for 600 ft. (180 m).

---

24. About 40.88677, 14.13304.

Day 1: Puteoli to Capua 43

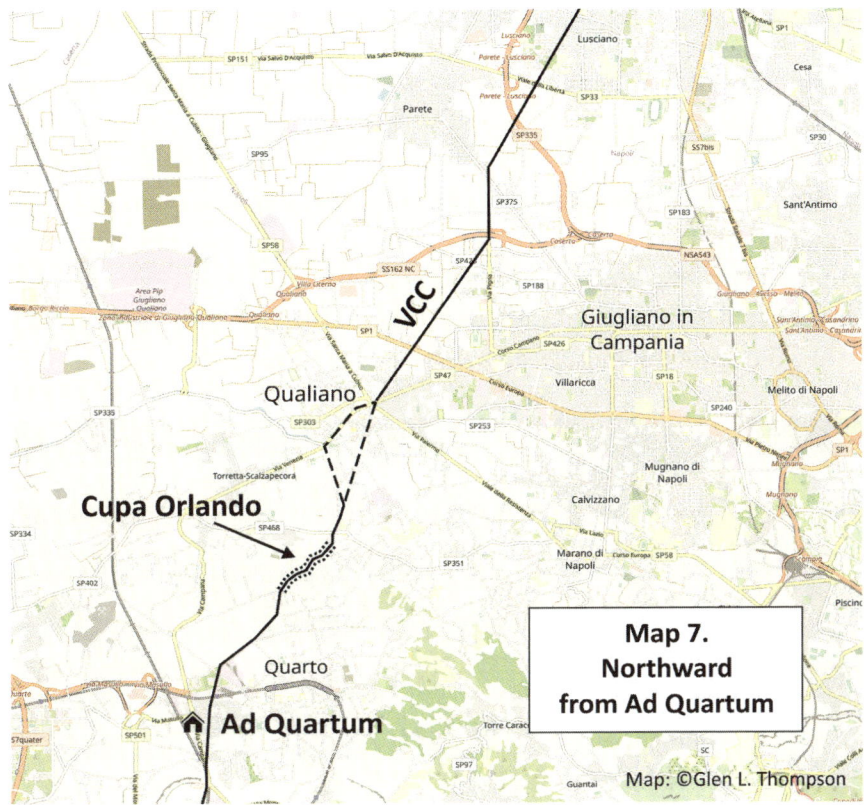

Map 7. Northward from Ad Quartum

There, about 1.3 mi. (2.1 km) northwest of Quarto, is a narrow lane, today called Cupa Orlando*, which snakes between high ground on both sides (fig. 9). Vestiges of *opus reticulatum*, curbing, and even paving can be seen along its 0.7 mi. (1.15 km) length. This narrow ravine, ranging from 10 to 20 ft. (3–7 m) wide and often with precipices of 33 ft. (10 m) on both sides, most likely was used as a passage already in pre-Roman times and incorporated into the later VCC. From the northern end of Cupa Orlando the road must have continued largely in a northerly path for another 1.5 mi. (2.4 km) to the center of modern Qualiano.

The path of the VCC is most uncertain at this point, and maps such as Rizzi-Zannoni's, mentioned earlier, make it clear that the road had disappeared centuries earlier. It apparently ran beneath the current Via San Rocco and then the current VCC for the first 2460 ft. (750 m). But its route from that point[25] is uncertain. It may have turned northeastward beginning under the current Strada Vicinale and then continued straight into Qualiano. Others have suggested that it turned northward and followed current tree lines to the southwest edge of Qualiano where it crossed the current Ponte di Surriento into the city. Our examination around the bridge (today a viaduct) was unsuccessful in discerning evidence of an ancient structure. These two alternatives are shown on map 7. In either case the route becomes clear again in central Qualiano.

**Figure 9.** Cupa Orlando

From the center of Qualiano*, at the intersection of Corso Campano and Via Antica Consolare Campana, the ancient VCC continued northeast under its modern namesake and across fields and countryside for

---

25. About 40.90660, 14.14725.

*Day 1: Puteoli to Capua*

some 5.2 mi. (8.35 km). At first the VCC follows the modern Via Antica Consolare Campana for 0.62 mi. (1 km) until it ends at the SP1. The ancient road apparently continued on the other side for another 1.25 mi. (2 km) as indicated by dirt tracks and tree lines today until it intersects with the present Prolungamento Via Pigna. It then seems to have turned due north following that road and a tree line after its end for a total of 0.7 mi. (1.15 km) before it disappears (40.95180, 14.17450). It then turns northeast across a field for 984 ft. (300 m) before following the course of a dirt road called Via Campana, then a series of paved roads—Via Guglielmo Marconi, Via Fiume, Via della Resistenza, Via Cottolengo, Via Enrico Altavilla, and Via San Lorenzo in Aversa. However, there are short breaks between some of these where no modern connecting road exists. It then turned slightly more to the east and ran almost perfectly straight for 10.33 RM (9.5 mi./15.3 km) to the south side of ancient Capua.

Although much of this route is no longer discernable under the modern street plan, after 2.67 mi. (4.3 km) a straight section passed in front of the abbey church of San Lorenzo ad Septimum*. The modern road bends a bit northward just to the south while the ancient road continued straight under the Benedictine monastery, then passed some 490 ft. (150 m) in front of the church's main entrance.[26] *Ad Septimum* was the name of a *statio* along the VCC. Excavations in the 1980s under the church courtyard uncovered a paved section of the VCC approximately 26 ft. (8 m) wide (fig. 10).

---

26. Many of the abbey buildings now house the Department of Architecture and Industrial Design of the University of Campania "Luigi Vanvitelli."

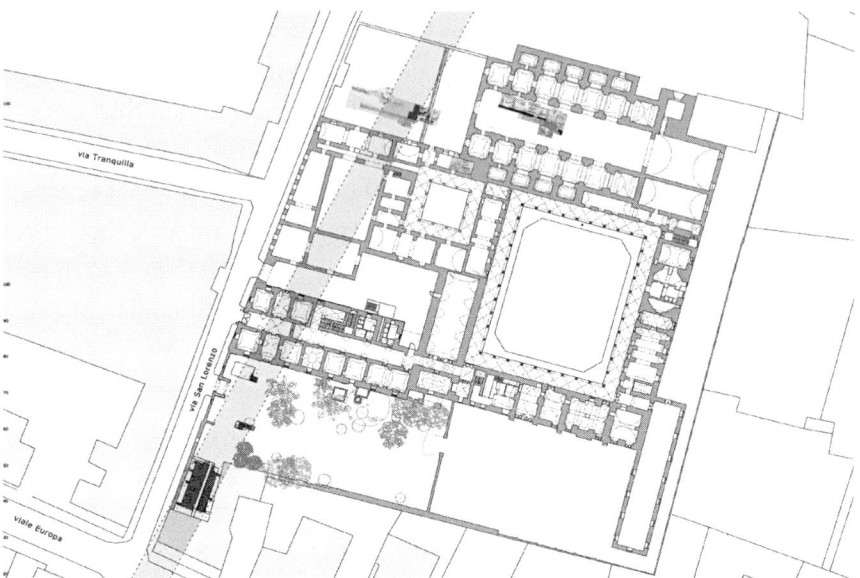

**Figure 10.** VCC at S. Lorenzo ad Septimum. The shaded area indicates the VCC's path through the monastery's courtyard. (Pasquale Argenziano [Melillo Faenza, Jacazzi, and Argenziano 2009, 213])

Previously, two milestones were discovered in the area, dating to the reigns of Vespasian and Antoninus Pius. Burials nearby make it clear that a road was present already in the fourth century BC. The latest excavations suggest that, while the road was not yet paved in the time of Augustus, it was carefully constructed and not just beaten earth (Melillo Faenza, Jacazzi, and Argenziano 2009, 218–21).[27] Further excavations under the church have revealed a structure from the Augustan period that perhaps was part of the *statio* of *ad Septimum* (Melillo Faenza, Jacazzi, and Argenziano 2009, 221). Paul and his party, after traveling some 13.5 RM (12.4 mi./20 km) from Puteoli, stopped perhaps for another rest at *ad Septimum*, which one day would become a place of worship for the Lord. The church and monastery date to the ninth or tenth century, by which time the road had fallen into disrepair.

---

27. The excavators Melillo Faenza, Jacazzi, and Argenziano (2009, 221) describe the unpaved road as "a conspicuous glare section of the Via Campana ... consisting of a first layer, perfectly compacted of sandy pozzolana mixed with pumice, gravel, pieces of lava stone, limestone flakes, limestone pebbles, and brick fragments, under which a well-compressed yellowish soil mixed with minute limestone flakes was exposed. Finally, this layer rests on a very thin layer of compact laminated sandy pozzolana, followed by coarse volcanic sands with pumice" (our translation).

Day 1: Puteoli to Capua

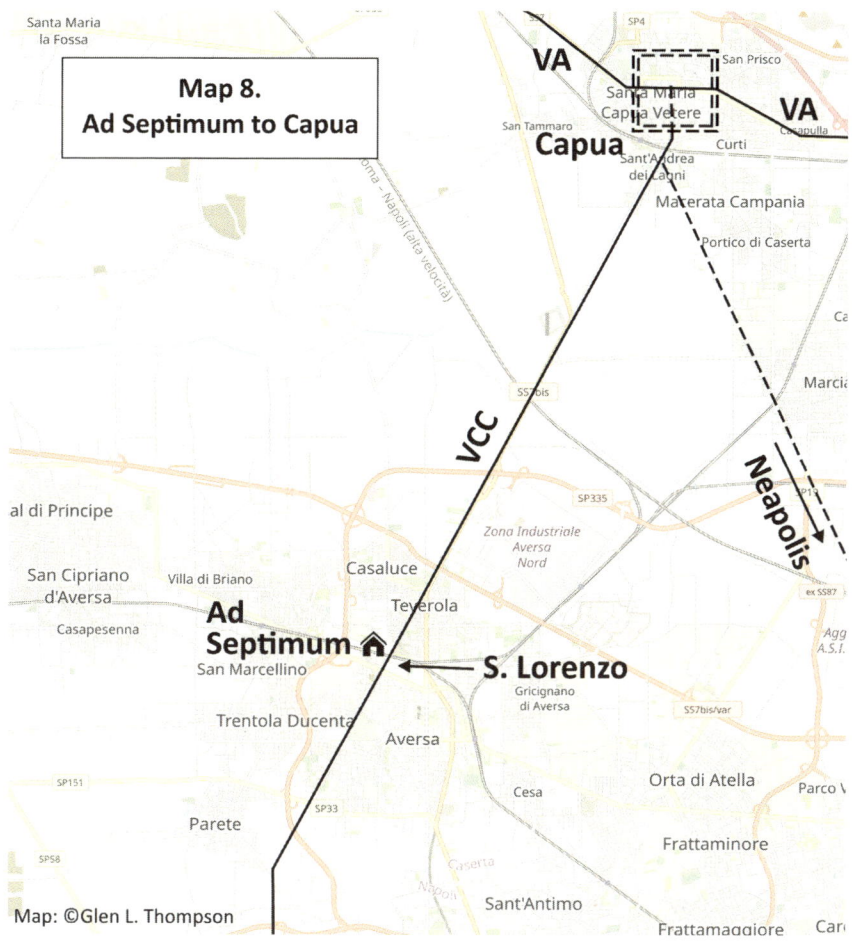

## Ad Septimum to Capua

After a rest, our travelers still had a walk to Capua of some 7 RM (6.5 mi./10.5 km), hence the name *ad Septimum*.[28] Unlike much of their journey thus far, this was mostly a straight, flat landscape (map 8). About halfway to Capua, they crossed a bridge over the Clanium (Clanio) River,

---

28. Our reconstruction of the distance from San Lorenzo to Capua's southern gate is actually a bit more than 7 RM (6.4 mi./10.4 km). *Stationes* and *mansiones* were not necessarily situated to coincide with milestones, but their location was often determined by other considerations such as existing settlements, crossroads, or water.

then continued through the Campanian countryside. At the north end of modern Sant'Andrea dei Lagni, the VCC intersected with a second road coming from Neapolis (Naples)*. Together the roads continued northeast to the southern gate* of Capua, probably just north of the current intersection with Via Giuseppe Avezzana in modern Santa Maria Capua Vetere.[29] From the Porta Campana in Puteoli to this gate in Capua Paul's party had traveled almost exactly 21 RM, the distance given on the Peutinger Map.[30] After passing through the gate, they continued north on Capua's *cardo maximus*,[31] mostly aligned with the current Via Albana. About 2625 ft. (800 m) later, they set foot for the first time on the VA (today Via Aldo Moro and SS7), the road that would take them to the capital. Their first act, however, would be to find lodging for the night.

Capua is an Etruscan name meaning "city of marshes." It had become an important urban center in the region of Campania already by the sixth century BC. Its central position soon made it a trading center between the local Etruscans and Oscans, the Greek cities of southern Italy, and the Samnite hill tribes. In 423 BC it was captured by the Samnites who soon controlled most of Campania. As Rome was expanding a century later, it established friendly relations with the Capuan aristocracy, giving them a form of citizenship (*civitas sine suffragio*) in 343 BC. Soon Capua was "the largest and richest city in Italy, with a very productive country near the sea" and "the granary of Rome" (Livy, *Hist.* 7.31.1). By the late Republic it was sometimes called the "second Rome" (Cicero, *Agrarian Law* 2.86;

---

29. Visitors today are often confused by the modern names of these cities. In AD 841 Roman Capua was destroyed by the Saracens. Only the Basilica of Santa Maria Maggiore, built around 497, was spared. When a new city was built in 856, it was situated nearby on the site of the earlier Roman city of Casilinum (see map 10), but renamed Capua to preserve the larger city's memory. As a settlement began to rise again around the basilica where the "old" (*vetere*) city had once been, it became known as Santa Maria Capua Vetere.

30. The distance from Puteoli's Porta Campana to the Quarto *mansio* was 3.78 RM (3.5 mi./5.6 km), from the *mansio* to San Lorenzo ad Septimum was 9.73 RM (8.9 mi./14.4 km), and from San Lorenzo to the southern gate of Capua was 7.5 RM (6.9 mi./11.1 km), totaling 21.01 RM.

31. The *cardo maximus* was originally the main north–south path through the middle of a Roman army camp while the *decumanus maximus* was the east–west path. These names came to be used of the main streets of a Roman colony or city, even when their orientation was not directionally true. This was the case in several of the cities Paul traversed on his journey where the VA became the main axis for urban development.

*Philippics* 12.7). That is why, already in 312 BC during the Samnite Wars, the censor Appius Claudius Caecus constructed a military road to join the two cities, a distance of 132 RM (121.4 mi./195.4 km; Uggeri 1990, 21; fig. 11). An inscription (*CIL* XI.1827), found in the forum of Arezzo and now in the Archaeological Museum of Florence (MCR 102), identifies Appius Claudius as the builder of the VA.[32]

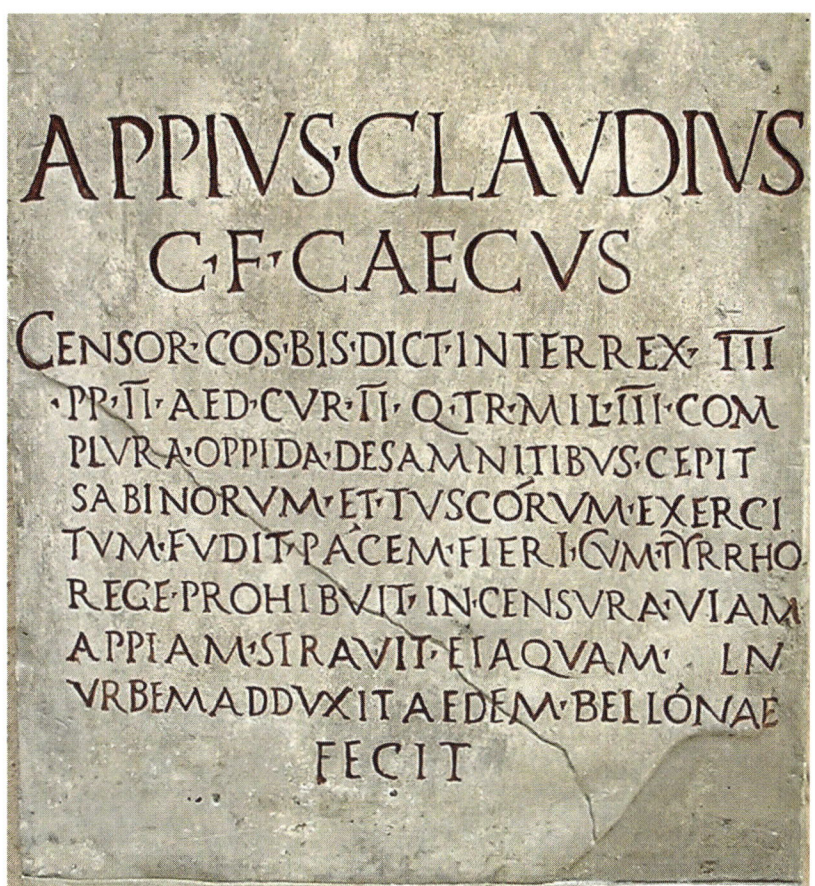

**Figure 11.** Appius Claudius inscription

---

32. The Via Latina already connected the two cities via a central route, but this passed almost entirely through Samnite territory. The more coastal route of the VA avoided that. For a discussion of the construction of the VA, see Quilici (2009, 554–59). The road is named in the inscription *CIL* 1².21.

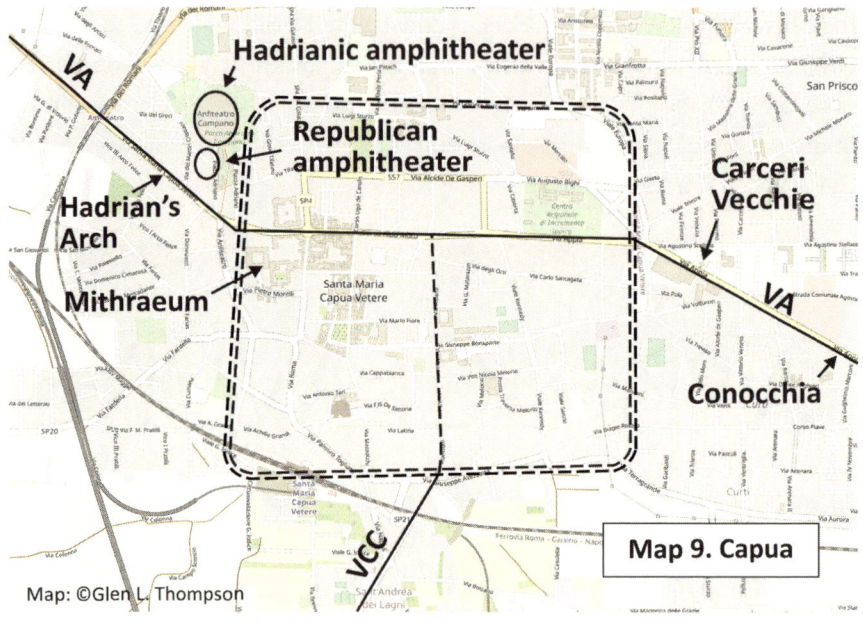

Map 9. Capua

In 216 BC, during the Second Punic War, the city defected to Hannibal and was subsequently besieged and recaptured by the Romans. After the war Capua and its surrounding territory, the *ager Campanus*, were confiscated by the Romans who then made a total geographical reorganization. By the 170s BC this new public land of the Roman people (Lat. *ager publicus populi Romani*) had been surveyed, centuriated, and allotted to farmers (Livy, *Hist.* 42.1; De Caro 2012, 68–69). In 83 BC the future dictator Sulla defeated the consul Norbanus here, the first battle following Sulla's return to Italy. For this victory he gave generous benefactions to the temple of Diana just north of the city.

At Capua Paul saw another Roman amphitheater* rising outside the city wall and 500 ft. (152 m) north of the western gate where the VA left the city and turned to the northwest (map 9).[33] Although not as large as the

---

33. For the location of the ancient city walls, see De Caro (2012, 36, fig. 2).

well-preserved early second-century AD amphitheater* visible today just to its north, the earlier Republican structure still measured an impressive 365 × 265 feet (110 × 80 m; De Caro 2012, 40–46). Here Spartacus and other members of Capua's famous gladiatorial school performed before their revolt in 73 BC. Peter Stothard (2012, 60) muses: "For the gladiators of Capua in 73 BC, objects of both amusement and money-making for the politically neutered local populace, the Via Appia meant much less, almost nothing. Once they were out of the school, the road was merely a means to a possible end—escape, escape to anywhere." Despite Spartacus's army growing rapidly to seventy thousand men before gradually losing momentum, only six thousand survived the final battle, only to be crucified "along the entire length of the road from Capua to Rome" (Appian, *Civil Wars* 1.14.120). That road was the VA, and travelers a century before Paul would pass forty-five crucifixions per RM—one every 130 ft. (33 m)! Needless to say, the public demonstration of such a cruel punishment was meant to deter future uprisings, especially among slaves.

In 59 BC Julius Caesar reorganized Capua as a Roman colony, adding twenty-two thousand Roman citizens to its population (Dio Cassius, *History* 38.7.3). A Hadrianic inscription found at the amphitheater's south gate and now in the Museo Provinciale Campano in Capua mentions its name: *Colonia Julius Felix Augusta Capua* (CIL 10.3832). Throughout the Imperial period, the city continued to be an inland commercial hub, now centered around two markets—Albana and Seplasia. Here merchants came to purchase slaves as well as spices, perfumes of wild roses, and olive oil. The city was also noted for its Campanian baskets and as the supplier of the cordage (*spartum omne*) used by Italian ropemakers (Cato, *On Agriculture* 135.2–3). Because of its wealth, Capua became known proverbially for its luxury and extravagance (Athenaeus, *Deipnosophists* 12.36). A painted Mithraeum* dating to the second century AD can be found below ground near the archaeology museum.

East of the amphitheater, Via Dianae (SP 4), a major north–south *cardo*, continued through the north gate to the *Pagus Dianae* on the western slope of Mons Tifata. This temple of Diana Tifatina* was famous throughout the Roman world (Pobjoy 1997, 59). Only 2.5 mi. (4 km) north of the

VA, the temple's accessibility ensured a regular stream of visitors. The Greek travel writer Pausanius (*Description of Greece* 5.12.3) reported that he saw the skull of an elephant there, certainly a victim of the *venationes* in the Capuan amphitheater. An inscription in a mosaic pavement, now in the floor of Sant'Angelo in Formis, mentions that the Diana temple was repaired in 108 BC, confirming that this late-antique Christian basilica was built over the temple's remains.

The main pre-Roman east–west road, running for just under 1 mi. (1.6 km) through the city, became the colony's *decumanus maximus* and later was incorporated into the VA. Although Capua became a Roman colony, its pre-Roman layout was for the most part preserved during the Roman period. Thus, not all of its streets were perfectly straight or oriented at ninety-degree angles to each other. While reconstructions show the path of the VA following a nearly straight, almost east–west path through the city, outside the city walls to the east and west it was oriented northwest to southeast. The Via Dianae served as a *cardo* principally to the north of the VA. Some 650 ft. (200 m) farther east another *cardo* stretched to Capua's southern gate where the VCC from Puteoli entered the city. At the eastern gate, formerly visible near the intersection of the SS7 with Viale Trieste, the VA turned southeastward toward Beneventum and its terminus at Brundisium. Confirming the first portion of that route today are two large and well-preserved Imperial-period funerary monuments known as the Carceri Vecchie* and the Conocchia*.[34]

In the archaeology museum's garden are displayed two VA milestones discovered in the plain to the west—both for the same mile, CXX (120), but dating to different periods.[35] During his land travels in Italy Paul regularly saw milestones. He was familiar with them because they lined the major roads in the eastern provinces as well. Those along the VCC were

---

34. The former received its name from a local legend that identified the tomb as a prison for gladiators. Conocchia came from its resemblance to the distaff used to spin wool; see Emmerson (2013, 353–54).

35. A sign in Italian provides the Latin text of each milestone—one dates to Nerva (r. 96–98) while the other to the period of the Tetrarchy (293–305). Quilici Gigli (2022, 198) proposes that the former milestone evidences *damnatio memoriae* with the name Domitian chiseled away above the CXX.

Day 1: Puteoli to Capua                                                                                   53

numbered from Capua (*CIL* 10.6941, 6944). On the milestones of the VA, the mileage from Rome was of course given. The inscriptions also named the Roman officials responsible for paving the road or making improvements to it. The VA was the first Roman road to feature milestones. While these initially may have had a propagandistic purpose, especially after the Samnite revolt in 311 BC, by Paul's day they had just become part of the odological landscape.[36] No stones exist from the VA's original phase; the oldest known milestone was MP LIII (53) found near Mesa (*CIL* 10.6838 = *CIL* 12.21). On its top surface are the names of two aediles, P. Claudius and C. Furius.[37] This milestone has been dated to 255/253 BC or 184 BC under the consul Gaius Claudius.[38] Milestones dating from the second century BC typically mention the builder's name in the nominative case. In 20 BC Augustus assumed the *cura viarum* ("management of the roads") so he began to inscribe his name in the nominative on milestones, even though the actual work was entrusted to an administrator (*curam viarum*; Suetonius, *Augustus* 37). Next came abbreviations of the powers and titles of Augustus. That no Augustan milestones have been found west from Capua does not indicate his lack of involvement in the VA, for Stefania Quilici Gigli (2020, 201) writes that "it cannot be excluded that Augustus had already made decisive plans for the road in order to facilitate transport from the port of Pozzuoli, passing through Capua." After the emperor's name came that of the provincial governor, the actual official involved in the construction or restoration. Subsequent emperors such as Domitian followed the same practice when he built the Via Domitiana.[39]

---

36. Kolb (2019, 12) perhaps overemphasizes their propagandistic aspect: "Their purpose was thus not purely practical, but also to immortalise Roman rule on stone columns along the Empire's main lines of communication. Ancient travellers were thus constantly confronted with Roman power, as well as the Empire's capacity for organization and public welfare." While familiarity may not breed contempt in this case, it would probably breed indifference.

37. For a discussion and illustrations of the milestone, see Buonopane (2011, 35–46).

38. For 255/253 BC see Ventre (2004, 120, 144 n. 38); for 184 BC see Laing (1908, 16).

39. In their homage to milestones Hamblin and Grunsfeld (1974, 80–81) eulogize: "No matter where they are, or how much they have been defaced, damaged, reused, the milestones manage to tug at the heart. ... Were they apprehensive, as Paul must have been as he neared Rome and his audience with the emperor? ... They speak so clearly of the coming and going, of the farewell and reunions, of those ancient people we almost know, so nearly can remember."

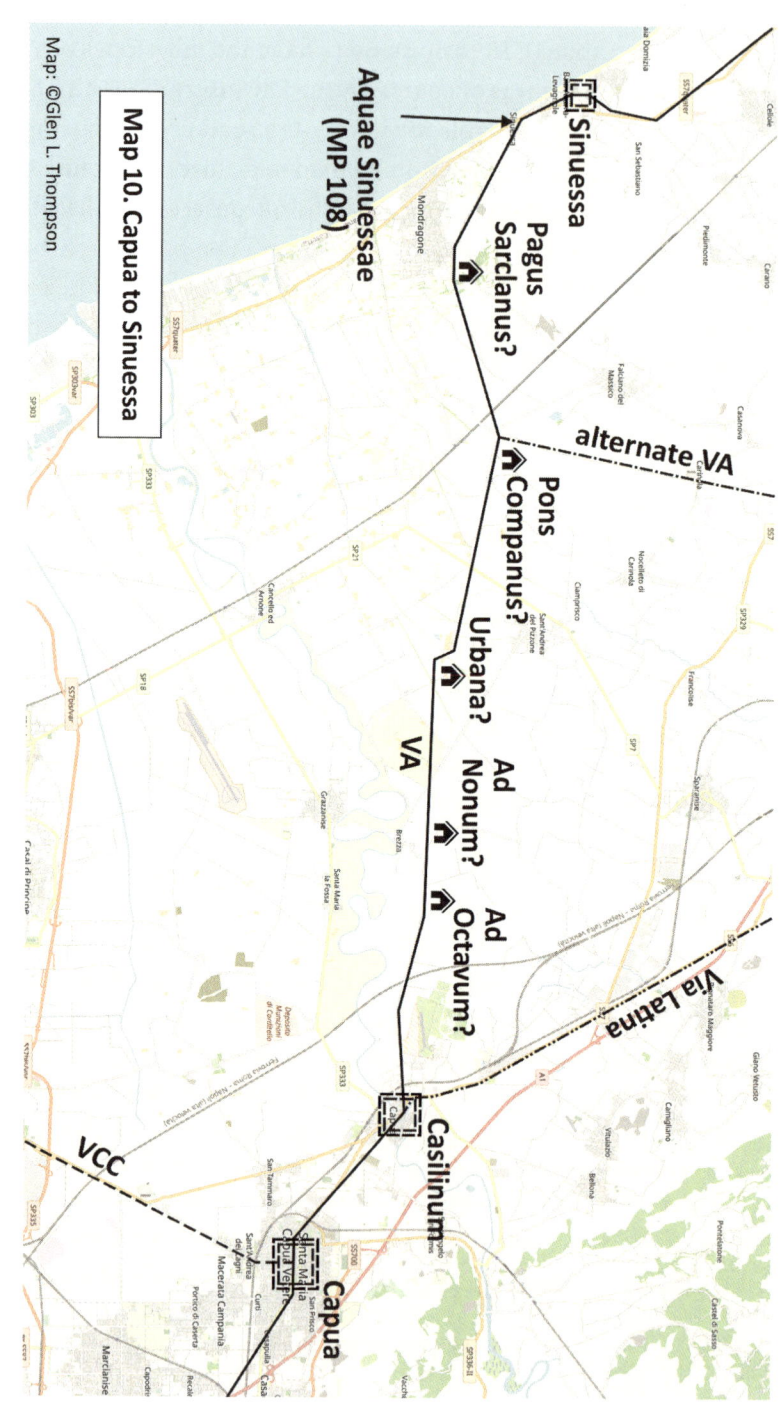

DAY 2

# Capua (RM 132) to Sinuessa (RM 107)

At Capua, Julius and his entourage prepared for their main overland journey to Rome. The VA left Capua through its western gate, the Porta Romana*, located about 650 ft. (200 m) southeast of the Republican amphitheater.[1] Just outside this gate, no longer in existence, the VA veered northwest running 2.86 mi. (4.6 km) to Casilinum (modern Capua). About 1000 ft. (300 m) after the turn, travelers today come upon the single surviving arch of the so-called Arch of Hadrian* (fig. 12). Originally a triple-arched triumphal structure made of brick and clad with marble, it was erected in honor of the second-century emperor. Nearby, the travelers passed MP 132, reminding them of the distance yet remaining to Rome. The VA lies beneath today's SS7 for 0.93 mi. (1.5 km) after the arch before continuing straight beneath fields and suburban housing for another 1.4 mi. (2.25 km). Within an hour the party entered Casilinum at today's Porta Napoli roundabout*. A short walk of 1650 ft. (500 m) brought them to the Volturnum (modern Volturno) River and its great bridge.

---

1. While there are no visible remains at this point, the map of Werner Johannowsky in his *Capua Antica* (1989) shows the city wall passing just east of the amphitheaters and crossing the VA near the current Piazza Adriano. The map is reproduced by Della Valle (2010, 25); see also the map of De Caro (2012, 37).

**Figure 12.** Hadrian's arch at Capua

**Figure 13.** Bridge over Volturnum River at Casilinum (post-WWII)

Casilinum was originally nestled in a bend of the Volturnum, which gave it protection on three sides. This caused Hannibal's army considerable problems when he attacked the city in the winter of 217–216 BC. In 59 BC Julius Caesar converted the city into a Roman colony, and this status was reconfirmed by Mark Antony in 44 BC (Cicero, *Philippics* 2.102). Although always overshadowed by nearby Capua, Casilinum had expanded to both sides of the river by the time Paul crossed the Volturnum River on the VA. The impressive bridge as rebuilt by Trajan, with four large and two smaller arches, continued in use until it was destroyed in 1943 (Quilici Gigli 2022, 196). The current bridge, with its three spans, piers, and cutwaters of large, squared stone, was built on the same spot; blocks from the old bridge lay submerged in the riverbed (fig. 13).[2]

Today on the western side of the river, the road passes a monumental gate tower first erected in 1239 by Frederick II, king of Sicily and Holy Roman emperor. A moat surrounded this tower and, according to Colin O'Connor (1993, 73, fig. 30), one of the bridges over this moat appears to be Roman. A few hundred paces after the river near MP 129, the VA intersected* with another famous Roman road—the Via Latina.[3] This artery provided a more northerly inland route to Rome, passing Teanum, Casinum, Aquinum, Fregellae, Frusino, Anagnia, and Tusculum. The two roads then rejoined 2300 ft. (700 m) from the VA's beginning at Rome's Porta Capena.

## Campus Stellas and Falernian Plain

At the fork, Paul's party remained on the more westwardly VA and began crossing the *campus* Stellas (map 11). This fertile plain spanned both sides of the Volturnum and had become a bone of contention in mid–first-century BC Roman politics (Cirillo et al. 2014, 269–75).[4] In

---

2. See the description and photograph in Quilici (1989b, 38–39).

3. For a map of the intersection of the two roads in Casilinum and a photograph of the prewar bridge with five arches, see Quilici (1989, 38–39, figs. 26–27).

4. Cirillo et al. (2012, 741–42) also note that northern Campania was "greatly transformed by one of the most powerful works in that time: the Appian Way." While later centuriation of the area

the closing days of 64 BC, a bill had been introduced in the Senate to appoint a board of ten commissioners to distribute plots of ten and twelve *iugera* of the *ager Campanus* and the *campus Stellas* (*Stellatis* or *Stellatinus*) to some five thousand colonists—army veterans and members of Rome's urban poor (Cicero, Agrarian Law 2.76, 78, 85, 96). Cicero successfully sidetracked the scheme, arguing that the colonists might become an army loyal to the commissioners who had allocated the land (3.16). Similar bills were introduced in 60 and 59 BC (Sumner 1966, 570–71). Eventually, however, the land was distributed, and its new owners continued to cultivate this area famous for its productivity. Strabo (*Geogr.* 5.4.3) lauds this fertility saying, "It is reported that, in the course of one year, some of the plains are seeded twice with spelt, the third time with millet, and others still the fourth time with vegetables." Olives and grapes were also produced in abundance, most of which were exported to Rome and its provinces. Paul's party now passed large and prosperous farms and country estates (*villae rusticae*), some owned by senators who normally resided in Rome. The intensive farming that has continued over the centuries accounts for the VA's disappearance, making this the most difficult stretch to reconstruct today.

---

did use the VA as a basis, northern Campania was less impacted by the VA than many other areas along its route.

## Day 2: Capua to Sinuessa

Our most detailed sources on the route of the ancient VA come from the surviving lists of rest stops and official inns (*mansiones* or *stationes*) that were made either by Roman officials or by private travelers along the major roads. Several of these have survived. Mitchell (1976, 127) writes of the word *mansio* that "from the early empire on it is much more commonly used to denote a designated resting or stopping place, precisely translated by σταθμός [*stathmos*] or, later, by μόνη [*monē*]. As such it became a technical term for the halting places of the imperial post and transport system, found above all in the surviving itineraries of the third and fourth centuries." The so-called Antonine Itinerary lists the important way stations and the distances between them in the late second or third century. A second itinerary, known as the Bordeaux or Jerusalem Itinerary, is the record of a fourth-century Christian pilgrim who traveled from France to Jerusalem, recording the stops along the way. Also of use is the earliest surviving map of the Roman road system, the previously mentioned Peutinger Map. Though the sole surviving manuscript dates from the thirteenth century, it seems to record the first-century road system, with some revisions made in the fourth or fifth century (fig. 14).

Day 2: Capua to Sinuessa

**Figure 14.** VA on the Peutinger Map

However, while the information given by these ancient itineraries about the VA is extremely valuable, it is also challenging to reconcile them since they mention different stopping points along the road and sometimes disagree on the distances between them. The VA between Capua and Sinuessa is a case in point. The Antonine Itinerary lists no intermediate *stationes* between Sinuessa and Capua and gives the distance as 16 RM, far too short. The original reading must have been 26 RM, the distance given by the Jerusalem Itinerary, which lists two intermediate stations—*ad Octavum* (8) and the *Pons Campanus* (9). The Peutinger Map gives the intermediate stops (east to west) as Casilinum (3), *ad Nonum* (6), Urbana (3), and *Pons Campanus* (3), but provides no distance for the final stage to Sinuessa.⁵ Figure 15 compares the information provided by these three sources for the VA from Capua to Rome. Errors in the manuscript transmission (Roman numerals are notorious for being miscopied in Latin works) and changes in the preferred stations are the most likely causes for the inconsistency in their evidence.⁶ However, with the help of road traces, aerial and satellite images, and the findspots of several surviving milestones, we are able to calculate the approximate path, distances between the *stationes*, and an overall distance of 25 RM between Capua and Sinuessa.⁷

---

5. For the itineraries, see Cuntz (1929, 15 [Antonine Itinerary], 101 [Jerusalem Itinerary]). For a comparison of these itineraries with the Peutinger Map, see Talbert (2010, 160, tab. 1, tronco Capua–Roma). The Jerusalem Itinerary states that the distance from Capua to Rome was 136 RM and that there were fourteen *mutationes* and nine *mansiones* along the way. After combining these three ancient sources, our chart shows seventeen stops.

6. While distances are always given in whole miles, the stations were often located between mileposts. This could also factor into the variation in distances recorded by the itineraries.

7. Our reconstruction of the VA's route synthesizes the three most detailed studies of the VA between Sinuessa and Capua: (1) Johannowsky (1975, 3–38); (2) Cirillo et al. (2012, 741–42); and (3) Zannini (2014b, 51–62). Our route also agrees with but is more detailed than map 44 in *The Barrington Atlas of the Greek and Roman World* (Talbert 2000, 44). After we completed our research, Stefania Quilici Gigli (2020b; 2022) shared two recent articles in which she discusses the route. Her conclusions about the path are virtually identical with ours.

Day 2: Capua to Sinuessa

|  | MP | Reconstructed | Peutinger | Antonine | Bordeaux/Jerusalem |
|---|---|---|---|---|---|
| Capua | 132 | - |  |  |  |
| Casilinum | 129 | 3 | 3 | - | - |
| ad Octavum | 124 | 5 | - | - | 8 |
| ad Nonum | 123 | 1 | 6 | - | - |
| Urbana | 119 | 4 | 3 | - |  |
| Pons Campanus | 115 | 4 | 3 | - | 9 |
| Sinuessa | 107 | 8 | (9) | (26) | 9 |
| Minturnae | 98 | 9 | 9 | 9 | 9 |
| Formia | 89 | 9 | 9 | 9 | 9 |
| Fundi | 75 | 14 | 13 | 13 | 12 |
| Tarracina | 62 | 13 | 13 | 14 | 13 |
| ad Medias | 51 | 11 | - | - | 10 |
| Forum Appii | 43 | 8 | ? | 18 | 9 |
| Tres Tabernae | 33 | 10 | 10 | 10 | - |
| ad Sponsas | 24? | 9 | - | - | 7 |
| Aricia | 16 | 8 | - | 17 | 14 |
| Bovillae | 12 | 4 | 6 | - | - |
| ad Nonum | 9 | 3 | - |  | 7 |
| Rome | 0 | 9 | 10 | 16 | 9 |
|  |  | 132 | 94 | 132 | 125 |

**Figure 15.** Ancient itineraries: Capua to Rome

## Ad Octavum to Pons Campanus

In typical Roman custom, the road westward across the plain from Casilinum followed a straight path, passing just above the northernmost bends of the serpentine Volturnum River. Although nothing is visible of the *stationes ad Octavum\** and *ad Nonum\**, they must have been located about 1 RM apart, the former about 1 mi. (1.6 km) northeast and the latter 0.5 mi. (800 m) north of Brezza.[8] Since two proximate stations

---

8. We place *ad Octavum* near MP 124 (about 41.11611, 14.12680) and *ad Nonum* near MP 123 (about 41.11674, 14.10927). Pagano (1978, 229–30) writes that MP 126* was found along the current

were unnecessary, they probably did not operate contemporaneously. For some reason one was replaced by the other in late antiquity. Paul's party probably had a brief rest at one of these *stationes*, having by then come 8 to 9 RM from Capua, as their names suggest.[9]

The VA was probably aligned with the path of SP1 until *ad Octavum*, at which point the modern road veers southward while the ancient road continued westward. After *ad Nonum* the road continued almost straight for 4 RM (3.67 mi./5.9 km) before reaching Urbana*.[10] After a short jog to the north, Paul's party continued straight across the bottom of the famous Falernian Plain for another 4 RM before crossing the Savo (modern Savone) River at *Pons Campanus* (MP 115; map 12). Roman surveyors used this section of the VA to centuriate the Falernian Plain north of the road.[11]

---

Capua to Brezza road (SP1), 2.2 mi. (3.5 km) west of the bridge in Casilinum and 787 ft. (240 m) east of the entrance to the Parco della Nunziatella, which no longer exists. Citing nineteenth-century testimonies to a visible stretch along the then highway, Pagano puts the VA on the path of the current SP1. Johannowsky (1975, 17–18) believed it was not in situ at that location and that the road went a little farther north. See also the map in Humm (1996, 716, fig. 11) and De Caro (2012, 155, fig. 171).

9. On the basis of the discrepancy between the Peutinger Map and the Jerusalem Itinerary, Zannini (2014a, 127–29) has suggested that, due to the encroachment of swamps, the actual route of the VA changed in this area.

10. Our reconstruction of the VA's path between its junction with the Via Latina at Casilinum (41.11092, 14.20471) and the Torre del Paldino (41.12971, 13.93736) can be defined by connecting these with the following five intermediate locations where changes of direction take place: (1) 41.10886, 14.17045; (2) 41.11573, 14.13548; (3) 41.11921, 14.04642 (Urbana); (4) 41.12252, 14.04402; and (5) 41.13430, 13.96720 (*Pons Campanus*).

11. For the centuriation, see Libertini (2019, 141–44, figs. 24 A–D). Later the Savo River marked the boundary between Campania and Latium.

## Day 2: Capua to Sinuessa

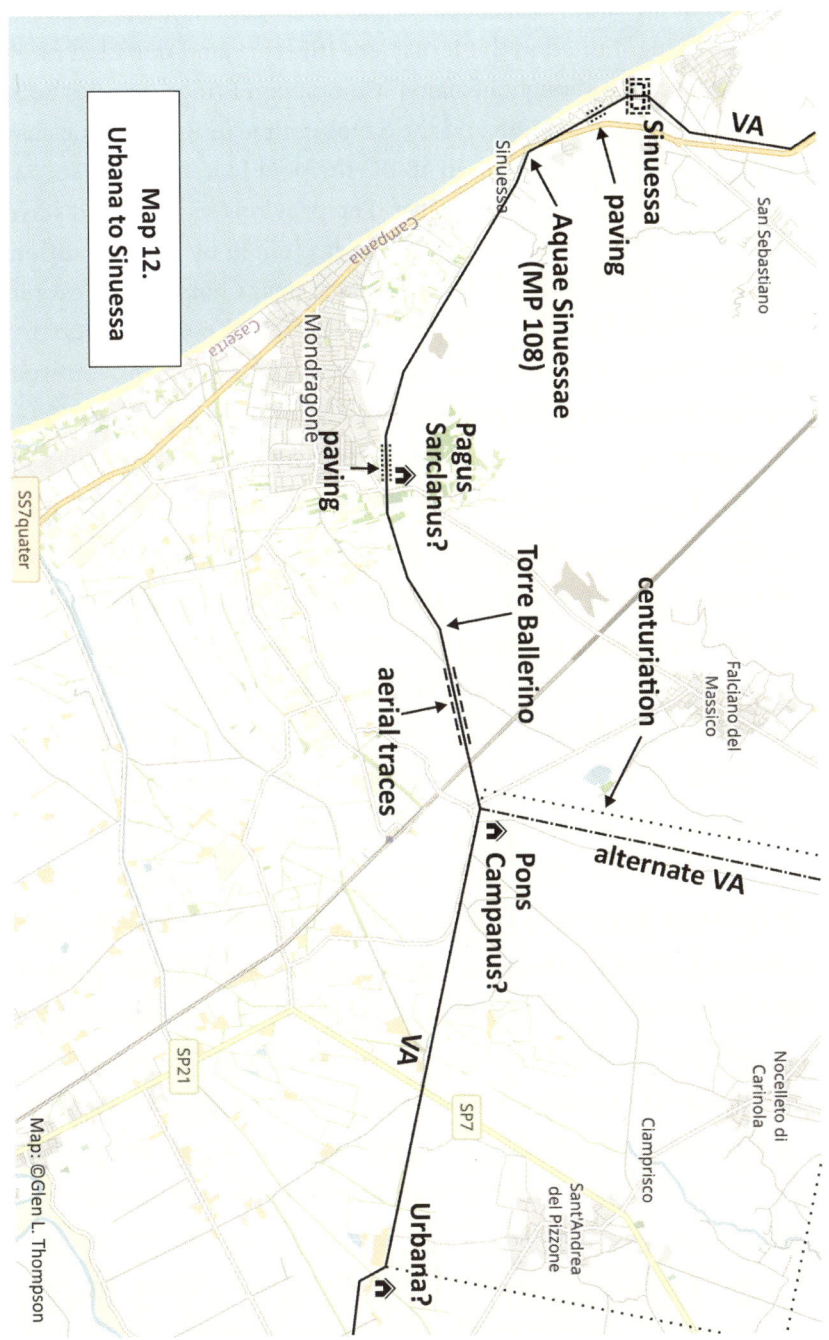

Map 12.
Urbana to Sinuessa

Located at the southwest corner of the Falernian Plain, the *statio Pons Companus*\* is mentioned in the Jerusalem Itinerary and depicted on the Peutinger Map. Even though the name "Campanian Bridge" implies both a bridge and a river, its location and the Savo's course in Roman times have not been definitively identified. In 38 BC the poet Horace (*Satires* 1.5.45) spent a night in a villa near the bridge. The previous night he had stayed with friends in or near Minturnae, then was joined by some additional traveling companions in Sinuessa, arriving at *Pons Campanus* by evening, a journey of 17 RM. Paul's party probably rested also at the *statio* or in the shadow of the bridge over the Savo. Although they had now traveled 17 RM, they still had another 8 RM to reach Sinuessa.

If Campania as a whole was the veritable breadbasket of Roman Italy, the Falernian Plain was its Napa Valley. Falernian wine became proverbial as among the best in the Roman world (Pliny the Elder, *Nat.* 14.8.2). As Paul Arthur (1995, 242) notes, the land "was intensively farmed by slave-run villas, at this time, and the main produce appears to have been wine." The slaves who worked the vineyards were brought from Gaul, where they were exchanged for Falernian wine—one slave worth approximately sixty amphorae of ordinary wine. An advertisement found in a bar in Pompeii underscores this point: "You can drink here for one *as*. If you give two you will drink better; if you give four you will drink Falernian" (*CIL* 4.1679).[12] Martial (*Epigrams* 13.111, trans. Bohn) likewise celebrates the wine produced on the southern sides of the two mountains that overlooked the plain—Mount Massicus and Mount Falernus: "This Massic wine comes from the presses of Sinuessa. Do you ask in whose consulate it was bottled? It was before consuls existed."[13]

---

12. Quoted in Cooley and Cooley (2014, 235).

13. Martial (*Epigrams* 13.108, trans. Bohn) also mentions that Attic honey was combined with Falernian wine to produce a drink which "deserves to be mixed by Ganymede."

Day 2: Capua to Sinuessa                                              67

## Pons Campanus to Sinuessa

Just after *Pons Campanus*, the VA turned slightly southwestward to head for the coastline around the southern end of Mount Massicus (modern Massico), whose rocky summit loomed to the northwest. Rising some 2625 ft. (800 m) above the plain, the mountain divided the region of Latium from Campania, forcing the VA to arc around its southern flank. At an early date an alternate paved road turned north near *Pons Campanus* and went around the eastern and northern sides of Massicus. Passing south of the Roman colony of Suessa (modern Sessa Aurunca), this alternate path then descended and rejoined the coastal VA just east of Minturnae.[14] Perhaps this route was constructed to provide a safer alternative during coastal flooding.[15]

Even if this alternate route existed by the mid-first century, we presume Paul's party used the easier coastal route. Continuing from *Pons Campanus* to the southwest the group observed a large funerary monument on the north side of the road at MP 113. The circular tower, on a base 26 ft. (8 m) square, dates to the first century BC and is today called the Torre Ballerino* (or Torre del Paladino).[16] The village (*vicus*) of Caedicius, mentioned in Pliny's description of Falernian wine as being 6 RM from Sinuessa (*Nat.* 14.8.2), may have been located in this vicinity.[17] About 2.5 RM farther, halfway between MP 110 and 111, the road passed another *mansio*\*. Although unmentioned by the itineraries, its existence has come to light through excavations (Ruggi D and Castaldo 2007, 40–41). It lies just west of the cemetery of Mondragone at the

---

14. Walker (2008, 187) maps Paul's final approach to Rome on such a route entering Mintura (*sic*) from the east. However, he shows it running north from Capua, something no Roman road did in antiquity. Perhaps Walker means to show the Via Latina that ran northwest from Casilinum to Teanum before turning westward toward Suessa and Minturnae.

15. That is the theory posited in a poster showing this route (but without extensive documentation) by Zannini et al. (2012). On the dating of the inland route, see page 76, note 4.

16. The tomb's inscription (*CIL* 10.4727) is said to be in nearby Carinola where it was reused in the church's belltower. We were unable to confirm this during a visit to the village, although we discovered Falernian wine at a nearby winery fittingly called *Regina Viarum*.

17. De Caro (2012, 171) cites Johannowsky for this. The Caediciae were a local family mentioned in the inscription now in Carinola (*CIL* 10.4727) and by Festus (*On the Meaning of Words*, bk. 3) as having *tabernae in via Appia*; cf. the edition of Mueller (1880, 45).

northwest corner of a five-way intersection (De Caro 2012, 166–69). From nearby inscriptions this *mansio* has been tentatively identified as the *Pagus Sarclanus*. In front of the ruins is a section of the ancient VA* 165 ft. (50 m) long (fig. 16). It was excavated in 2002 and is still visible beneath the undergrowth. Another paved road can be seen intersecting it from the southwest.[18]

**Figure 16.** Paving near Mondragone cemetery

---

18. For the plan of the excavation, see Ruggi D and Castaldo (2007, 324, tab. 9–10). They speak of the two intersecting roads as being two phases of the VA, and they are followed by De Caro (2012, 169–70). We lean toward seeing the smaller road as a diverticulum.

Day 2: Capua to Sinuessa

After passing the *mansio*, our travelers followed the VA as it curved along the mountain's base for another 3 RM. During this stretch Paul began to see the Tyrrhenian Sea in the distance. The party arrived at the coast just after passing MP 108*.[19] To the south ran the direct coastal road to Cumae and the Bay of Naples. As noted earlier, it was only upgraded with paving a half century after Paul's time, at which point it became known as the Via Domitiana.[20]

## Sinuessa

The junction was near the famous hot springs, Aquae Sinuessae (Waters of Sinuessa), which attracted visitors for their healing properties.[21] Pliny the Elder (*Nat.* 31.4.1) noted that the waters cured barrenness in women and insanity in men. Shortly before Claudius was poisoned to death by his wife Agrippina, Tacitus (*Ann.* 12.66) reports that the emperor "had an attack of illness and went to Sinuessa to recruit his strength with its balmy climate and salubrious waters." Martial (*Epigrams* 11.82) mentions a Philostratus who nearly lost his life falling down a flight of stairs after drinking too much wine at a feast in Sinuessa; he should have drunk of its waters instead!

---

19. On the recovery of MP 108 and 109 (*CIL* 10.6870), see Pagano (1991–1992, 109–10; also 117, fig. 1).

20. Today the name Via Doimiziana is given not only to the coastal road SS7qtr, which roughly follows the ancient road between Mondragone (Sinuessa) and Puteoli, but also to the coastal road between Formiae and Sinuessa.

21. Two milestones, MP 108 and 109, were found along this stretch of road, the former at Aquae Sinuessae. Zannini (2014b, 51–52) used these findspots as reckoning points for his reconstruction of their positions both to the north and south.

**Figure 17.** Paving south of Sinuessa

Day 2: Capua to Sinuessa

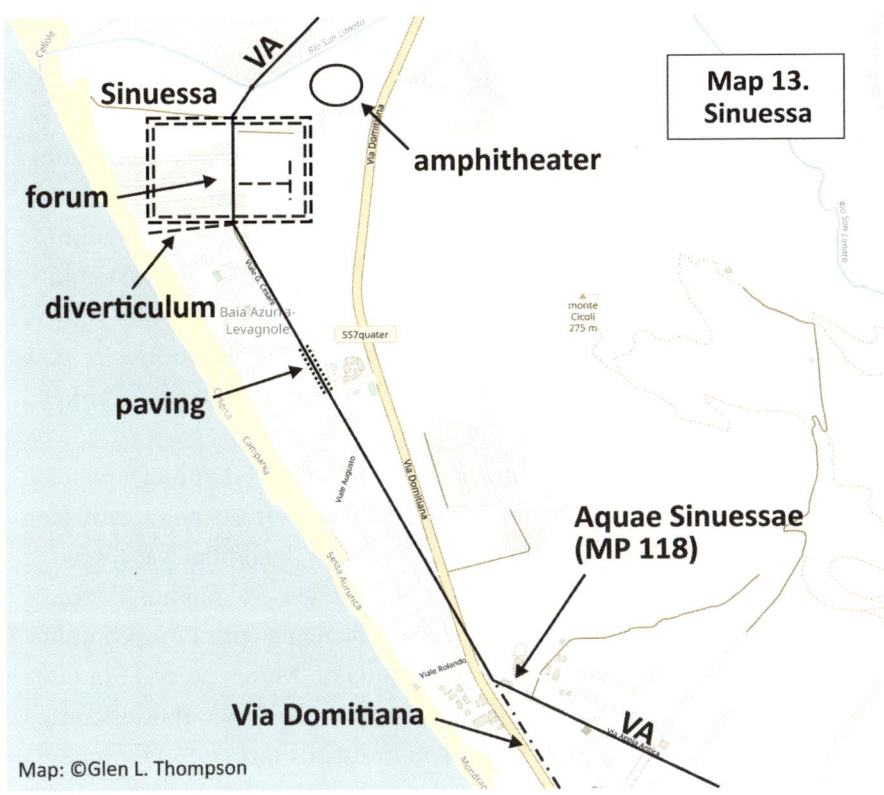

Map 13. Sinuessa

At Aquae Sinuessa the road turned northwest to parallel the coast for 1 RM (0.96 mi./1.55 km). Along this stretch ancient paving* 492 ft. (150 m) long is still visible (fig. 17).[22] The road then veered almost due north just past MP 107 to enter the walls of the Roman colony founded in 296 BC (De Caro 2012, 162–70; map 13). Together with Minturnae, Sinuessa was intended to protect the area (Livy, *Hist.* 10.21.7–8) and the VA that passed through this narrow strip of land, scarcely more than 325 ft. (100 m) in width, between Monte Cicoli and the Tyrrhenian Sea. Pliny

---

22. This curbed section is parallel to and just east of Viale Augusto in the housing development of Baia Azzura-Levagnole.

the Elder (*Nat.* 3.9.5) reported that the site had previously been occupied by a Greek settlement called Sinope, but this has not been confirmed archaeologically. The colony was laid out as a rectangle on the plan of a *castrum* (army camp) with its walls encompassing about 1750 × 1000 ft. (530 × 300 m). An amphitheater* lay to the northeast; its remains are in *opera quasi quadrata* with a trace of a corner wall (Quilici 1989b, 36).[23] The VA served as the *cardo maximus* for the new colony, running from northeast to southwest through its eastern section. A diverticulum* ran from outside the southern gate* to the harbor. A section is still visible north of Baia Azzurra.[24] The road, whose other sections are now underwater, once provided access to the city's port facilities (Pennetta et al. 2016, 198–99).[25]

The colony has an interesting history. In 217 BC Hannibal advanced into the region, burning the farmsteads of the colonists and destroying Aquae Sinuessae. Despite reaching the city gates, Hannibal was forced to retreat because of the advances of the Roman general Fabius Maximus (Livy, *Hist.* 22.13–14). In 49 BC during his struggle with Pompey, Julius Caesar traveled this route arriving in Capua on March 26 and Sinuessa on March 27 before meeting the Senate on the VA outside Rome's boundaries on April 1 (Cicero, *Letters to Atticus* 9.15.6–16.1). Sinuessa was also the site of a major slave uprising in 133 BC. It ended with the crucifixion of about four thousand slaves there and five hundred more at Minturnae (Orosius, *History against the Pagans* 5.9.4). The apostle to the gentiles, a δοῦλος (*doulos*, "slave") of Christ Jesus, now arrived in Sinuessa as a prisoner. As a Roman citizen, his trial would not end in crucifixion, but it might well end in death. Tired from a day's journey of 25 RM (23 mi./37 km) and after eating an evening meal with some

---

23. Pagano (1995, 67, fig. 3, B) mentions streets excavated within the city walls of Sinuessa, which are depicted on map 13.

24. The road is heavily overgrown but still visible today (also on map 13). For a photograph of the diverticulum outside the wall, see Ruggi D'Aragona and Cascella (2017, 11, fig. 1).

25. For a map of the urban plan of Sinuessa transected by the VA, see Ruggi D'Aragona and Cascella 2017, 29, fig. 3.1. The labels for the (ancient) VA and the (modern) Strada Domiziana on their map on page 12, fig. 3 are, however, depicted incorrectly and should be reversed.

famous local wine, he said his prayers and slept well to the sound of the sea lapping the nearby shore.

Day 3

# Sinuessa (RM 107) to Itri (RM 83)

The next morning Julius led his group outside the north gate* of Sinuessa where the VA angled inland northeast for about 1.6 mi. (2.5 km) before veering northwest to parallel the coast of the *Sinus Amyclanus* (modern Gulf of Gaeta) for the remainder of the 9 RM to Minturnae.[1] This took the party across the fertile Caecuban plain. Despite being marshy in spots, its soil nourished a tree-climbing vine that produced superb wines (Strabo, *Geogr.* 5.3.5). The marshy terrain is probably why the engineers sited the VA 1.4 mi. (2.25 km) from the present coastline. Constant farming over past centuries has erased all traces of the road. Its track most likely lies beneath or near the present SS7qtr/Via Domiziana.

A century earlier in 44 BC, Cicero made a similar trip, although he was carried in a litter or rode in a cart. "On November 9, I got up before daybreak, left Sinuessa, and just before dawn reached the Teretina bridge at Minturnae" (*Letters to Atticus* 16.13.1).[2] Paul's walk took the same path across the Teretina

---

1. The route is shown on two maps in Pennetta and Trocciola (2017, 12, fig. 3; 29, fig. 3.1); however, the path of the VA is not the same on both. The latter map shows the VA continuing straight through the current Villaggio Le Perle. We prefer the depiction on page 12 in which the road veers northeast after crossing a small fossa and follows the approximate track of the modern road that borders the southeastern side of Villagio Le Perle. It then continued straight following the current tree line until it headed north again with the track of SS7qtr at the entrance to Baia Felice. This is the route also depicted in the maps of De Caro (2012, 162, fig. 176) and Pagano (1995, 67, fig. 3).

2. Cicero wrote two days earlier from Sinuessa (*Letters to Atticus* 16.10). He mentions other places on this stretch of the VA: "On the 7th [of November] I arrived at my lodge at Sinuessa. That same day the common talk was that Antony was going to halt at Casilinum. So I changed my plans. I had decided to go straight home along the Via Appia, but Antony would have easily caught up to me; for they say he travels with 'Caesarian rapidity.' So I turned off at Minturnae onto the road to Arpinum."

bridge.³ Approaching the bridge over the Liris (modern Gargliano) River, they passed the junction where the road branched eastward to the nearby Roman colony of *Colonia Julia Felix Classica Suessa* (modern Sessa Aurunca) founded in 313 BC. As previously mentioned, this road continued past Suessa and across the northern end of Mount Massico before it cut south to rejoin the VA near *Pons Campanus*. Several miles past Suessa a branch of the road continued eastward to join the Via Latina. T. P. Wiseman (1970, 130) suggested that this inland road was the original route of the VA since it passed through Suessa, which had been founded the year before the VA was constructed. Werner Johannowsky (1975, 15) and Cascella (2016, 24 with map), along with the majority of scholars, read the archaeological remains at Suessa as showing that this was clearly a later imperial route.⁴

## Minturnae

In 295 BC Rome established the colony of Minturnae (*Colonia Minturnensis*) to secure passage over the Liris River, still the southern boundary of Latium (modern Lazio). Founded at the same time as Sinuessa, it secured the VA coastal route to the south (Velleius Paterculus, *Roman History* 1.14.2). According to Strabo (*Geogr.* 5.3.6), Minturnae lay midway between Formiae and Sinuessa, 80 stadia/10 RM (9.2 mi./14.8 km) from each. The original *castrum* was situated on the river's northwest bank. From its north gate another road crossed a causeway above marshy ground and led northward some 30 mi. (50 km) to Arpinum (Arpino). On his trip of 44 BC mentioned above, Cicero took that road to reach Arpinum, his hometown.⁵

---

3. While the manuscripts of Cicero's letters give the bridge's name as Tirenum or Tiretium, these names are mentioned nowhere else. At its foundation in 295 BC Minturnae was "enrolled in the Roman tribe Teretina," which occupied the lower Liris River Valley. Freier (1969, 510–12) argues this became the name of the bridge, then was later corrupted in the manuscripts.

4. Sergio Cascella confirmed in an email to Thompson (July 27, 2021) that the inland route dated later. Neither the section of pavement visible in Sessa Aurunca (41.22833, 13.92601) nor the twenty-one-span Roman bridge referred to as the Ponte Ronaco (41.22306, 13.91761) were part of the main inland route from Minturnae to the *Pons Campanus* and Via Latina, despite that claim by the Caserta website (https://caserta.italiani.it/la-storia-del-teatro-romano-di-sessa-aurunca/). Instead they were part of the road that led from Suessa's southern gate to Sinuessa and the VA; so Cascella (2016, 103). O'Connor (1993, 9, fig. 1; 72, figs. 28, 29) has fine images of the paving and bridge near Suessa but again incorrectly identifies them as part of the VA. Note that none of the extant ancient itineraries substitutes the route through Suessa for the coastal route through Sinuessa.

5. Freier (1969, 511 n. 9) places the turnoff to Suessa along the Arpinum road, but this would require yet another bridge. It is more likely that the road to Suessa intersected the VA directly on

Archaeologists have discovered the stumps of over 150 oak piles and some submerged concrete rubble that remain from the *Pons Teretina*\* used by Cicero and Paul to cross the Liris. This wooden bridge took the VA across the river about 330 ft. (100 m) south of the reconstructed nineteenth-century iron suspension bridge—Ponte Real Ferdinando II di Borbone—that still graces the site. The wooden bridge remained in use until the sixth century AD and was never replaced by a masonry structure. Some 2400 Roman coins along with a large deposit of metal objects were found in the river near the wooden piles. Many were votive offerings such as medical or cosmetic instruments, styli, enameled plaques, and cheap jewelry (Ruegg 1983, 207–14). As Alan Brookes (1974, 46) notes, "The Romans are thought to have thrown objects into rivers when crossing them as offerings to river deities."[6] Despite being 1.3 mi. (2.1 km) from the sea, Minturnae had a harbor, the Portus Lirensis, accessed by the navigable river. It became a major shipbuilding center, particularly for vessels carrying large storage jars (*dolia*), several of which are displayed near Minturnae's theater (Bellini 2007, 22). The city soon expanded to its eastern bank, though that area has been little explored by archaeologists.

**Figure 18.** Paving in forum of Minturnae

---

the east side of the Liris River.

6. For a map showing the nineteenth-century bridge and its relationship to the original Pons Teretina, see Brookes (1974, 42).

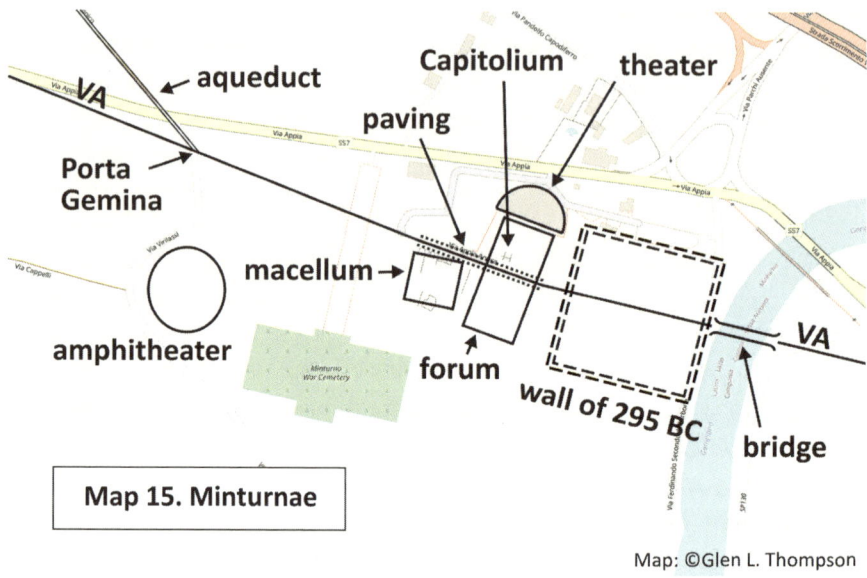

Map: ©Glen L. Thompson

Minturnae was long held in honor by the Romans. When Gaius Marius fled Rome in 88 BC, its citizens first provided him with a haven and then a means of escape from certain death at the hands of Sulla's henchmen (Cicero, *For Plancius* 10). He was taken by the river road past the temple of the sea goddess Marica, mother of Latinus, whose ruins are still visible about 1300 ft. (400 m) from the river's mouth. At the coast a ship was provided to carry Marius into exile in Africa.[7]

From the bridge, the VA continued across Minturnae's forum and served as the city's *decumanus maximus* (map 15; fig. 18). On its north side, the Republican Capitolium was built of tufa in 191 BC. After a major fire

---

7. The event is portrayed by the French artist Germaine-Jean Drouais who in 1786 painted "Marius in Minturnae," now hanging in the Louvre. It depicts the moment when Marius reaches out to the young soldier about to execute him and asks, "Would you dare kill Marius?" Unable to face the general, the soldier steps back and pulls his cloak over his face. As the soldier fled, he cried out, "I could never kill Marius!" (Plutarch, *Marius* 37–40). The painting can be seen at: https://collections.louvre.fr/en/ark:/53355/cl010064837.

Day 3: Sinuessa to Itri

devastated the forum in the mid-first century BC, Minturnae experienced renewal and expansion under Augustus, who rebuilt the central area with limestone. Also on the north side of the VA was the theater* seating 4600 persons. The rebuilt Capitolium* and a temple for Augustus* were sited behind the porticoes that then lined the VA. On the south side were an addition to the forum*, a *macellum*\* ("market"), a basilica, and a Roman bath. Outside the wall about 328 ft. (100 m) south of the western gate stood an amphitheater*.[8]

## Minturnae to Formiae

Traversing the city on the VA, Paul's party left Minturnae by passing though the monumental arch of its western gate, Porta Gemina*. An exedra with a niche stood on its left side. It was covered with marble and supported the statue of a cuirassed member of the imperial family. On the right side was a nymphaeum that monumentalized the terminus of the Augustan aqueduct* constructed of *opus reticulatum* (Pagano 1995, 55).[9] It brought water from Monti Aurunci 7 mi. (11.3 km) to the northeast. The aqueduct is still a stunning sight today with about 120 arches remaining.[10] A milestone with RM 98 was found in the area.[11]

From here the VA continued straight northwest for the next 5 RM (4.6 mi./7.4 km). Today it lies beneath the current SS7qtr/Via Domitiana south of modern Minturno.[12] Toward the end of this stretch, the hill of Gianola* came into view on the left near the sea. The structures atop it were perhaps

---

8. The arc of the current Via Pantano indicates the approximate location.

9. For an illustration of the statue, see Pagano (1995, 65); for a map of Minturnae, see page 66. See also Richmond (1933, 154–56), particularly page 155, fig. 5, for a drawing of the gate and arch.

10. For a discussion of the history and archaeology of Minturnae, see Ferrante and Mastrorilli (2016, 87–98). For their map of Minturnae's territory, see page 90, fig. 86. A digital reconstruction of the city's monuments can be seen at https://digilander.libero.it/buro61/minturnae/Capitolium.htm. Modern visitors should also visit the British World War II cemetery just southwest of the excavations.

11. It was published by Maximilianus Ihm in *Ephemeris epigraphica*, a supplement to *CIL* 10 (1899, 220, no. 901) as *columna mill. rep. Minturnis contrada Virilasci in fundo Francisci Iannazzi*. Pagano (1995, 110 n. 7) cites that publication and states the milestone was found near the northern gate of Minturnae. If this were the case, it could not have been in situ. Ihm (1899, 220), however, says it was seen along the VA between Minturnae and Sinuessa. Unfortunately, its exact findspot remains a mystery.

12. About 800–1000 ft. (250–300 m) west of the gate at Minturnae, the VA again becomes virtually contiguous with the SS7. It then seems to have continued for 4.5 mi. (7.3 km) until, if the SS7 follows

used as warehouses or waypoints for navigators. Garrisons might even have used this elevated vantage point to monitor traffic either on land or sea. A century before Paul passed this way, Mamurra, the Roman knight whom Julius Caesar tasked with building a fleet for his invasion of Britain (Caesar, *Gallic Wars* 5.1), spent time in his luxury seaside villa here. Horace (*Satires* 1.5.37) referred to nearby Formiae as the city of the Mamurra family.

Here at modern Scauri, the coastline turns west above a small bay—*Formianus Sinus* (modern Gulf of Formia). The VA also turned and ran westward parallel to the coast for the next 3.1 mi. (5 km) before turning southwest to Formiae. Modern construction has obscured any traces of the road, but it probably lay beneath the SS7 for most of this section. After the first 2.1 mi. (3.4 km) of this stretch, an imposing Roman funerary monument*, marked "Sepolcro Romano," is seen standing on the north side of the SS7, confirming this as the track of the VA. The Torre di Mola*, dating from the thirteenth century AD, stands 1.2 mi. (2 km) farther on the south side. This tower was built above Roman baths whose tepidarium and caldarium are visible beneath the glass floor.

## Formiae

Formiae (modern Formia) was tucked into a narrow coastal strip beneath the southern end of the Aurunci Mountains, a massif that encompassed some 150 sq. mi. (400 sq. km.) and whose highest peaks rose to 5000 ft. (1525 m). Since only 10 RM (9.2 mi./4.8 km) separated it from Minturnae, Paul and his party arrived after a couple hours of walking. Following the Latin War (340–338 BC), Formiae came under Rome's rule, and its inhabitants were given partial rights as citizens (*sine suffragio*). However, full suffrage only came in 188 BC when it was enrolled in the tribe Aemilia (Livy, *Hist.* 8.14.10; 38.36.7–9).

---

its path, it bent slightly more to the north for a final 985 ft. (300 m) before a major turn to the west at the current roundabout. See also the maps in Libertini (2019, 157, figs. 27A, B; 159–60, figs. 27E, F).

## Day 3: Sinuessa to Itri

The construction of the VA in 312 BC divided the city into an upper sector with an acropolis and a lower, southern sector along the sea (map 16). Within the city walls, the VA also served as the *decumanus*, about 0.6 mi. (1 km) long.[13] Its eastern half is not easy to discern, but the western part lies under the SS7.[14] When Paul passed through Formiae, it had not yet become a colony; only under Hadrian in the second century AD did it become *Colonia Aelia Hadriana Augusta*.[15] Its harbor offered a favorable layover for ships on their way to Ostia (Strabo, *Geogr.* 5.3.6). Martial (*Epigrams* 10.30.1, 11–15) exults in its delightful setting and climate: "O Formiae, sweet and mild shore; ... a gentle breeze skims the water's face, yet it awakes and with its sultry waves gently rocks a skiff, like the flickering of a purple fan cools a lass from oppressive heat" (trans. Thompson). It owed its prosperity not only to its port but also "to its situation on the Via Appia, its abundant water, and the excellence of its agriculture, especially its fruit, and its attractions as a resort" (L. Richardson 1976, 334). Pompey and other Roman elite built villas along the seaside stretching westward as far as Caieta (Gaeta), which was connected to the VA by a diverticulum.

---

13. The eastern gate was perhaps near the junction of Via Anfiteatro Romano and Via Ferdinando Lavanga; the western gate was apparently near the junction of the SS7 with Via Olivetani.

14. Heading west from the roundabout, the road apparently followed the path of Via Abate Tosti, then through the current large parking area to Via Ferdinando Lavanga and on to Via Angelo Rubino.

15. This summary is based on Lacam and Vella (2016, 47–57). Figure 55 is an archaeological map of Formiae.

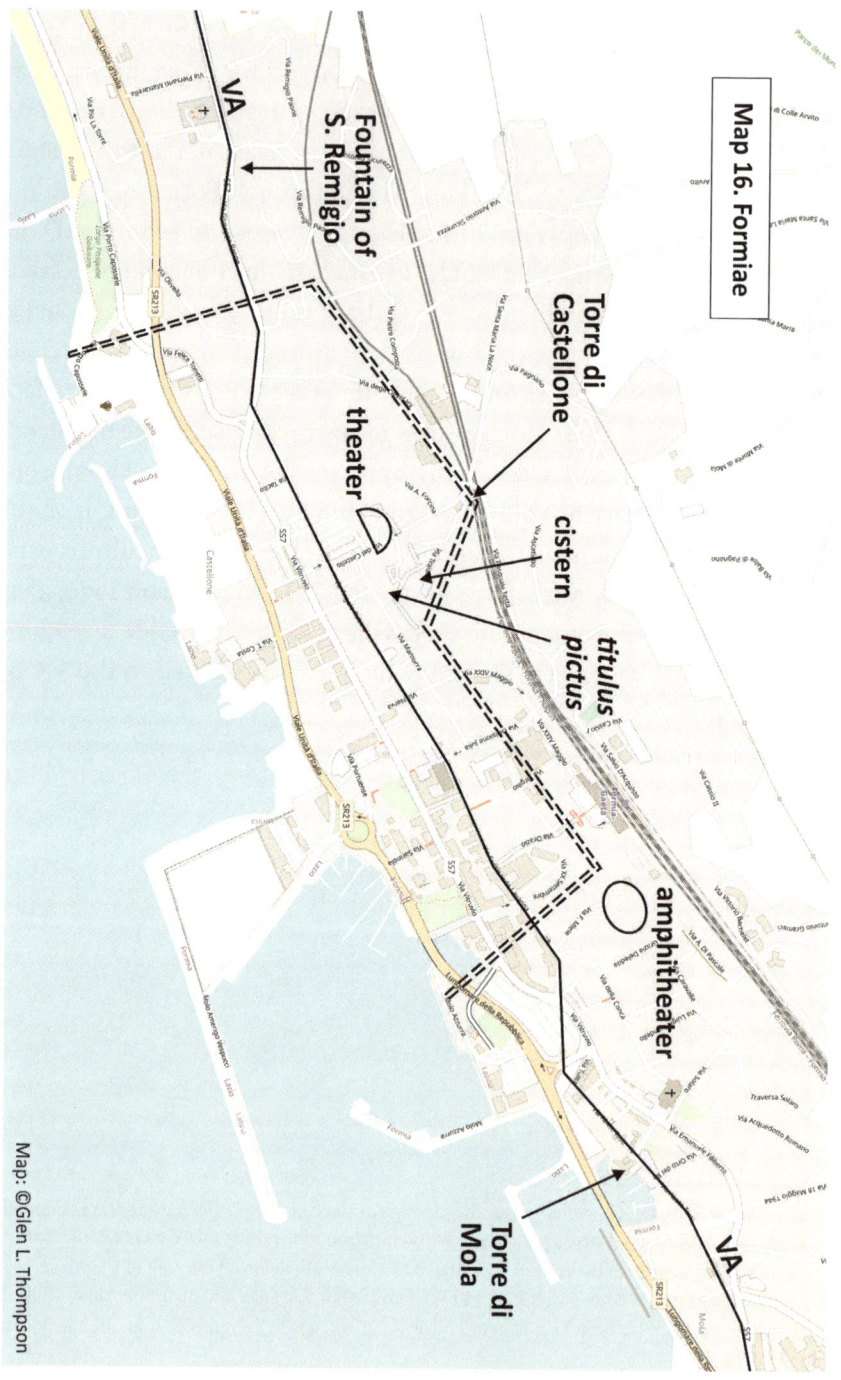

## Day 3: Sinuessa to Itri

Where today the ancient city wall crosses Via Mamurra, a room was found containing an inscription in red on a plastered wall, now known as Titulus Pictus*. It lists about thirty Roman legionaries by rank—*centurio, cornicularius, actarius, tesserarius*—all of whom belonged to the Gens Valeria. In the Castellone section are the remains of the Roman theater* now turned into apartments for local residents. The Torre di Castellone*—built on a polygonal base during the Republican period—has an octagonal tower built atop a Roman arch. Nearby is a large Roman cistern* which distributed water throughout Formiae, especially to its fountains. As Paul passed through the city gate and continued westward, he perhaps stopped for a drink and to refill his water skin from the fountain today called Fontana San Remigio* (fig. 19). Water issued through two theater masks—anthropomorphic figures of the moon and the sun. Unfortunately, only the sun figure is visible today. The fountain also featured a water trough for thirsty horses and other livestock traveling along the VA. In front of the fountain a wide and well-preserved section of basalt paving merged seamlessly into the VA.[16] As the VA continued west under the current SS7, the remains of a substantial Roman tomb* are visible on the right about 560 ft. (170 m) past the fountain. Local tradition has connected it with the noted Roman architect Marcus Vitruvius Pollio, possibly a native of Formiae (L. Richardson 1976, 334). His treatise *On Architecture*, still widely read today, served not only as a guidebook for Roman builders but also greatly influenced Renaissance building.

---

16. Regarding the use of basalt, Kaster (2012, 23) writes: "The stone was quarried in pyramidal chunks, each chunk with a rounded base a foot or more across and an apex of perhaps half that. Set in the gravel with apex down, base up, and fitted together." He notes that Procopius had written that the blocks did not look so much fitted together as grown together.

**Figure 19.** Fountain of San Remigio in Formiae

On the left 0.6 mi. (1 km) farther, the road passes an enormous cylindrical funerary monument* linked with the famous first-century BC Roman orator, Cicero. Cicero (*Letters to Atticus* 1.3.2) had two villas on the gulf—one traditionally at Villa Rubino and the other 3 mi. (4.5 km) southwest in Caieta.[17] At the instigation of Mark Antony, this Roman orator, statesman, and author was assassinated on December 7, 43 BC while attempting to flee from one of these villas (Plutarch, *Cicero* 47.4–48.4). Leaning out of his litter, Cicero presented his head for decapitation. Antony also instructed the assassins to cut off Cicero's hands, for they had written the fourteen speeches known as the *Philippics* in which Cicero had condemned Antony after Julius Caesar's assassination. Cicero's head and hands were taken to Rome where they were nailed on the rostra in the forum (Seneca the Elder, *Suasoriae* 6.18–20). According to tradition, Cicero's corpse, minus head and hands, was buried in a chamber in this tower, which rises 80 ft. (24 m) from a square limestone base (fig. 20).

---

17. The Villa Rubino is in the center of Formiae's coastal area (41.25247, 13.60023).

Looking down from a hill north of the road is a smaller tomb believed to be that of Tullia or Tulliola, the pet name given by Cicero to his beloved daughter.[18] Although neither tomb is proven archaeologically, Cicero and his family remain irrevocably linked with Formiae.[19]

**Figure 20.** Tomb of Cicero (?) near Formiae

---

18. Photographs of this and many other Roman remains in Formiae and the surrounding area can be found at: https://www.formiae.it/siti/tomba-di-tulliola-in-acerbara/.

19. In early church history Formiae also gave rise to a famous bishop named Erasmus, martyred by Diocletian in 303. Also known as Saint Elmo, he became the patron of sailors. He is said to have continued preaching even after a thunderbolt struck the ground near him. Thus, sailors in danger from sudden storms and lightning began to invoke Elmo's assistance. Electrical discharges on the mastheads of ships, read as a sign of his protection, became known as St. Elmo's fire. His relics were removed from Formiae's cathedral after it was razed by the Saracens in 842 and relocated to Gaeta. Currently they are in the Cathedral Church there. His feast day is celebrated annually on June 2, the anniversary of his martyrdom.

**Figure 21.** MP 85 and 84 south of Itri

About 1 RM (0.96 mi./1.55 km) west of Formiae, just past Cicero's tomb, the VA bent slightly northwestward as it moved farther from the coast. The road thus avoided the Aurunci massif to the east and the hilly area above coastal Caieta and the coastal marshes farther to the west. Instead, it ran parallel to the coast but about 5 mi. (8 km) inland. Again, the SS7 preserves the approximate track of the ancient VA. This is shown by a number of traces, including several small Roman bridges and viaducts in the vicinity.[20] Further confirmation is provided by two surviving

---

20. A local historian, Raffaele Capolino, has identified these and posted photographs on a website that features Formiae and its antiquities (https://www.formiae.it/siti-presenti-sul-territorio/).

# Day 3: Sinuessa to Itri

milestones (fig. 21). The first MP bears the number LXXXV (85)* and can be seen on the east side of SS7 775 ft. (240 m) before it crosses under a railway bridge.[21] A half mile (800 m) after the railway, on the west side of SS7 above the Itri train station, the second MP is visible with the number LXXXIIII (84)*.[22] Since the distance between their present positions is only 0.7 RM (0.64 mi./1.03 km), both cannot be in situ. Measuring from the in-situ MP 43 in Forum Appii (see day 5 below), MP 85 should have stood about 328 ft. (100 m) south of where MP 84 stands today. Thus, while both milestones are genuine, it appears that they were both moved at some point to their present positions.[23]

## Itri

From Formiae the easy walking on the coastal plains had been left behind. Fields of grain had given way to vineyards and flocks of sheep as Paul's group began to traverse more hilly country. From MP 84, the VA followed the east side of a ravine northward beneath SS7 for another 0.8 mi. (1.3 km). Where SS7 then turns northeastward, the VA continued straight and then arced northwestward to hug the hillside for another 2800 ft. (850 m) under Corso San Gennaro. This becomes Corso Appio Claudio when it enters the medieval city of Itri (map 17).

---

By email he has provided their measurements; each is about 33 ft. (10 m) long, 7.9 ft. (2.4 m) high, and 9.8 ft. (3 m) wide.

21. The SS7 runs just west of where MP 85 now stands. The highway then bends further to the west and back eastward to pass beneath the railroad tracks. The ancient VA instead appears to have continued straight, and thus would have passed on the east side of MP 85.

22. The numbers were badly weathered already when the stone was first documented. It is either CIL 10.6859 or 6861. CIL 6859 was read as LXXXIII but LXXXIIII is clearly seen in our photograph (fig. 21).

23. Our calculations put MP 84 originally at 41.28411, 13.53862, and MP 85 originally at 41.27207, 13.54577. Zannini (2007, 75) assumes that 85 is in situ and matches perfectly with his calculation northward from MP 108 in Sinuessa and 88 in Formiae. Our own calculations starting from his location of MP 108 put MP 85 about 655 ft. (200 m) south of its current location.

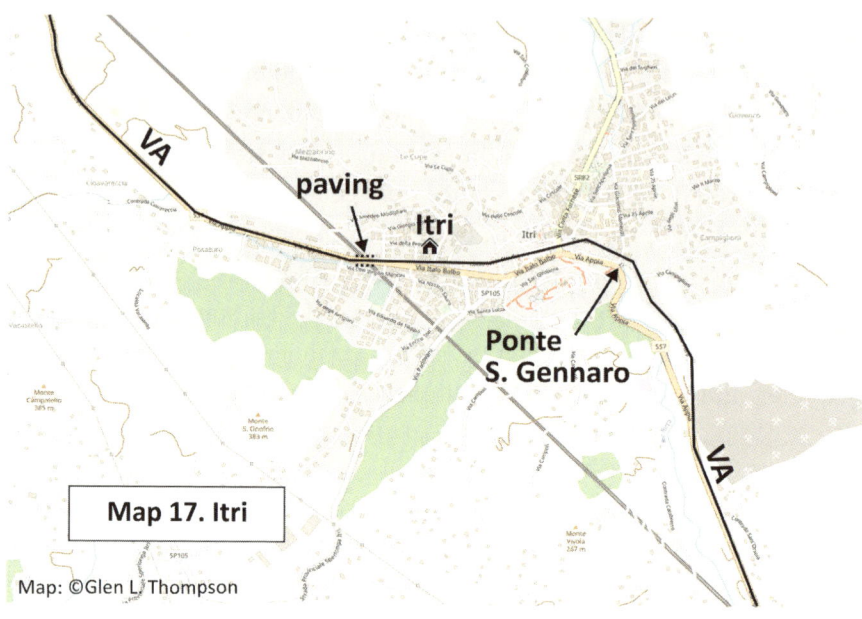

Map 17. Itri

Map: ©Glen L. Thompson

In antiquity Itri was part of Formiae's territory, apparently receiving its name from the VA since *iter* means "route" or "way." No ancient city is ever mentioned at this location, so the site probably developed as a way station providing food and equipment for travelers and their livestock. Although not mentioned in the itineraries, it lies almost halfway between Formiae and Fundi, and thus would be a natural place for a *mansio*. Soon *tabernae* and other support services for travelers would develop around it. When Paul arrived, it was probably little more than a rest station. The modern Ponte di San Gennaro* has a well-preserved stretch of the Roman drainage system that channeled water coming from a ditch upstream of the VA.[24] From the western end of Via San Genarro, the VA ran beneath

---

24. Our description of the path is that proposed by Addessi and Baldanza (2014, 173) who also provide a photograph of the structure (fig. 3); cf. Humm (1996, 712, figs. a–b).

*Day 3: Sinuessa to Itri*

today's aptly named Corso Appio Claudio.[25] In Itri a section of original paving* 200 ft. (60 m) long is visible where Corso Appio Claudio merges again with SS7 on the town's western edge. Julius and his party spent the third night of their journey at the *mansio* here, according to our hypothetical reconstruction.

---

25. Others have suggested that the VA, coming from the south, crossed the deep valley spanned by a viaduct, whose remains are still visible (41.286094, 13.537016). Its incline of 15–20 percent would have been barely passable for travelers and carts. If this route goes back to Roman times, it must have been a diverticulum from the VA.

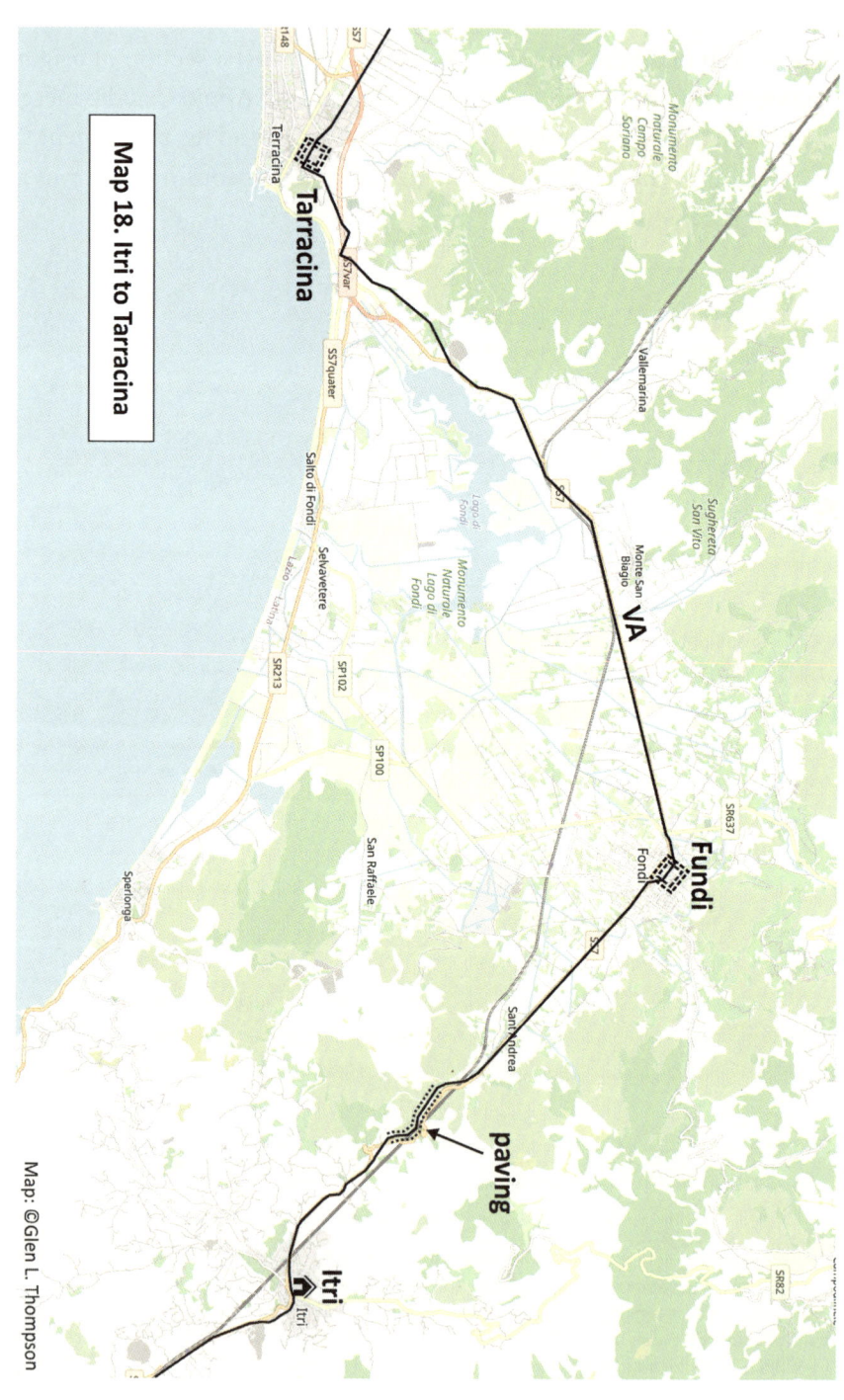

DAY 4

# Itri (RM 83) to Tarracina (RM 63)

## Valley of Sant'Andrea

Leaving Itri, Paul's party continued northwestward along the path of SS7 for about 2.8 mi. (4.5 km) before reaching the entrance to a narrow pass where a stream crossed to the northwest over the southwestern flank of Monti Aurunci.[1] Historically the pass held a strategic position. With a length of 2 mi. (3.2 km), it is known today by the picturesque name of Gola (*throat* or *gorge*) di Sant'Andrea. Here, because the engineers of SS7 chose a route 175–325 ft. (50–100 m) away along the northern side of the pass, a section of the VA\* has been preserved 1.9 mi. (3 km) in length (fig. 22). Part of the Monti Aurunci National Park, it is here that modern travelers can best experience an extended walk along the path that Paul traveled.[2] Access is easiest from the north where a partially paved bridge spans the stream, and a parking lot is provided for vehicles.[3] Numerous signs in Italian provide excellent maps and explanations of the repair work done during the various periods of the road's history over the past two thousand years. The surface was first paved with calcareous

---

1. More precisely, from the end of the ancient pavement in Itri at the east end of the Corso Appio Claudio, the ancient route follows SS7 closely for 1.6 mi. (2.6 km). Then, at 41.39461, 13.49954, the SS7 veers west to begin a hairpin turn and descent into the valley. The VA continued straight another 1800 ft. (550 m) to about 41.30775, 13.49463 before beginning a 325 ft. (100 m) arc to the west where it crosses SS7 and joins the beginning of the preserved stretch signposted in the park.

2. A detailed brochure about the park can be downloaded from its official website at: https://www.parcoaurunci.it/luoghi/appia-antica/.

3. The FIRB research project has been doing systematic archaeological and topographical research on the VA in the area of the pass: http://firb.appiantica.itabc.cnr.it. Drone footage of this section of the VA can be viewed on their website.

breccia that was replaced with limestone during the Augustan period. In AD 216 Caracalla had this resurfaced with volcanic basalt brought from Roccamonfina or Vesuvius. Curbs and sidewalks were added at that time, traces of which still remain. Later repairs were made by Philip II of Spain in 1568 a few years after adding "king of Naples and Sicily" to his titles, and in the eighteenth century when the Bourbons controlled the area.

As one proceeds into the valley from the south, an ancient quarry becomes visible that contains a wall later faced with *opus reticulatum* and used as a rest station\*. Halfway through the pass a temple of Apollo\* was built during the Republican period. Although situated on a hilltop, the temple with its Corinthian pillars was built on a platform that itself was 46 ft. (14 m) above the valley floor. By the time Paul passed, the sanctuary complex had spread to the north side of the VA as well. More than five hundred years later, Gregory the Great (*Dialogues* 7.3) told the story of a Jewish traveler heading toward Rome on the VA a century or more earlier. He was still in this valley (4.5 mi./7.25 km from Fundi) when it became dark, so he was forced to spend a sleepless night in the ruins of the deserted temple. The next day he continued to Fundi where he met with Bishop Andrew and was converted to Christianity. By the high Middle Ages a chapel for Saint Andrew (the apostle) was built on the site, hence the modern name, Gola di S. Andrea (St. Andrew's Gorge).[4]

---

4. We follow the majority opinion that the ruins here belong to the Apollo temple mentioned by Gregory, although Nicolai has found a dedication to Mercury Invictus in the same area. Carlo Labruzzi sketched the ruins in the late 18th century before Napoleon's troops demolished it to build a fort. The first specific mention of the church as S. Andrea in Silice is in a papal bull of 1158. On the temple and its identification, see the lengthy article by L. Quilici (2003) and the more recent summary of Lacam and Quadrino (2016, 30–34).

**Figure 22.** Paving in Sant'Andrea Valley

**Figure 23.** *Opus reticulatum* wall outside Fundi

About 750 ft. (225 m) after crossing the still-extant Roman bridge\* at the northern end of the pass, the VA veered to the northwest, rejoining the path of the SS7. Paul's party now had nearly a straight and level path for the remaining 3.61 mi. (5.82 km) to the outskirts of Fundi (modern Fondi). That the modern road preserves the path of the VA is confirmed by a wall in *opus reticulatum*,\* 740 ft. (225 m) long, lining the eastern side of SS7 as it enters Fondi (fig. 23). It was probably the wall of a Roman country villa. Near this spot Paul's party passed a junction with a road built in 184 BC by the censor L. Valerius Flaccus. It ran south to the coast at Sperlonga, then continued to Caieta. Known as the Via Flacca, it is more properly called the Via Valeria (Livy, *Hist.* 39.44.6). In Sperlonga, Tiberius had a magnificent villa built on a rocky promontory projecting into the sea, and on its grounds was a *spelunca* ("grotto"). Once when Tiberius was dining in its elaborate triclinium, the roof collapsed and Tiberius was miraculously saved by his praetorian prefect Sejanus (Tacitus, *Ann.* 4.59).[5]

The road to Sperlonga passed through the Caecuban Plain, which Strabo (*Geogr.* 5.3.6) praised for producing excellent wines whose fame was widespread.[6] Years of neglect and the construction of Nero's canal, fed by the marshy water in the plain, caused the destruction of its single vineyard (Pliny the Elder, *Nat.* 14.8.61; Tacitus, *Ann.* 15.41).

## Fundi

Fundi sat inland, although its *territorium* included much of the Sperlonga area. Together with its neighbor Formiae, it did not fight against Rome in the Latin War of 338 BC and, as a result, had been awarded citizenship *sine suffragio*. In 330, however, a leading citizen, Vetruvius Vaccus, joined

---

5. The briefer description by Suetonius (*Tiberius* 39) of the same incident places it more ambiguously "near Terracina." Sperlonga is about 10 mi. (16 km) from Tarracina. The marble used for the remarkable Sperlonga statue group discovered in 1957 was brought from the Docimium quarry near Afyon, Turkey. These statues are now displayed in the Archaeological Museum of Sperlonga; see Bruno, Attanasio, and Prochaska (2015, 375–94).

6. Called a "generous wine but overpowering and strong" by Athenaeus (*Deipnosophists* 1.27a), the Caecubian wine took many years to mature. Its vineyard was situated on marshy ground at Amyclae, somewhere near Sperlonga, where the vines were trained to climb poplar trees (Martial, *Epigrams* 13.115).

*Day 4: Itri to Tarracina*

a revolt by the nearby city of Privernum (modern Priverno), thereby eliciting Roman retaliation. The city fathers diverted much of the punishment, however, by convincing the Roman consul Lucius Plautius Venox that Vaccus had acted on his own initiative and that the rest of the city had always remained loyal to Rome (Livy, *Hist.* 8.19). In 188 BC, Fundi's citizens received full suffrage and were enrolled in the tribe Aemilia (Livy, *Hist.* 8.14.10; 38.36.7–9). Because of the marshy ground running northward from the coast and Fundi's importance in the area's Romanization (demonstrated during the Latin Wars), the VA was laid out to run northeast from Tarracina to Fundi before continuing southeast to Formiae, rather than following a more direct path along or nearer the coast.

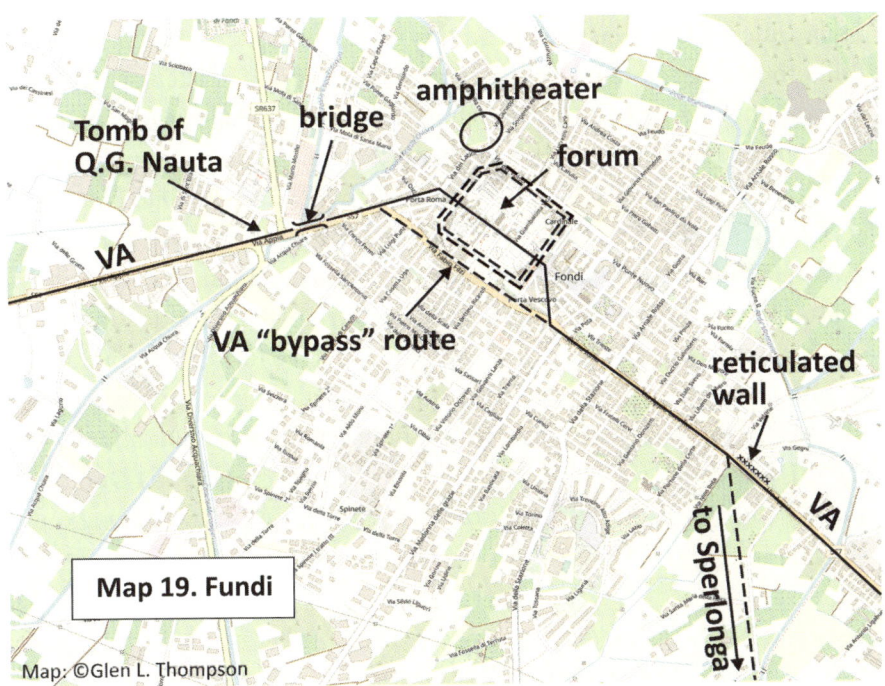

Map 19. Fundi

Map: ©Glen L. Thompson

The ancient city plan, still surviving today, dates somewhere between the late fourth and early second centuries BC (map 19). However, more precise dating is controversial.[7] The plan is shaped like a Roman castrum in which the VA of 312 BC served as its *decumanus maximus*, similar to Capua, Sinuessa, Minturnae, and Formiae. It runs beneath the current Corso Appio Claudio from the eastern gate, the Porta Capuana*, to the western gate, the Porta Romana*. At the Porta Romana the original polygonal walls, built into modern structures, are visible.[8] Via Giuseppe Mazzini and Via Vitruvius Vacca mark the *cardo maximus*. Within the city walls were seven lesser *decumani* and six lesser *cardines*, most still discernable. These are in near perfect alignment, all at thirty degrees east of north.[9] So was the city built around the VA, or vice versa? Some have argued that the city was moved from a nearby location after the VA was built; others that it was rebuilt on this plan after the city was destroyed. Still others suggest that the city plan was already in existence, and the VA was engineered to pass through its center (C. di Fazio 2012, 16–20).

Complicating the discussion further is that the VA from Itri approached Fundi on a path almost exactly parallel to the *decumanus maximus*, but 460 ft. (140 m) to the southwest. Therefore, it had to angle up to the eastern gate, probably beneath the current Corso Italia. Then, after transiting central Fundi, the VA passed through the Porta Romana and continued another 250 ft. (75 m) before making a forty-degree turn to the southwest. At some point, however, perhaps already in Paul's day, a "bypass"* came into use by which travelers from Itri continued straight, passing about 65 ft. (20 m) outside the southern city wall. This follows roughly Via Damiano Chiesa and Via Fabio Filzie (Rumiz 2017, 306).[10] Although saving only

---

7. What follows relies considerably on the fine study of C. di Fazio (2012, 15–41); her fig. 2 (p. 19) reconstructs the position of the ancient walls of Fundi. See also Lacam (2016, §15).

8. For a photograph of the walls at the Porta Romana as well as a diagram of the city walls with gates, see Quilici and Quilici Gigli (2013, 53, fig. 4; 58, fig. 9).

9. Vitruvius (*On Architecture* 1.6.6–8) says that this orientation avoided direct exposure to the winds. This is cited by C. di Fazio (2012, 17, n. 21). *Decumani* is the plural form of *decumanus*; *cardines* the plural of *cardo*.

10. The path is shown in C. di Fazio (2012, 18).

about 360 ft. (110 m), this bypass avoided the crowded streets in the city center. However, its dating is also controversial.[11]

Both routes may have been available to Julius.[12] If the central route was chosen, his party passed MP 75 just inside the eastern gate. The forum* was located on today's Piazza Santa Maria. Since the city has remained occupied without interruption since antiquity, there has been little opportunity for substantial excavations in its center. Only a few remains from the Roman period have been identified with numerous smaller finds exhibited in the archaeological museum. Suetonius (*Tiberius* 5.1) informs us that Tiberius, perhaps born in Fundi, had the Senate erect a statue of Fortuna here in his honor. It was likely placed in a prominent location, and Paul may well have seen it as he passed.

Outside Fundi's western gate, the VA turned southwestward, again under SS7, to begin its extended run straight toward Tarracina. Nearby is a pedestrian bridge over the Acqua Chiara canal, built perhaps over remains of the original VA bridge*. As elsewhere, tombs lined the road outside the city. One impressive circular tower* remains today, attributed dubiously to Gavius Quintus Nauta.[13] It is partially hidden behind the old church of Santa Maria del Soccorso on the north side of SS7. About 1300 ft. (400 m) later, the travelers passed MP 74. The party were now just over halfway to Rome on their journey of 153 RM from Puteoli.

---

11. One factor not mentioned by C. di Fazio (2012) is the centuriation remains studied by Libertini (2019, 150). These show that the agricultural land surrounding Fundi has three different centuriation patterns, the last in connection with the settlement of veteran soldiers by Augustus. The earliest seems to be aligned with the city plan, but unfortunately its date is also unknown. The entry in the *Liber colonarium* reads: "Fundi, fortified town surrounded with a wall. No right of way is due to the community. Its cultivated land by order of Augustus was allocated to veteran soldiers: the rest <of the territory> reverted to its jurisdiction and to public control"; see Libertini (2019, 149).

12. Besides the short bypass, there may have been a longer bypass that ran approximately 1.5 mi. (2.4 km) south of the *decumanus maximus* and followed the railway line from 41.35125, 13.35902 to 41.33320, 13.46314. It was 0.73 mi. (1.18 km) shorter than the route through Fundi. This seems to be the only route across the plain that would fit the topography and still avoid the marshes. However, we are unaware of any evidence of such a route during the Roman period.

13. An inscription found nearby belonged to a tomb of this aedile from Fundi (*CIL* 12.1719 = *ILLRP* 601). A large piece of the monument collapsed in 2019, and the site is now scheduled for restoration; https://www.latinaquotidiano.it/fondi-crolla-una-parte-della-tomba-di-gavio-nauta-de-meo-sara-messa-in-sicurezza/.

For the next 7 RM the VA was engineered to stay on the higher ground along the northern edge of the plain, thus avoiding the marshy coastal area which today has become the Lago di Fondi.¹⁴ The first 4 RM ran in a straight line slightly south of west and still under SS7 until it entered the shadow of the Ausoni Mountains (modern Monti Ausoni). Milestone 71 (*CIL* 10.6854) was removed at some point from the roadside and placed in the porch of the cathedral of Monte San Biagio* where it can still be seen (fig. 29).¹⁵

About 1000 ft. (450 m) after passing MP 70 and just after the VA curved southwest around the foot of Monte San Biagio, travelers today arrive at a medieval tower. Called Portella*, it stands on the north side of the road. In early modern times, this tower was connected by an archway to a similar one on the south side. This formed a fortified gateway that marked the border between the kingdoms of Naples and the Papal States. The VA passed beneath the gate until 1933, and a small stretch of ancient paving can still be seen running from the surviving tower toward the west.

It has been suggested that the path of the VA over the following miles may in places have been closer to Via Bufalari rather than SS7 (Rumiz 2017, 308–9). However, the surviving remains all seem to border SS7. These include the remains of a wall* on the north side, just before the cemetery of Monte San Biagio. Some 2625 ft. (800 m) farther is the quadrangular mausoleum of Sestus Julius Frontinus*, a patrician who maintained a majestic villa in the area. Almost hidden by trees along the north side, the mausoleum has a square shape with sides measuring about 105 ft. (32 m), while its height is 33 ft. (10 m). It was formerly thought to belong to Galba, who was born in a villa between Fundi and Tarracina in 3 BC (Suetonius *Galba* 8). Galba briefly reigned as the first emperor of AD 69, the famous Year of the Four Emperors.

---

14. A satellite photograph of Fundi and its surroundings with arrows marking the VA is found in Quilici and Quilici Gigli (2013, 56, fig. 7).

15. See the photograph in Carbonara and Messineo (1998, 126).

*Day 4: Itri to Tarracina*

After another 0.6 mi. (1 km), Paul's party saw yet another large tomb on the right. In the sixteenth century it was turned into a fortification by adding a tower, so today is known as Torre dell'Epitaffio* ("Tower of the Epitaph"). It alerted travelers heading south that they were leaving the Papal States and would soon, at the aforementioned Portella, enter the Kingdom of Naples.[16] Originally, however, it was a Roman tomb, once thought to be that of Tullia, Cicero's only daughter who died in childbirth in 45 BC. When Cicero's young and jealous second wife Publilia refused to show sufficient grief for Tulliola ("little Tullia"), he divorced her. We have already noted that another tomb overlooking the so-called Tomb of Cicero west of Formiae is also named as her resting place. Cicero was truly grief-stricken at her death, but it probably led him to build one substantial tomb rather than two. Here the medieval tower is connected by a round arch to a surrounding wall that stretches along the mountain above the VA. Traces of a retaining wall built into the hillside are still visible while proceeding toward Tarracina (modern Terracina). Near the tomb is a sign waymarking the Via Francigena, a hiking trail with some sections paralleling the VA from Rome to Minturnae.[17]

Some 1300 ft. (400 m) after passing MP 67, and just over 1 RM (0.96 mi./1.55 km) beyond the monumental tomb with an epitaph, the remains of a monumental Roman exedra* are hidden in the foliage on the north side of SS7 (fig. 24). At this point the original route of the VA left the plain and began to climb through a pass in the Volscian Hills toward Tarracina. Later the exedra would mark the place where the VA split, for a second coastal route was built later to avoid the ascent into the city.

---

16. Perhaps the 1.9 mi. (3 km) between the Portella and this tower were a neutral buffer zone between the two kingdoms.

17. The Via Francigena was the medieval pilgrimage trail running from Canterbury, England, to Rome. It has now been extended southward beyond Rome; see https://www.viefrancigene.org/en/the-via-francigena-in-italy/.

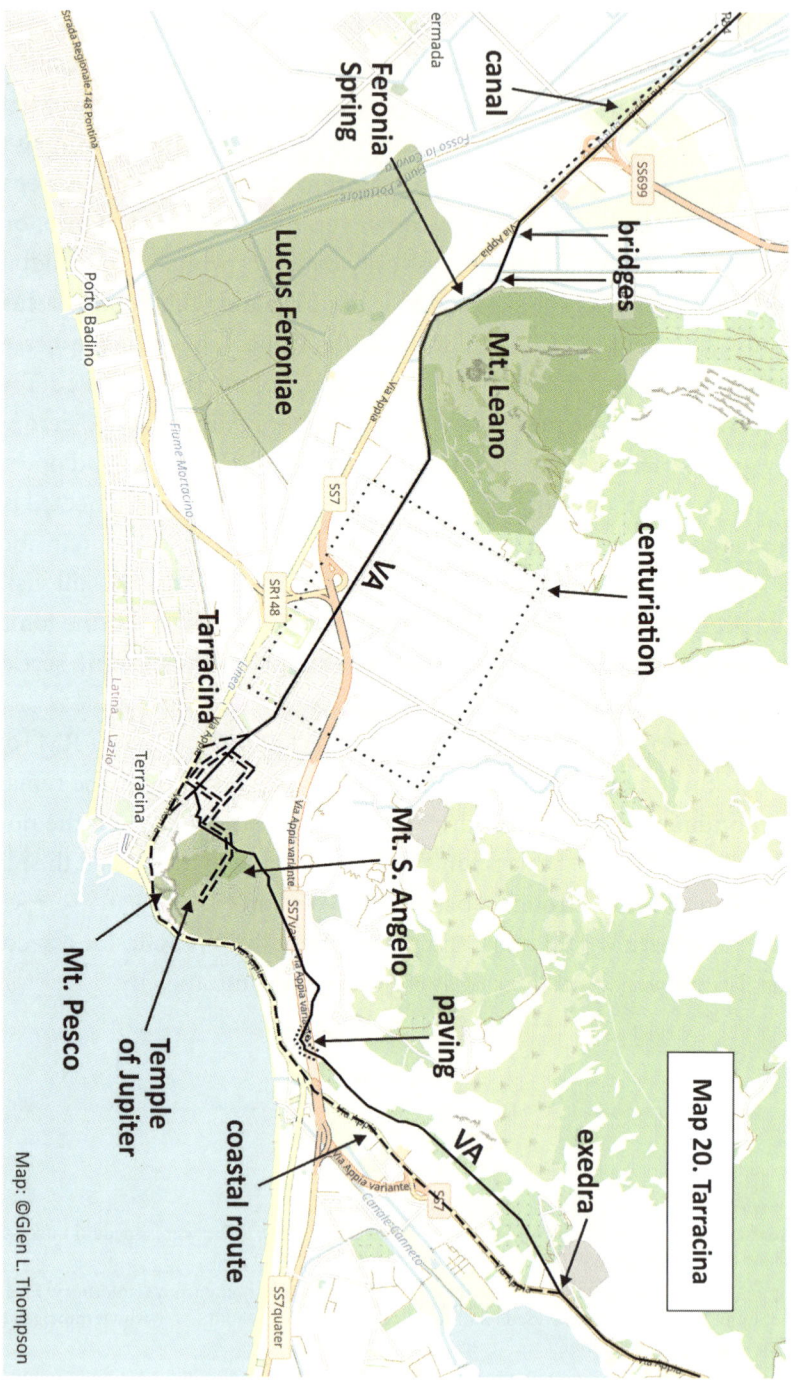

Map 20. Tarracina

Day 4: Itri to Tarracina

## Trajan's Coastal Route

Because the mountain (modern Monte Sant'Angelo) lying on the south side of Tarracina descended to the sea, early travelers could not pass beneath it along the coast. In 179 BC, on the coast to the west of the mountain, Marcus Aemilius Lepidus, consul in 187 BC, built a breakwater to improve the small harbor. However, even with the upgrade, it was apparently insufficient for the anchorage of larger ships and served more for Lepidus's personal use, hence the criticism by Livy (*Hist.* 40.51.2) for building it at public expense. Some trade goods were apparently imported through this port (Laurence 1999, 105), but it was not until the second century AD that the Emperor Trajan engaged in a major upgrade of Tarracina's harbor.

**Figure 24.** Exedra east of Tarracina

The accepted opinion is that his engineers simultaneously cut a seaside route for the VA.[18] This allowed travelers both to bypass the city center and to stay on level ground by avoiding the steep climb through the pass farther north. The Roman engineers cut vertically along the coastal side of the tall rock formation called Pisco Montano to create the passage still followed by the modern highway.[19] The chiseled rock face* is marked by Roman numerals set in *tabula ansata* that start at X and descend every ten Roman feet with the lowest being CXX (*CIL* 10.6849).[20] The entire height of the modification is thus 128 Roman feet (125 ft./38 m). The rock removed from the face was used to rebuild the harbor. A stele found there depicts a group of workers in various activities of harbor-building directed by a seated individual dressed in a *paladumentum*, a cloak or cape worn by military commanders.[21] Whether this depiction dates to Trajan's reconstruction is debatable. However, the scene is certainly suggestive of how the modification of the Pisco Montano resulted in a new harbor as well as facilitated the rerouting of the VA past the port. In any case, the seaside route was not yet an option in Paul's day.[22] For a comparison of the length and difficulty of the two routes using digital map modeling, see appendix 2.

---

18. Some scholars have argued for an earlier date for this reengineering of the road. However, the consensus remains that the modification at Pisco Montano was initiated by Trajan. The dedicatory inscription for Trajan's column in Rome indicates that the Quirinal slope was similarly cut to provide space for the Forum and Markets of Trajan. The column's shaft was an artificial unit of 100 Roman feet that was increased and adjusted by the pedestal and other elements. As Jon Coulston (n.d.) notes, "A contemporary parallel to this concern for topographical modification, and its metric expression, is provided by the Pisco Montano road cutting for the Via Appia at Terracina (Italy)."

19. SS7 now bypasses the center of Terracina through a tunnel under the mountain.

20. For a close-up of seven of these numerals, see Staccioli (2003, 78–79, figs. 60–66).

21. For an illustration of this relief, see Huissen (2020, Photo 14).

22. On the two VA routes at Tarracina and the related road system, see particularly Malizia (1988, 73–86) and the map on page 81, fig. 32. Interestingly, a color drawing of the VA leading to the walls of COLONIA AXVRNAS found on fol. 89r of Vatican manuscript Pal. lat. 1564 (ninth century)—a copy of Hyginus Gromaticus's *Agrimensores* ("surveyors") which was written by him during the reign of Trajan—still has only one route of the VA leading to the city; see at https://digi.ub.uni-heidelberg.de/diglit/bav_pal_lat_1564/0205. The rest of the illustration, however, does not match the city's geographical situation and centuriation, so it is not conclusive evidence.

Day 4: Itri to Tarracina                                                   103

## Tarracina

From the exedra Paul's party began the moderate climb up Monte Sant'Angelo that would take them the final 3.7 mi. (6 km) to the forum of Tarracina (map 20). For the first 1.2 mi. (1.9 km) the track of the VA has been lost, but the route of much of the following 1.75 mi. (2.8 km) is preserved by Via Piazza Palatina.[23] This section of road widens and served as a rest stop, today known as Piazza Palatina*. Here a beautiful vista was offered of the sea below and the Temple of Anxur above. At various points along this stretch, ancient paving stones, curbing, and support structures are visible today (fig. 25). After catching their breath and appreciating the view, the group continued to climb the remaining 0.9 mi. (1.5 km) to the top of the pass where the modern Via Piazza Palatina ends.

**Figure 25.** Paving on Via Piazza Palatina

---

23. The VA must have passed under the parking lot of the marble quarry and made a gentle arc uphill through the fields, paralleling the main quarry road but about 410 ft. (125 m) to its south for about 2953 ft. (900 m). Then (c. 41.31539, 13.29158) it bent to parallel SS7 about 1150 ft. (350 m) to its north for another 3280 ft. (1000 m). It cut across the terrain and steadily climbed until it reached Via Piazza Palatina where that modern road bends ninety degrees to connect with the old SS7 below (41.30810, 13.28360). Via Piazza Palatina ends at 41.29674, 13.25796.

The group had climbed some 500 ft. (150 m) since leaving the plain. Nearby a sacred road led onto a promontory rising above the sea where the famed Temple of Jupiter Anxur* stood. This impressive complex of the Republican period was constructed on an arched podium between 150–50 BC over an earlier–fourth-century-BC sanctuary. It soon became the religious focus of the city, which lay below to the northwest. Just beyond the Anxur temple the remains of a temple dedicated to a Greek deity have been discovered. Built in the second century BC, it is the earliest Hellenistic structure of its type in Latium and perhaps the first terraced temple in the region.[24] Paul's party continued to follow the VA as it turned south and then crossed the broad pass before snaking down the steep hillside and passing through the northeastern gate* to the forum and the center of Tarracina.[25]

Probably first an Etruscan settlement, Tarracina later became a city of the Volsci who named it Anxur after the eponymous deity of the city (Diodorus Siculus, *Library* 14.16.5).[26] Strabo (*Geogr.* 5.3.6) wrote that the Roman name Tarracina was perhaps a Latinized version of the Greek *Trachina*, from τραχύς (*trachys*) meaning "rugged." The Romans founded a small colony here in 329 BC. Seventeen years later the VA was routed through the city to provide a ready link to Rome. In 217 BC the Roman consul Minucius was able to hold the pass against Hannibal's army, thus preventing the Carthaginians from using the VA to advance on Rome (Livy, *Hist.* 22.15). After Germanicus died in Antioch in AD 19, his body was returned to Italy. His adoptive brother Drusus the Younger and his younger brother, the future emperor Claudius, traveled down the VA to Tarracina to meet the general's widow, Agrippina. Together they

---

24. Excavations by German and Italian archaeologists have revealed this temple; see https://disci.unibo.it/en/research/archaeological-missions/archaeological-missions-italy/terracina-latina-sanctuary-monte-sant-angelo.

25. The gate was about 1395 ft. (425 m) past the end of Via Piazza Palatina and 2380 ft. (725 m) from the forum. According to the oft-reproduced 1926 map of Lugli, reprinted by Carbonara and Messineo (1998, 102) and Coppola (1984, 327), the VA, after entering the gate, ran straight and did not have the large bend that Via Anxur follows today. It ran several hundred yards/meters inside the city wall, which was to its right. Its path nearer the forum is more difficult to determine.

26. The Emperor Augustus was descended from the Volscians with his paternal family coming from nearby Velletri (Suetonius, *Augustus* 1).

*Day 4: Itri to Tarracina* 105

accompanied the urn with his ashes back to Rome (Tacitus, *Ann.* 3.2). In AD 68 after Nero's suicide, the city initially supported their native son Galba. However, after his death on AD January 15, 69, Tarracina then supported Vespasian in his successful bid to become emperor (Tacitus, *Histories* 4.3).

The VA's path is not totally clear as it descends from the east into the city, but it is thought to approximate the path of Via Panoramica, then turn into Via Anxur, then into Via San Francesco Nuova, and finally leveling just southeast of the forum, a distance of 0.7 mi. (1.15 km).[27] Here it ran through a monumental gate* characterized by four large arches arranged on a square plan (*arco quadrifonte*). One arch remains amid a cluster of nearby archaeological ruins, including a wall of mixed construction styles, the so-called temple of Vicolo Pertinace, and an entrance to the theater* from a stepped alley. Just above the arch is the podium upon which rose a tetrastyle of Tiberius and Livia (Malizia 2020, 19–24).[28]

Near the *quadraporticus* and still outside the forum, a road descended to the original harbor, following the path of today's Via Annunziata and Via Roma. It was probably built in conjunction with Trajan's modifications to the Pisco Montano and the harbor. The new coastal bypass route of that period passed the Bath of Neptune and a later Forum of Severus. A fragment of the route of this lower VA* is nicely preserved inside the walls of the Villa Salvini.[29] The canal that ran from Forum Appii to Tarracina was not extended to the harbor until the end of the eighteenth century.

---

27. Coppola (1984, 373) specifically supports Lugli's reconstruction of the VA's path with its *doppia curva* ("double curve") up the hill of San Francesco.

28. For photographs and drawings of this area, see Malizia (2020, 30–32, figs. 5–10).

29. Visits to the site can be arranged by appointment through the Circolo Legambiente Terracina "Pisco Montano."

**Figure 26.** Pavement in forum of Tarracina

Upon reaching the city center, the VA turned northwestward and entered the forum* (fig. 26). Denoting either its date or its benefactor, it has been called both the Republican Forum or the Forum Aemilianum.[30] The distinctive paving of the VA* still crosses the northeast side of today's city square. The pavement on the rest of the forum was built upon a series of supporting arches to provide a broad, level surface. This suggests that the site was chosen to ensure that the city's central space was contiguous to the VA.[31] Travelers passing through the city center were somewhat shielded from the hustle and bustle of the crowds in the forum by a row of curbstones and statues. This layout may have been in response

---

30. Hesberg has reconstructed the quadrangular plan of the earliest colony in relationship with the later plan. His map is reproduced by Pagano (1995, 68, fig. 5).

31. This site was chosen over others closer either to the temple of Jupiter Anxur or to the harbor just because it was on the VA; so Laurence (1999, 156–57). Likewise, when the alternative coastal route of the VA was completed together with the redevelopment of the harbor area in the second century AD, the lower forum along the route of the new VA route was greatly remodeled; see Malizia (1988, 73–82) and Laurence (1999, 154–56).

## Day 4: Itri to Tarracina

to legislation passed in the reign of Claudius which attempted to balance the tension between the traveler in a hurry and the inhabitants of Italian towns (Suetonius, *Claudius* 25.2). The law stipulated that travelers were not permitted to bring their carriages into towns, but required either to walk or be carried by litter through them. This slowed their speed so that they would not hit pedestrians. However, the slower pace would also allow the city's monuments, statues, and inscriptions to impact travelers visually. Here an inscription still embedded in the paving announces: "Aulus Aemilius paved this" (*Aulus Aemilius stravit*, CIL 10.6306). Laurence (1999, 154–56) viewed Tarracina as a case study for Claudius's urban legislation. Nevertheless, since this was the only route to the south at Paul's time, we are left to wonder how a traveler passing through could get his carriage from one end of Tarracina to the other.

The forum in Paul's day was about twice as big as today's Piazza Municipio, extending farther to the northwest and some 100 ft. (30 m) farther to the southeast. At the northwest end the medieval cathedral, the Duomo di Terracina, stands upon the site of a Roman temple*, also built by the same local benefactor, Aulus Aemilius, and dedicated to Rome and Augustus (CIL 10.6305). Some of its ancient columns were incorporated into the cathedral's walls. To the north just outside the current piazza, the Capitolium*, dating to about 40 BC, and another temple, thought to be dedicated to Minerva, flanked the route of the VA. On the northeast, just across the VA a portico lined the road beyond which a theater*, dating to the time of Sulla (138–78 BC), was built into the hillside. Other unidentified public buildings lined the western and southwestern sides, where today the city's archaeological museum looks out over the lower city. The layout of these public buildings may well have reminded Paul of Minturnae. Our reconstruction of Paul's itinerary posits that, after their fourth day of traveling another 20 RM, Paul and his party found food and lodging somewhere near or at Tarracina.[32]

---

32. Horace spent his fourth night at Tarracina where some friends joined him. The city thus was a popular stopping point. In his *Tales of a Traveller*, Washington Irving also provides a colorful account of his stay in the chapter entitled "The Inn at Terracina" (1824, 261–76).

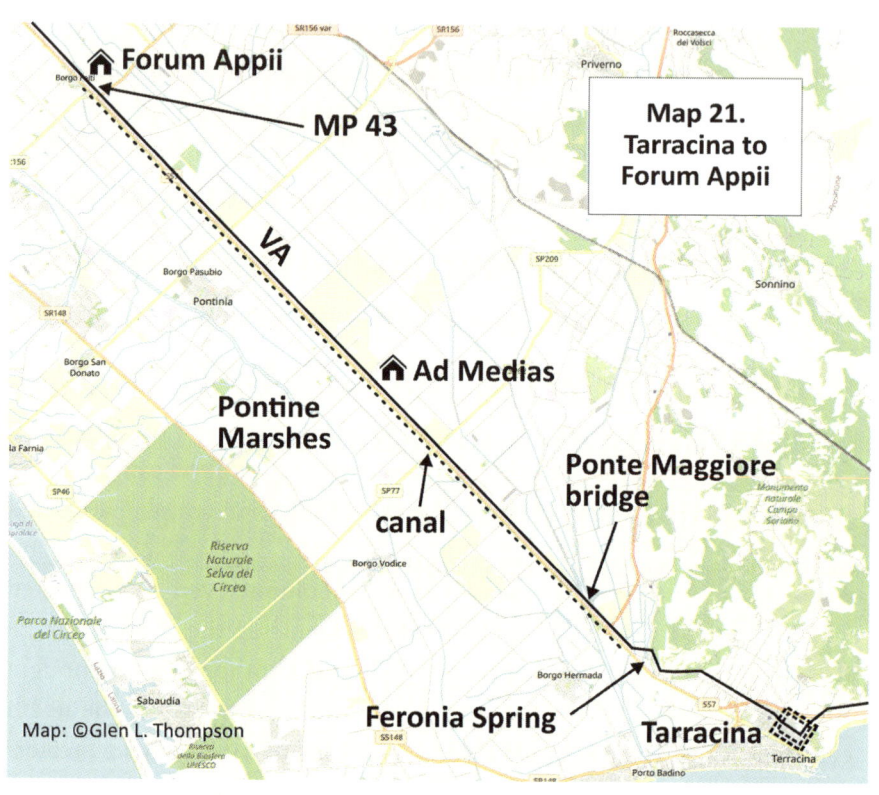

DAY 5

# Tarracina (RM 63) to Forum Appii (RM 43)

The VA served as Tarracina's *decumanus maximus*. Six hundred feet (185 m) after leaving the forum, it passed through the northwest gate* in the city wall, in medieval times known as the Porta Maggio or Porta San Lorenzo. The actual gate was moved in the late eighteenth century some 725 ft. (220 m) farther down the VA where it is today called the Porta Romana*. This rebuilt gate features an ancient tower with a base of polygonal stonework and is surmounted by a wall built in *opus incertum*. The wall has four ancient arched windows now walled up. The VA continued straight down the Via Porta Romana another 440 ft. (135 m) to Piazza Quatro Lampioni*. From this point a road ran down the hill, approximately preserved by Via dei Volsci, and on to the harbor and the Trajanic coastal road. This bypass allowed travelers to avoid the crowded forum area. However, Paul and his party continued straight on the VA, which ran beneath Via della Stazione. After about 400 ft. (120 m) they passed MP 62.[1] Then some 500 ft. (150 m) later, the road swung to the left, paralleling the railroad beyond, and continued straight for another 1.5 mi. (2.4 km) under Via Appia Antica to the foot of Monte (Mount) Leano.[2] This

---

1. The distance from Rome to Tarracina given in the Antonine and Jerusalem Itineraries is 61 RM. It was actually somewhat over 62 RM to the northwestern city gate and almost 63 RM to the southeastern wall. The distance traveled along the VA to get from one side of Tarracina to the other was apparently not considered when the itineraries calculated their distances. This may be one factor in the inconsistencies between them.

2. About 650 ft. (200 m) after the turn, an ancient arch (41.29800, 13.24000) is visible on the right between the modern road and the parking lot of the railroad station. Although no documentation on the

stretch, as depicted on the maps of Libertini (2019, 230, figs. 40a, 40c) and others, formed one of the *decumani* of the centuriated agricultural land of Tarracina.³

**Figure 27.** Spring of Feronia

The VA then arced westward around the base of Mount Leano for 1.1 mi. (1.8 km) before veering northwest and descending a final 1800 ft. (550 m) to the plain. Though Paul's party was going downhill steadily over this stretch, travelers from Rome found it a somewhat arduous climb. Horace (*Satires* 1.5.24) describes the ascent as a crawl of three miles. The path of the VA here is confirmed by various remains. On the north side of modern VAA are the brickwork of a funerary monument and the channel of a low aqueduct. Along Strada Provinciale 73 is a water monument believed to be the spring of the goddess Feronia* (fig. 27) whose temple was situated

---

arch was found, there must have been a second arch to accommodate the width of the road if it preserves the path of the VA.

3. See also Cancellieri (1990, 69, fig. 6) and Di Rosa (2018, 198, pl. 1).

Day 5: Tarracina to Forum Appii                                         111

in a nearby grove. Vergil (*Aeneid* 7.799–800, trans. Williams) says this area is where Jupiter Anxur stands guard and where "forests green make fair Feronia glad." Horace (*Satires* 1.5.24) washed his face and hands in Feronia's stream before starting his three-mile climb to Tarracina.[4] Two ancient bridges are still found along the Strada Ponte Alto. About 985 ft. (300 m) after the spring of Feronia, a single-arched bridge* crosses the Fosso dell'Acqua Traversa. Called the Ponte Antico, it was built with ashlars of local limestone and a retaining wall of *opus reticulatum* (O'Connor 1993, 71). Some 1310 ft. (400 m) farther and about 500 ft. (150 m) before the Strada Ponte Alto ends at SS7, another Roman bridge*, probably the eponymous Ponte Alto, is incorporated into the current road. The long, ramped bridge of local limestone—20 ft. (6 m) wide with a span of the same size—was built during Trajan's reign, although a bridge to cross the marshy ground certainly existed here earlier. Its single arch features roughly cut voussoirs (wedge-shaped stones used in arches) that were not well-shaped to its curve (Quilici 2009, 557).[5]

## Pontine Marshes

Arriving on the plain*, the VA immediately enters a large rectangular marshy area extending some 15.5 mi. (25 km) from northwest to southeast and about 10 mi. (16 km) in width. It is bounded by the sea to the west, by Mount Leano to the east, and by the Lepine Mountains to its north. This vast marshland prompted Livy (*Hist.* 4.59.4) to describe Tarracina as *urbs prona in paludes* ("a city surrounded by marshes"). Known as the Pontine, or Pomptine, Marshes, this area was an ongoing challenge not only for agriculture but also for transportation. Roman engineers

---

4. M. Di Fazio (2012, 344, fig. 5) reproduces Carlo Labruzzi's 1789 sketch of the sanctuary remains. It is also found in Malizia (2017, 8, fig. 2) together with other illustrations of the Tarracina area by Labruzzi.

5. Regarding the inscription probably related to this bridge (*CIL* 10.6846), Ballance (1951, 100) writes, "On both the Appia and the Flaminia there is a marked lack of Augustan inscriptions recording any kind of repairs, and it is not until the time of Trajan that these become even comparatively common."

sought to drain or divert the water but were never entirely successful.[6] Only in the twentieth century was the area more permanently drained by constructing numerous drainage channels and canals. The VA's construction actually increased the drainage issues, so ongoing maintenance was necessary. For "the marshes became dammed up behind it and the bridges were too small to take the force of the storm waters" (Dilke and Dilke 1961, 173).[7]

At some point in the Republican period, workers dug a substantial trench along the west side of the VA, from the turnoff toward Tarracina to Forum Appii, a distance of 15.75 RM (14.9 mi./24 km).[8] Earth from the trench was used to raise the VA above the surrounding area to make it more impervious to flooding. The trench was then converted into a canal to improve drainage and to provide transport (fig. 28). Strabo (*Geogr.* 5.3.6) describes the canal:

> Near Tarracina, as you go toward Rome, there is a canal which runs alongside the Appian Way, and is fed at numerous places by waters from the marshes and the rivers. People navigate the canal, preferably by night (so that if they embark in the evening they can disembark early in the morning and go the rest of their journey by the Way), but they also navigate it by day. The boat is towed by a mule.

---

6. Using metrology, Peterson (2015, 448) has suggested that the surveyors for the VA began at the northwest end of the Pontine plain: "It is the end nearer to Rome and it might be expected that surveying would start at the city and proceed southeastwards."

7. See also the map of the VA around Tarracina in Dilke and Dilke (1961, 174).

8. Horace implies that in his day the canal began near the current bridge in Borgo Faiti, about 985 ft. (300 m) north of MP 43. Later it may have been extended toward Tres Tabernae. It initially ended near Ponte Alto, for Horace disembarked at the spring of Feronia and started his three-mile climb to Tarracina from there. Today its later extension ends in Terracina at the junction of Via Appia Nuovo and Via Gregorio Antonelli (41.29075, 13.24728).

Day 5: Tarracina to Forum Appii    113

**Figure 28.** Canal along *decennovium*

Horace (*Satires* 1.5.11–23) provides an amusing account of his trip on the canal a century before Paul passed this way. He and his companion Heliodorus hired a barge so they could sleep while being pulled overnight from Forum Appii to Tarracina. Despite pesky gnats, they did get some sleep, but so did the bargemen. When they awoke the next day, they had not made any progress. A question to consider: Did Paul travel from Tarracina to Forum Appii by land or by boat, since both modes of transportation were available? Since Luke says nothing about traveling by barge, Julius apparently chose to keep his party on the VA alongside the canal.[9]

---

9. Leonard (1961, 30), however, takes the opposite view, saying that it was "probable" that they took a boat. Laurence (1999, 92–93) tries to generalize about travel speeds using Horace's journey from Rome: "He breaks off from his journey at Aricia, a mere sixteen miles from Rome. Next day he travels to Forum Appii, covering the distance of twenty-seven miles by the evening. He states that the journey from Rome to Forum Appii could be completed in one stage, but he had chosen to take his journey on the Via Appia at a slow pace. This would suggest that a normal pace for the journey would be forty-three miles for the first stage to Forum Appii, where a barge would take the traveller the eighteen miles to Tarracina overnight. Thus, over a period of twenty-four hours a distance of fifty-one miles was covered. Horace's journey features stages of under twenty miles, as

Paul was now entering Latium proper, the *suburbium* of Rome. Some 384 country villas have been documented in this region along with around forty towns. Population estimates in the early empire suggest that Latium was occupied by about 350,000 people, half as many residents as Rome itself (Smith 2020, 87). Yet the majority of people lived in the hill country east of the VA and much farther to the north. For despite the attempts at mitigation, the Pontine Marshes remained an inauspicious place for habitation. Paul and his party made good time because the road was straight and flat. In fact, there was not the slightest bend for the next 40 RM (37.75 mi./60.8 km).[10] For the entirety of the Pontine Marshes, the SS7 lies atop the VA which itself was renovated between 1777 and 1784 under the auspices of Pope Pius VI.

Whether knowingly or not, the pope, for the road from Tarracina to Forum Appii, was imitating Trajan who repaved this section in the early second century. Several surviving milestones display both the normal numbering from Rome (on the lower part of the column), but also a second number (near the top) aligning with the 19 RM in this stretch called the *decennovium* ("the nineteen") that ran from MP 42 to 63 (fig. 29).[11] Further evidence of Pope Pius's work can be seen in the regular layout of the road system in this area. Secondary roads and canals branch at right angles from the VA/SS7 at intervals of almost exactly 1 RM (0.96 mi./1.55 km). They are also named Strada Migliara 57, Via Migliara 56, and so on. These reflect quite accurately where the ancient milestones were placed—from MP 58 in the south, 0.6 mi. (1 km) before the road leaves the plain for Tarracina, to MP 41, 1.67 mi. (2.7 km) north of Forum Appii.[12]

---

well as those in the region of thirty-nine miles during the later stages towards Brindisi." A "normal" pace of 43 RM per day would be exceptional since a pedestrian generally averaged 20 RM per day.

10. The stretch of SS7 that begins just south of Cisterna and ends at Terracina, atop the VA the entire way, remains the longest straight road in Europe.

11. Figure 29 includes MP 48 (*CIL* 10.6833) and MP 49 (*CIL* 10.6835), which are marked as MP 5 and 6 respectively of the *decennovium*, both viewable in front of the posthouse at *ad Medias*. See the map in Humm (1996, 725, fig. 14).

12. These sideroads are not spaced precisely at a distance of 1 RM from each other, at least according to the modern consensus that 1 RM = 0.92 mi. or 1.48 km. The sideroads match almost

## Day 5: Tarracina to Forum Appii

Although such past and modern road renovations have validated the VA's path, they have also destroyed almost all visible traces of the historic road and its accompanying artifacts except for the canal. About 1.1 mi. (1.76 km) after starting across the plain, the party crossed two rivers. The first was the Amasenus (modern Amaseno), which the Volscian king Metabus and his daughter miraculously crossed with the aid of the goddess Diana (Vergil, *Aeneid* 11.532–567). The second was the Aufentus (modern Ufente) River. The confluence of these rivers and several drainage canals reflects the need for a multiarched bridge* in antiquity (cf. Strabo, *Geogr.* 5.3.6). The existence of such a bridge is confirmed in the name of the nearby village, Ponte Maggiore. One of the semicircular arches had a height of 35 ft. (10.5 m) to permit navigation beneath. Part of the Roman structure survived until it was demolished by German forces during World War II.

---

exactly our calculations for MP 42, 43, and 44, but then each of the *strada migliaria* to the south tend to be located about 33 ft. (10 m) short of one RM from the previous one. By the time Via Migliara 58 is reached it is some 360 ft. (110 m) short of where MP 58 was located. Pius VI's engineers thought they had found MP 42 and 46 in situ. Dividing by four from those positions, they calculated the RM to be 658.5 *canne* (rods), i.e., about 10 m shorter than the modern consensus. It was on this basis that they laid out the sideroads and canals (Nicolai 1800, 365–66).

**Figure 29.** MP 48 and 49 (Ad Medias), MP 43 (in situ at Forum Appii), MP 71 (Monte San Biagio)

Day 5: Tarracina to Forum Appii 117

The next stop was *ad Medias**, a *mansio* midway (hence the name) between Tarracina and Forum Appii—about 9.5 RM. *Ad Medias* along with Forum Appii "were presumably founded in the late 4th century (contemporaneously with the construction of the VA). Both sites were certainly active during the Republican and early Imperial periods; after this *ad Medias* probably disappeared, whereas *Forum Appii* continued to exist for several centuries" (De Haas et al. 2017, 510). The approximate location of *ad Medias* is marked today by Casale di Mesa where two milestones from Trajan's reign, not in situ, are displayed in front of a building (fig. 29). They record the distances both from Rome (48 RM and 49 RM) and from Forum Appii for the *decennovium* (5 RM and 6 RM).[13] North of the milestones on the east side of SS7 are the remains of the first-century BC podium and tower of the mausoleum of Clessipus Geganius*.[14] According to legend, he was an ugly humpback slave freed by his mistress for his amatory skills. After inheriting her fortune, he built this monument in memory of his benefactress (Garland 1999, 52–54, 190).

---

13. On the milestones, see note 11 above. Cooley (2012, 160) mistakenly gives the distance from Tarracina, not Forum Appii. Her discussion on pages 160 and 162 has informed our text. Assuming the *decennovium* ran from MP 43 at Forum Appii to MP 62 at Tarracina, *ad Medias* was located not quite "at the middle." Casale di Mesa is 1500 ft. (450 m) south of where MP 51 would have stood, that is, a bit more than 8 RM from Forum Appii.

14. The inscription naming Clessipus Geganius (*CIL* 1².1004) is installed high on a wall in Casale's courtyard. For a description, photo, and plan see Carbonara and Messineo (1998, 97–98).

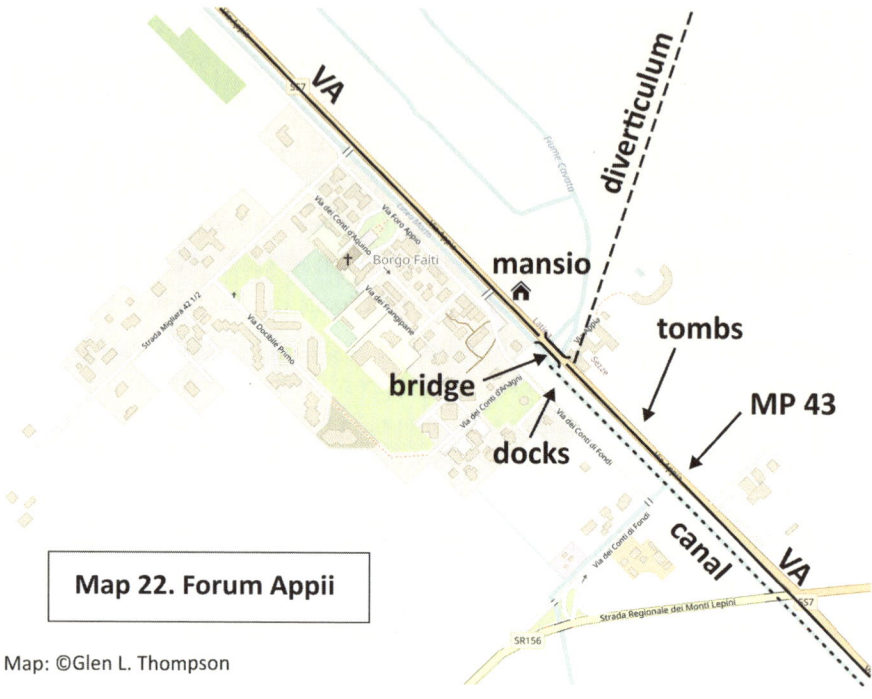

Map 22. Forum Appii

Map: ©Glen L. Thompson

## Forum Appii

Little else survives in the northern half of the *decennovium* until it ends at MP 43 in Forum Appii (modern Borgo Faiti). Here the Cavata River flows into the canal and is where the canal apparently started. The name indicates that it was established as a forum by Appius Claudius at the time of the VA's construction. By the first century BC it may have become a formal *municipium*, functioning as a local market and administrative center.[15] Horace (*Satires* 1.5.4) recalls that Forum Appii was "crammed with boatmen and stingy tavern-keepers." Topographic surveys by Gijs

---

15. For a summary of recent archaeological research around Forum Appii, see Tol and Borgers (2016, 353–54); see also De Haas et al. (2017, 508–10).

Day 5: Tarracina to Forum Appii

Tol and his team have mapped a number of Roman structures including a large building, presumably the ancient *mansio**, remains of two side roads, storehouses, and traces consistent with a landing place and dock for barges on the south side of the canal (see map 22). Remains of a one-arched Roman bridge* are visible beneath the SS7 bridge (fig. 30). Evelien Witmer of the Groningen Institute of Archaeology has recreated a nice visualization of what Forum Appii may have looked like in antiquity (Tol, De Haas, and Anastasia 2019, 39, fig. 10).

Inscriptions and votive material show that several cult places were also located in the area. On the hills above Forum Appii were the vineyards that produced the celebrated Setinum wine. Pliny the Elder (*Nat.* 14.8.61) relates that Augustus and the emperors who followed him preferred it because it did not cause indigestion. Tasting like figs, it was served chilled and diluted with snow (Martial, *Epigrams* 13.23, 112).

**Figure 30.** Bridge at Forum Appii

**Figure 31.** Artistic reconstruction of Forum Appii (Evelien Witmer, from Tol, De Haas, and Anastasia [2019, 39, fig. 10]).

Milestone 43* (fig. 29) is located about 900 ft. (275 m) south of the bridge in Forum Appii. As late as 2010 the stone still protruded some 5 ft. (1.5 m) above ground with much of its text still legible. Since then, vandals have broken it, leaving a mere stump 1 ft. (0.3 m) high.[16] It and MP 19 are the only milestones of the VA between Rome and Capua still virtually in situ. We have used these two stones along with Google Maps and Google Earth to calculate the approximate locations of the remaining milestones.

Although Paul was still 43 RM (39.5 mi./63.6 km) from Rome, he received an encouraging surprise at Forum Appii.[17] Acts 28:15 tells us that a delegation of Christians came from Rome to meet and welcome him here.[18] This was an unprecedented act of honor, since delegations of Roman senators and officials would rarely go such a distance from Rome to meet a returning emperor at his *adventus*![19] As Bruce (1990, 536) has aptly noted, Paul "had told the Roman Christians of his longing to see them when he wrote to them some three years before (Rom. 1:11–15; 15:23); now his prayer was granted and, in circumstances unforeseen when he sent his letter, he saw them face to face." The encouragement Paul had given the Romans through his letter was now reciprocated by their two-day walk to greet him.

When Luke writes that believers "traveled from Rome to meet us, some at Forum of Appius and others at Three Taverns," several commentators

---

16. *CIL* 10.6825 at 41.46493, 13.00011.

17. A plaque dating from 1961 on the front of Borgo Faiti's Vergine del SS. Rosario Church (41.46821, 12.99385) commemorates the visit of Paul nineteen centuries earlier. The village regularly organizes a reenactment of the meeting between the apostle and the Roman Christians complete with sets, costumes, and food of ancient times.

18. Dalby (2000, 44) suggests they stopped at Forum Appii because if they had gone farther "the two parties could have missed each other." Their failure to connect might occur only if one group walked while the other went via barge on the canal. Since even these routes were parallel, it hardly seems possible they could have missed each other. It is more likely that Forum Appii was simply a more comfortable and convenient place to wait.

19. The delegation in AD 19 that went all the way to Tarracina to escort the body of Germanicus back to Rome was mentioned by Tacitus (*Ann.* 3.2) because it was so exceptional. In the later empire when emperors seldom visited Rome, delegations might go farther to meet him. For example, in AD 357 senators went about 35 mi. (56 km) to meet Constantius II at Ocriculum; see Thompson (2005, 93).

have interpreted this to mean two separate groups. R. B. Rackham (1919, 498) suggested that perhaps one was a group of Jewish Christians, the other gentiles; however, nothing in the text suggests that. Others more plausibly have suggested that it was "the younger and particularly zealous Christians" who went the extra 10 mi. (16 km) to meet Paul at Forum Appii.[20] Although Luke provides no answers, among these groups were probably several who had been greeted by Paul several years earlier in his letter to the Romans (Rom 16:3–15). We can postulate that this informal delegation of Roman Christians resulted from the messenger(s) sent from Puteoli to inform the Roman church of Paul's arrival there. Perhaps those messengers accompanied these believers to Forum Appii and then afterward continued their journey back to Puteoli. In any case, despite both Paul's party and that from Rome each having spent a long day on the road, we can imagine that their conversations in the *mansio* of Forum Appii continued long into the night. Again Julius, the guards, and the other prisoners must have been astonished at the devotion that Paul engendered from his fellow Christians.

Here Luke provides a rare glimpse into Paul's inner state along the journey. As Paul approached Rome, he must have experienced some apprehension about what would happen upon his arrival. Where would he be imprisoned? And could he have contact with the Christian and Jewish communities there? Upon meeting the believers at Forum Appii and Tres Tabernae, he first thanked God and then took courage (θάρσος, *tharsos*).[21] Two years previously, while Paul was in custody in Jerusalem, the Lord had appeared to him and said: "Take courage [θάρσει, *tharsei*]! Just as you have testified concerning the things about me in Jerusalem, so also must you testify in Rome" (23:11, trans. Wilson). The courage needed when threatened with assassination by the Jews and imprisoned

---

20. Haenchen (1971, 739) cites this proposal and then dismisses it, saying that Luke simply "named the two best-known stopping places on the Via Appia between Rome and Naples." In reality, these were two lesser-known stops on the route!

21. Compare 27:35 for Paul giving thanks during the storm. In his letter to the Romans, Paul had written similarly: "First, I give thanks to my God through Jesus Christ for all of you, because your faith is being reported throughout the whole world" (Rom 1:8, trans. Wilson).

under two Roman governors had now brought him to the outskirts of the imperial city. Whatever fears and misgivings Paul might be experiencing dissipated after he saw his brothers and sisters from Rome. He again took courage, knowing that the Lord's promise about testifying in Rome was about to be fulfilled.

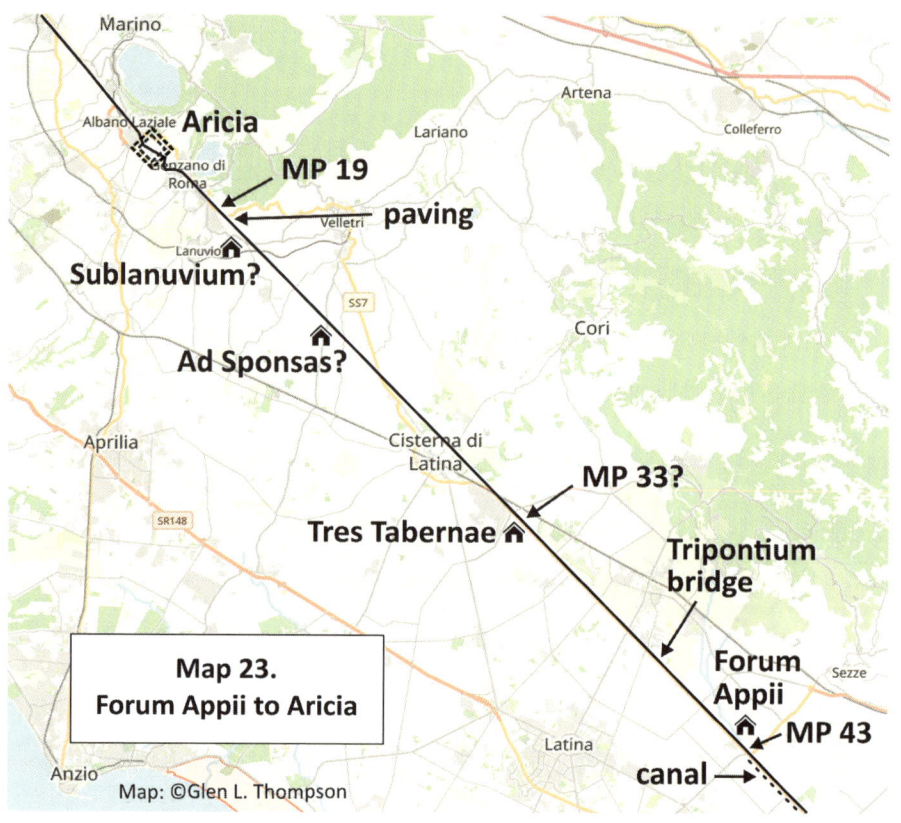

DAY 6

# Forum Appii (RM 43) to Aricia (RM 16)

Paul's party was back on the road the next morning as they continued northward 10 RM toward the next *mansio* at Tres Tabernae. But Paul had new traveling companions, for those who met him at Forum Appii had now joined the group. These brothers and sisters undoubtedly informed Paul that others were also coming from Rome to join the procession. It may have seemed to Julius that his file of prisoners was turning into a celebrity's *adventus*.

An hour and a half after leaving Forum Appii and just after passing MP 39, the group crossed the three-arched bridge of Tripontium*, still used by SS7. Its name is preserved by the modern town of Tor Tre Ponti that lies 2000 ft. (600 m) farther. Nerva began the renovation of an earlier Roman bridge around AD 97, and it was completed by Trajan as stated in a dedicatory inscription, still in situ, on the bridge's southern side (CIL 10.6819). In the village in front of the Church of San Paolo Apostolo, two milestones from the VA have been placed in the garden*.[1]

## Tres Tabernae

By mid-morning the travelers passed MP 33 and about 1000 ft. (300 m) farther approached the *mansio* of Tres Tabernae and its adjacent buildings on the west side of the VA. Here Paul met a second group of Roman believers who had traveled 33 RM (30 mi./48 km) to meet him. Apparently three *tabernae*, the Latin word for a small shop of any sort, were established here at a crossroads. The second road ran from the inland city of Norba (modern Norma) down to the

---

1. Milestone 39 (CIL 10.6820) dates to Nerva; the smaller one mentioning Antoninus Pius seems to be unpublished.

coast at Antium (modern Anzio).[2] Cicero had villas at Tusculum, Antium, and Formiae, so he often used the VA to travel from Rome to one of the latter two, or between them. On several occasions, he dispatched or received letters while at Tres Tabernae (*Atticus* 2.10, 12–13), presumably from one of the three *tabernae*. His letter of March 21, 59 BC was written at 10 AM from Forum Appii before leaving for Formiae. In it he mentions writing a letter to Atticus earlier in the day from Tres Tabernae. A second letter was written on April 19 when he was traveling through Tres Tabernae from his Antium estate. There he simultaneously met his friend Curio coming from Rome as well as received a letter from Atticus.[3] Writing to Atticus, Cicero (*Atticus* 2.12.1) thanked him for relaying some good news—using the Greek word εὐαγγέλια (*euangelia*). A century later Paul passed the same spot with a very different kind of good news—the gospel (εὐαγγέλιον, *euangelion*).

**Figure 32.** Excavations at Tres Tabernae

2. Anzio was the site of the Allied landing in 1944 after which a major military engagement ensued and is now the site of the major American military cemetery in central Italy. By the end of the second century AD a major road, the Via Severiana, linked Ostia to Tarracina, passing along the coast through Antium. This was designed specifically to haul cargo and thus alleviate some of the slower traffic on the VA.

3. Cicero's letters confirm other important uses for *mansiones* and *stationes*, namely as a staging area for meeting people coming from other directions and as postal stations for holding letters.

Day 6: Forum Appii to Aricia

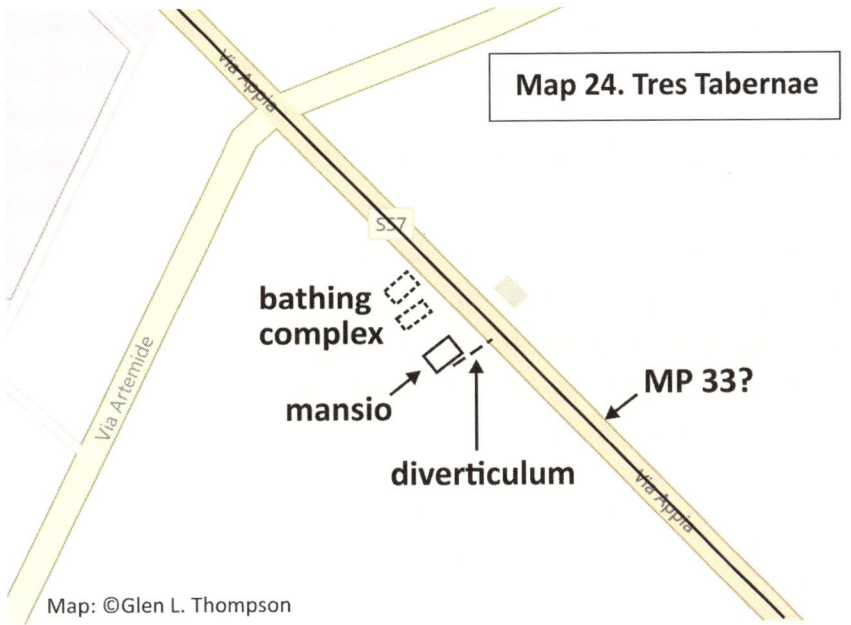

Map 24. Tres Tabernae

This crossroads settlement slowly grew into a regional agricultural center as well. Perhaps it was due to its association with Paul, however, that it became a bishopric by the early fourth century.[4] It continued as the main settlement in the area until it was destroyed by the "Saracens" in 868. The town was later rebuilt on higher ground 2.5 mi. (4 km) northwest to become Cisterna di Latina. As the centuries passed, all visible traces of the original site disappeared. In fact, its exact location was still a matter of speculation throughout most of the twentieth century. Only in the past two decades have archaeologists uncovered part of the ancient *statio* at KM 58.1 of SS7 (map 24; fig. 32).[5] Since 1993 several excavations

---

4. Bishop Felix from Tres Tabernae took part in the council at Rome in October 313 which condemned Donatus and absolved Caecilian of Carthage from wrongdoing. See Optatus of Milevis, *Against the Donatists* 1.24. Its last known bishop, Anastasius, is listed among participants at a council of Rome in 853.

5. 41.56184, 12.87495. This puts it about 5.65 mi. (9.1 km) north of the Trajanic bridge at Tore Tre Ponte and 0.68 mi. (1.1 km) north of the fascist-era bridge of Mussolini. This *casa cantoniera* was one of many built at intervals along the main Italian trunk roads in the early twentieth century to assure their maintenance.

and sondages have occurred at the site with others still ongoing.[6] A paved diverticulum* leading from the VA to the presumed *mansio** was uncovered just opposite a *casa cantoniera* on the east side of SS7.[7] Several additional buildings* with mosaic flooring as well as a bath complex stretch for 325 ft. (100 m) to the north.[8] The excavations are so recent that even preliminary reports of most finds remain unpublished. The site is normally closed to the public.

After another time of "meet and greet" at Tres Tabernae, the party, now augmented by the second group of Roman Christians, continued together toward Rome. Other travelers, seeing this large entourage, might have surmised that someone very important was arriving in Rome to warrant such a welcome. Julius, the guards, and the other prisoners again must have wondered who this man was to garner such attention and devotion and what sort of "bonds" connected him so strongly with people he had never met previously.

## Ad Sponsas and Sublanuvium

From Tres Tabernae the VA continued, still without the slightest curve, for almost another 15 RM (14.3 mi./23 km). The Pontine Marshes now lay behind, and the path ran a bit higher through well-watered, fertile agricultural land. In his day Edward Bunbury (1857, 1291) could write: "The ancient pavement is still visible in many places between Aricia and Tres Tabernae." However, centuries of farming, combined with modern development spreading from Rome, have erased most traces of the ancient route here. SS7, laid atop the VA since north of Tarracina, now continues

---

6. These excavations have prompted the erection of a sign visible from SS7 that this is the archaeological site of Tres Tabernae. Therefore, it is puzzling that Schmisek (2018, 231) writes that "modern scholars are unsure of the precise location of this ancient way stop."

7. See the summary in Fiocchi Nicolai (2015, 125–35). For a view of the excavated diverticulum, see page 135, fig. 3.

8. See Urbini et al. (2010, 43–49). Among the finds is a funerary inscription related to the senatorial Pinarius family (Cisterna di Latina, n.d., https://web.archive.org/web/20060513015431/http://www.cisterna.it/dettaglio.php?action=lista&location=227). See also the many photographs of the site posted on Google Maps at 41.56224, 12.87447.

## Day 6: Forum Appii to Aricia

only 1 mi. (1.6 km) past Tres Tabernae before veering west away from the ancient VA to parallel the railway and enter Cisterna di Latina.

However, the VA and Paul's party continued straight under the modern railroad tracks, under Via Bufolareccia, and then to the west of a monumental tomb* approximately 1650 ft. (500 m) past the railway (Cassieri 1990, 179–81). The VA continued beneath the northeast quadrant of Cisterna, leaving almost no trace.[9] North of Cisterna, it passed beneath the hamlet of Le Castella almost parallel to SS7, but 500–650 ft. (150–200 m) to its northeast. Here it passes near the Parish Church of San Giacomo Apostolo*, which still has ancient and medieval remains visible alongside. That church was built on the site of the important medieval church of San Andrea in Silice, whose name probably reflects the nearby remains of the VA. *Silice*, Italian for "flint," was often used to describe ancient paving stones (Lat. *silex*; cf. Livy, *Hist.* 10.47.4).

---

9. For some distance the VA ran parallel to Via Enrico Fermi but about 165 ft. (50 m) farther northeast on a modern property line with a row of trees. Then a stretch of unpaved road is very close, if not identical, to the ancient route (from about 41.59956, 12.82600 to 41.61475, 12.80639).

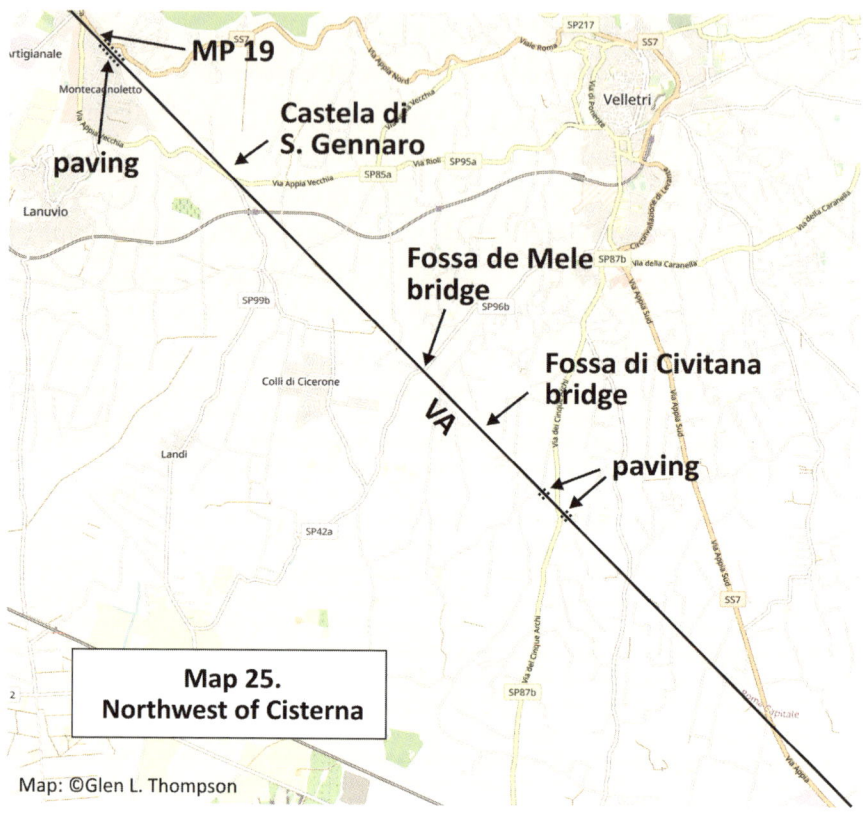

Map 25. Northwest of Cisterna

Map: ©Glen L. Thompson

Farther to the northwest, the VA crossed SS7 about 325 ft. (100 m) south of the turnoff, still marked as the Via Appia Antica. The latter road arcs to the north and west for 825 ft. (250 m) until it straightens after joining the ancient route. From this point forward it runs atop the VA for almost 4.3 mi. (7 km; map 25). Today, however, the road is little more than a track in some places and is best walked. It crosses five larger drainage canals (*fossae*), which required the Roman engineers to build bridges over some. These larger *fossae* were fed by an intricate system of smaller underground drainage tunnels (*cuniculi*) that predated the construction of the VA but were incorporated into it.[10] This system kept the ground

---

10. Until fairly recently the system was thought to be pre-Roman and to have been abandoned in the Roman period. This view has now been corrected and its construction seen as part of the

## Day 6: Forum Appii to Aricia

dry enough for agriculture and prevented it from becoming a swamp like the nearby Pontine area. Among the traces of the VA still visible are a stretch of ancient embankment and a small stretch of paving outside the Scuola (School) Sole Luna*.[11] In the early twentieth century travelers could still see its entire width together with sidewalks 6.6 ft. (2 m) wide on each side! Lorenzo Quilici (1989a, 85) posits that this was where the VA intersected with the Via Mactorina, which ran from Praeneste (modern Palestrina) and Velitrae (modern Velletri) down to the coast at Antium.[12] A century ago ruins, still identifiable as belonging to a *mansio*, were located nearby. Quilici (1989a, 84–85) asserts that this was probably *Ad Sponsas*, a *mutatio* mentioned in the Jerusalem Itinerary but which has proven hard to localize.[13]

Proceeding from the school across the intersection with Via dei Cinque Archi, one comes upon another short stretch of ancient paving* before crossing Via Soleluna. Then, about 0.62 mi. (1 km) from the school, the modern track peters out 395 ft. (120 m) before the ancient VA crossed the fourth ditch, the Fossa di Civitana*. The ancient bridge over it collapsed sometime in past centuries and has not been rebuilt. However, sources suggest that some bridge remains are still buried in the undergrowth. The modern road begins again 460 ft. (140 m) to the northwest and tracks with the VA for another 0.62 mi. (1 km). Here, at a four-way intersection, the VA crosses the final fossa, almost imperceptible to travelers today—the

---

Roman settlement of the region; see Quilici Gigli (2020a, §§9–26).

11. Outside the Sole Luna school are signs in Italian and English describing Roman road construction and the history of the VA. Also displayed on the school is a modern mosaic of Paul in chains looking at MP 24. Our calculations put MP 24 1100 ft. (340 m) to the northwest, 100 ft. (30 m) before Via Soleluna. There is also a plaque commemorating the apostle's passage on the VA during the Jubilee Year of Paul in 2008–2009 proclaimed by Pope Benedict XVI.

12. A third sign in Italian near the school describes a stele found nearby dating to the first half of the first century BC. It states that L. Octavius Onesimus had repaired damage to the Via Mactorina at his own expense. Google Maps still gives the best route from Velletri to Anzio as SP87b, which crosses the VA at this very spot.

13. The Jerusalem Itinerary places that *mansio* 7 RM from Forum Appii. That cannot be correct since it would then be located south of Tres Tabernae. The Pleiades website just as problematically places it between Cisterna and Tres Tabernae at 41.58389, 12.84611 (https://pleiades.stoa.org/places/422816). On the problems of the itineraries and the localization of the *mansiones* they mention, see Crogiez (1990, 100–102). Note that she built upon the work of de la Blanchère (1888, 54–68) and wrote before the excavations at Tres Tabernae had verified its location.

Fossa de Mele. The remains of the bridge, the Ponte di Mele*, are under the current one although the original single arch, 26 ft. (8 m) high and 13 ft. (4 m) wide, is now almost completely overgrown.[14] Quilici (1991, 326) surveyed the bridge in 1960 and concluded that the structure dated to the VA's original construction in the late fourth century BC, making it one of the oldest structures of its kind still preserved.

Continuing northwest along the modern road, ancient paving starts just beyond the bridge and continues for 1312 ft. (400 m) until Via Colle Ottone Basso. The track then dead-ends 1075 ft. (330 m) farther at a grove, resuming 300 ft. (90 m) later at the end of Via Palaggi. When Via Palaggi veers west 1950 ft. (600 m) later, the VA continued straight leaving no trace in the current farm fields for about 1.6 mi. (2.55 km). During this stretch it passes about 325 ft. (100 m) east of the San Gennaro train station and just a few yards/meters east of the current junction of SP95a and SP99b. For the next several hundred yards/meters, the traveler passes along the foot of a high hill on the right. While Roman-era ruins are to be found there, probably the remains of a villa, today they are surmounted by a medieval fortress called the Castello di San Gennaro*.

The VA continued straight (east of today's SP95a), and after about 655 ft. (200 m), an unidentified Roman building* has been incorporated into a modern structure. This stood about 160 ft. (50 m) southwest of the VA. A stretch of ancient buttressing* is located similarly between the ancient and modern roads 1230 ft. (375 m) farther northwest. While these may be the remains of a country villa, others have suggested they were part of a *taberna* along the VA and/or perhaps part of the *statio* of Sublanuvium ("below Lanuvium"), the hilltop Roman town 1 mi. (1.6 km) to the southwest (Quilici 1989a, 77).

Paul's party passed MP 20 about 500 ft. (150 m) farther, where the VA's path crosses the modern VAA.[15] From there, they faced another 2.6

---

14. Today the bridge is on private property and so is inaccessible. A local archaeology group—Gruppo Archeologico Veliterno—cleaned around the arch in 2014. For photographs see http://www.gruppoarcheologicoveliterno.it/site/appia-antica/ce-ancora-un-ponte-ovvero-ponte-sullappia-antica/.

15. 41.68369, 12.71604.

## Day 6: Forum Appii to Aricia

mi. (4.1 km) of straight but constantly rising road until the point where the ancient engineers were forced to deviate around the Alban hills on the northwest side of modern Genzano di Roma. Numerous traces of the ancient road survive in the first part of this stretch. A length of Roman terracing or substructure* is visible after the first 850 ft. (250 m). Then 1640 ft. (500 m) farther on the right, an ancient structure* has been incorporated into a modern house.

After an additional 1000 ft. (300 m), where Via Montecagnoletto 2° branches off to the southwest, the VA continued straight. The narrow lane preserves the ancient paving* for about 1050 ft. (325 m). An ancient wall on the left near the end hides ruins of an ancient structure. Quilici (1989a, 77) identifies these ruins as another possible location of the *statio* of Sublanuvium, but this is less likely than the site previously mentioned, which is more directly *sub Lanuvio*.[16] Here the VA parallels and briefly brushes the Via Appia Nord/SS7. However, after just a few yards/meters, the modern road veers at an angle to the north while the VA continued straight. About 442 ft. (135 m) after the ancient paving disappears, MP 19* still stands in the bushes on the north side below Viale Unione Sovietica (fig. 33).[17] This milestone has seemingly remained in situ since its erection during road renovations conducted under Nerva. Calculating from the Porta Capena, we have confirmed that this is within a few yards/meters of its expected location.

---

16. Severini (2001, 69) is equally noncommittal about the remains being those of Sublanuvium. We have been unable to identify the precise location or supply GPS coordinates for this structure, which may no longer exist or is inside private property.

17. 41.69319, 12.70368. As stated earlier, we have used MP 19 and MP 43 at Forum Appii as dead reckoning points for our milestone calculations.

**Figure 33.** MP 19 in situ

From here the VA continued straight, passing under Via Emilia Romagna. A few ancient paving stones are visible in the first 1150 ft. (350 m) as it enters Genzano di Roma. On his right, Paul would have seen the top of the crater containing Lake Nemi to the northeast. The VA ran about 35 ft. (10 m) southwest of the current roundabout with Via Luigi Longo, then continued straight while rising steadily as it passed beneath the streets of Genzano di Roma for the next 1650 ft. (500 m). It ran beneath Via Alcide de Gasperi, which turns into Via Romana for a final 2135 ft. (650 m). The intersection with Via Colle Fiorito ends the long, straight stretch that started just outside of Tarracina.

# Day 6: Forum Appii to Aricia

## The Deviation at Aricia

The VA had now reached an altitude of 1310 ft. (400 m), having climbed partway up the hill named Colle Pardo. The hill merged with the northwest rim of an ancient crater whose western outline can still be seen from the air. On the next hill to the north was Aricia. Below to the west was the floor of the crater, once containing a lake, Lacus Aricinus. The Roman engineers laid out a deviation* that descended the steep eastern side, crossed the plain, and then rose gradually up the western side, a distance of 1.7 RM (1.5 mi./2.5 km). Its terminus was the beginning of another straight stretch 12.7 mi. (20.5 km) long that led to the edge of Rome (map 26).

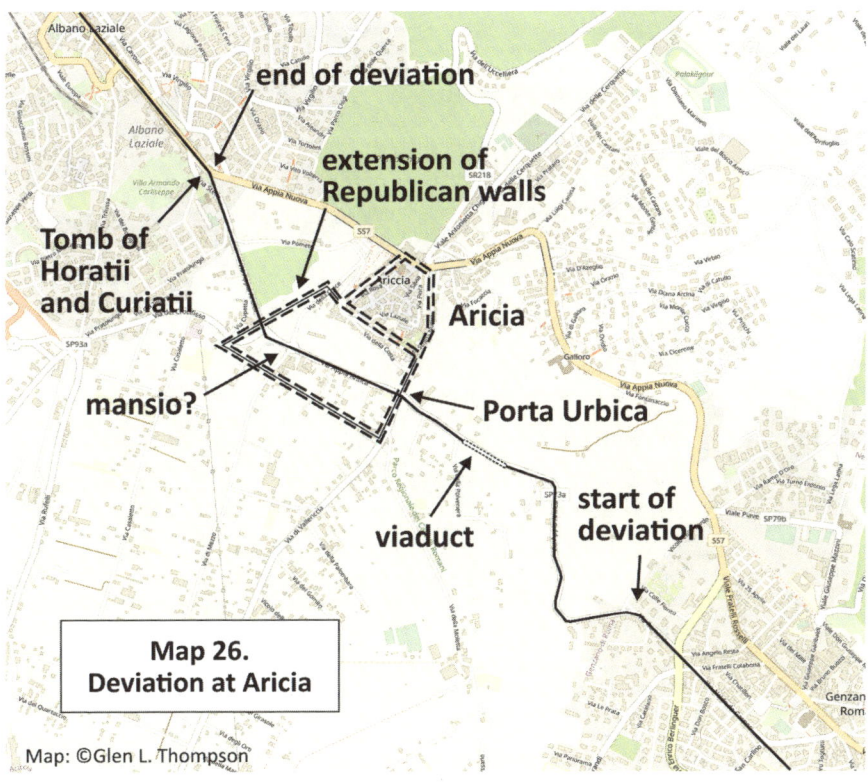

Map 26. Deviation at Aricia

Map: ©Glen L. Thompson

**Figure 34.** Viaduct at Aricia (Pirenesi, above; view today, below)

Day 6: Forum Appii to Aricia

About 150 ft. (45 m) before the end of Via Romana, the ancient road veered west for 650 ft. (200 m) before snaking down the side of the hill and arcing back north for an additional 1975 ft. (600 m). Where the road turned northwest again, the final 750 ft. (230 m) to the valley floor lies atop one of the most impressive and innovative engineering feats of the entire road—a massive viaduct*. Here is how Lorenzo Quilici (1989a, 73–74), the great scholar of the VA, describes it:

> It extends like a complete wall over 230 m long, 13 m high, and 8.2 m wide at the top; it was built of a concrete core covered with blocks of peperino rock in *opus quadratum*. A massive arch provided drainage for the waters of the ditch which passed under the middle of the structure, while a further arch in the first section formed an underpass for a road. Two more arched drains are beyond the main arch and at its end. This extraordinary road construction, which shows considerable reconstruction during the same ancient period, can be dated mostly between the late second century BC and the Augustan age.

While built against the hill in some spots, it appears that much of the viaduct was freestanding. It was similar to, but slightly less spectacular than, the nearby monumental bridge of the mid-nineteenth century that leads the Via Appia Nova into Ariccia today. Unfortunately, the ramp, sometimes referred to as the *pons* or *clivus Aricius*, is difficult to see today because of the thick vegetation growing along its side and the new housing on the hillside below it.[18] Engravings by Giovanni Battista Piranesi (1757; fig. 34) and Carlo Labruzzi (1789) show how impressive it once appeared.[19] Paul's party was able to descend the 200 ft. (60 m) into the

---

18. The identification of this ramp as the "*pons*" mentioned in Juvenal and elsewhere is now generally accepted. For the most complete study of the ramp, see Florescu (1925, 21–27). For an example of the earlier debate, see Haverfield and Owen (1900, 86–88), in which each author comes to the opposite conclusion. More recently, see the overview by Petrucci (2007, 52–57). The road atop the ramp today facilitates only one-way traffic coming from Genzano di Roma to Ariccia.

19. For images of these engravings, see Vincenti (2017, 155–56, figs. 15, 16). See also her photographs of the viaduct (155, fig. 15). Between 1894 and 1911 Thomas Ashby took several photographs of the structure, now online in the Ashby Collection of the British School at Rome (www.

valley quite comfortably. The descent was also famous for beggars who perhaps could profit along its length because of the slowed foot traffic.[20] One can picture Paul or his companions giving a coin to these beggars and then speaking a few words of the gospel to them. Riders, however, often dismounted to descend the viaduct.

While this practice of dismounting was likely due initially to the substantial incline, ancient writers said this was done in remembrance of the Greek hero Hippolytus (later Virbius to the Romans), who died after falling from his chariot (Vergil, *Aeneid* 7.761–782). According to the earliest stories, Hippolytus, the son of King Theseus of Athens, devoted his life to hunting and to Artemis/Diana, while spurning the advances of Aphrodite/Venus. Incensed by this, Aphrodite spooked the horses of his chariot; he was thrown out and his horses dragged him to his death. In later stories, however, he was resurrected by Asclepius. To prevent further retribution from Aphrodite, Hippolytus stole away to Italy where he became king of Aricia under the assumed name of Virbius and built a sacred precinct there to his goddess Artemis (Pausanias, *Description of Greece* 2.27.4–5). The temple and the more archaic sacred grove (*lucus*) with its ancient image of Diana Nemensis (Diana of Nemi or Diana of the Woods [Lat. *nemus*]) both overlooked the northern shore of Lake Nemi, about 1.9 mi. (3 km) northeast of the VA. The grove and sanctuary* were major pilgrimage and tourist sites in Paul's day (Strabo, *Geogr.* 5.3.12). The goddess Diana had been pictured in her Nemian grove on a denarius a century earlier in 43 BC in her threefold Greek form—the huntress Artemis, the moon goddess Selene, and Hekate goddess of the underworld (Alföldi 1960, 137–44).[21]

---

bsrdigitalcollections.it/). Other photographs taken by Ashby along the VA have been published in Le Pera Buranelli and Turchetti (2003).

20. Juvenal (*Saturnalia* 4.117–18) mentions this: "[Catullus] ... whose worthiest fate would be to run begging by the carriages on the road to Aricia and blow his fawning kisses to the chariot as it descends the hill." Martial (*Epigrams* 2.19) quips that the dinners at Zoilus's home are so bad that they would only please the people who "recline on Aricia's slope," i.e., the beggars. Martial (*Epigrams* 12.32.10) also disparages the quality of the personal possessions being moved by Vacerra as being equal to those one would expect on the hill of Aricia.

21. The coin can be seen at: https://commons.wikimedia.org/wiki/File:Diana_Nemorensis _denarius2.jpg. Alföldi has shown that the coin was minted by P. Accoleius, part of the *gens Accoleius*

Day 6: Forum Appii to Aricia                                                                      139

The myth of Hippolytus and Diana may well have been retold among Paul and his party as they descended the viaduct toward Aricia. Paul and his fellow Christians perhaps reflected further how they had now dedicated themselves to a completely different deity, not triform but triune—to the incarnated God-man Jesus of Nazareth who had participated in the creation of the sun and moon. He had died willingly and then gone to preach his victory over death in the underworld after which the Spirit raised him from the dead. Unlike Hippolytus, his resurrection had been confirmed by many witnesses. He had not been a hunter but a fisherman—of people. And he had called Paul and his friends to tell a different story, one rooted in historical events and not in myth.

## Aricia

Aricia (modern Ariccia) was an ancient town long an ally of Rome and known for its Voconian and Atian laws, famous magistrates, and brave knights (Cicero, *Philippics* 3.16). Nevertheless, it was despised by some Italians. Rivals of Augustus sought to disparage him by claiming his ancestors first ran a perfume shop and then a bakery at Aricia (Suetonius, *Augustus* 4). Among them was Antony who derided Atia, mother of the first emperor by mentioning Aricia as her birthplace (Cicero, *Philippics* 3.15, 17). Some 1300 ft. (400 m) after descending the viaduct and passing more tombs, Paul and his party arrived at the southeastern city gate. Part of the mostly buried arch is still visible, now the center of a roundabout at SP90b. Today it is called the Porta Urbica* or, because only the top of the arch is showing, the Basto del Diavolo ("saddle of the devil").[22]

The early Latin city occupied the hilltop several hundred yards/meters due north. Perhaps due to the VA passing through the valley

---

of Aricia. Diana of Nemi is mentioned by Ovid (*Fasti* 6.59), Lucan (*Civil War* 6.73–75), and Martial (*Epigrams* 13.19.1). Vergil (*Aeneid* 3.679–681) speaks of *coniferae cyparissi, lucus Dianae* and of *tergemina Hecate, tria virginis ora Dianae*; also, Catullus (*Poems* 34.9–13). Statius (*Silvae* 3.1.55–60) describes the annual August 13 festival that took place there: "Now the day was nearly come when Trivia's Arician wood, apt for runaway kings, makes smoke and the lake privy to Hippolytus shines with many a torch. Diana herself wreathes her veteran hounds and furbishes her darts and lets the wild beasts go in safety; all the land of Italy celebrates Hecate's Ides at its chaste hearths."

22. For a photograph of the remains of this gate, see Vincenti (2017, 142, fig. 12).

below, the city grew in this direction by spreading down the hillside so as to encompass both sides of the VA by Paul's day. The city wall was also enlarged to enclose the new area. The VA continued across the expanded lower city past a second roundabout at Via della Croce. It exited by a southwestern gate* located near the junction of the VAA with Via del Crocifisso, 1725 ft. (525 m) from the southeastern gate. Here the western wall reached the valley. A commercial forum was probably located within this stretch, perhaps on the northern side of the VA. Also nearby was the ancient *mansio* of Aricia in which travelers from Rome would often spend their first night. Here Horace, after departing Rome, stayed in a modest inn (*hospitium modicum*) on the trip immortalized in his famous *Satires* (1.5.1).[23] Quilici (1989a, 73) mentions the Roman remains built into a house* on the north side as its possible location;[24] others identify it with a structure called the Osteriaccia* on the south side just west of the Porto Urbico and still visible in the early twentieth century (Severini 2001, 53). A third candidate is the complex* found beneath a recently demolished early-modern structure on the south side about 250 ft. (100 m) inside the southwestern gate.[25] By our calculations, MP 16* was located at the modern roundabout just inside the ancient southwestern city gate. A milestone with that number, dating from the early fourth century and naming the Emperor Maxentius, was discovered in that area in the late nineteenth century and later moved to its present location in the park of Palazzo Chigi.[26]

We hypothesize that Julius halted for the night at the *mansio* in Aricia. The terrain had been fairly easy, despite the gentle ascent before Aricia. The party could easily have traversed the 27 RM (25.5 mi./41 km) from

---

23. Gowers (1993, 50) writes: "The journey is a milestone in Horace's book; it marks the half-way point in his 'Conversations,' Sermones." The placement of a journey in a literary work is significant, even as Paul's journey concludes the book of Acts.

24. However, Severini (2001, 52–53) identifies the structure as a small Tuscan temple.

25. The location was suggested by Francesco Petrucci in an email to Glen Thompson on March 22, 2021. See also the photos in Petrucci (2021).

26. For a photograph of this milestone, see Vincenti (2017, 149, fig. 7).

## Day 6: Forum Appii to Aricia

Forum Appii on day 6. This left only 16 RM for the final day, allowing for an early arrival so Julius would have time to transfer his prisoners to the appropriate authorities in the capital. Despite the long day's journey, the conversation and prayer among the Roman Christians with Paul and his companions probably extended far into the night.

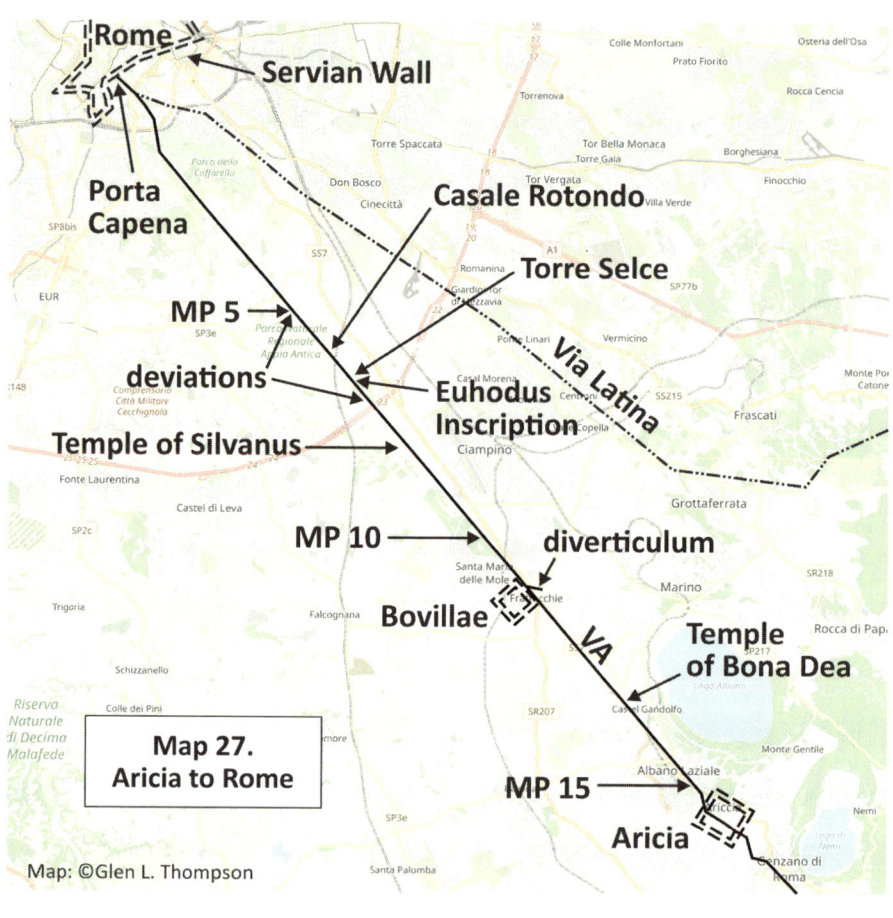

Day 7

# Aricia (RM 16) to Rome

The next morning the party exited the southwestern gate of Aricia and followed the VA northwest along the path of the VAA heading uphill. The deviation that started before Aricia ended after 2000 ft. (600 m) when the road veered to the left. Before that junction, Paul passed the most impressive tomb he had yet seen, today called the Tomb of the Horatii and Curiatii*.[1] The tall circular central tower was surrounded by thinner towers at its corners. The tomb evokes the story of the three Roman Horatii brothers who fought against the three Curiatii brothers from nearby Alba Longa. Volunteering as combatants in the mid-seventh century BC as proxies for their armies, all but one died. The one surviving Horatius was later condemned to death for killing his sister whom he had discovered mourning one of the Curiatii to whom she was betrothed. He escaped death, however, by appealing his case to the people. The tale, repeated by Livy (*Hist.* 1.24–26) and other Roman historians, may have been intended to explain the origin of the Roman citizen's right of appeal. This would make for lively conversation among the group, since Paul was traveling because of his direct appeal to Caesar. However, the tomb in Aricia more probably belonged to the patrician, Marcus Atius Balbus.[2]

---

1. The VA continued straight to the junction and did not follow the curve of today's Via della Stella. Paintings and etchings from the seventeenth and eighteenth centuries confirm that the VA passed east of the elaborate tomb. The VA can be seen in two of Carlo Labruzzi's paintings of the tomb on pages 83–84, figs. 20–21 of the exhibition catalog found at https://www.simondickinson.com/wp-content/uploads/2016/01/Labruzzi-Catalogue-2012.pdf.

2. Since other ancient funerary mounds closer to Rome have also been identified with the brothers, the conversation might have occurred several hours later. For the attribution to Balbus, see the study of Petrucci (2019, 161–77).

Whether it was the engineering of the VA and its viaduct, the magnificent tombs, or the stories about ancient heroes, goddesses, or political figures, Paul was becoming more aware that he was approaching the center of a great empire. From the turn beyond the monumental tomb, the VA levels and veers almost exactly northwestward, again coinciding with the path of the VAA. Paul was now on the home stretch to Rome, a straight line of 12.4 mi. (20 km) to the edge of the imperial city.[3]

Soon after the straight path to Rome began, Paul's group encountered a major road branching to the right. Its path ran northeast, first between two extinct volcanoes whose craters became Lake Albano and Lake Nemi and then toward Mount Albanus (Monte Cavo), the highest peak in the region. On its peak the sanctuary of Jupiter Latiaris* was located. Here the allied Latin cities celebrated sacred rites long before they were conquered by Rome. As was so often the case, the Romans subsequently incorporated these *Feriae Latinae* into their own calendar, with the consuls and praetors sacrificing a white bull there every April (Livy, *Hist.* 25.12). Thus the road became a *via sacra*, the name still used today for the several kilometers of well-preserved ancient paving on the mountainside. The importance of the site in Roman times was increased when it became an alternate site for Roman triumphs. It became a *via triumphalis* for generals such as Marcus Claudius Marcellus. When he was granted only the lesser honor of an "ovation" in Rome in 212 BC, he came here to lead his troops in a full triumphal procession (Plutarch, *Marcellus* 22.1; Livy, *Hist.* 26.21.7).[4]

Passing this *via sacra* Paul, with his "army" of Roman Christians, shared an almost expectant air of triumph, despite the apostle's possible death in Rome. Writing previously to the Corinthians, he used the imagery of a Roman triumph to describe his ministry: "But thanks be to God, who in Christ is always leading us in triumphal procession (θριαμβεύοντι,

---

3. While it is often stated that the VA was totally straight from Aricia to just outside Rome's city wall near the Church of Quo Vadis, there are in fact two very slight deviations in the final seven RM, one between MP 6 and MP 7, the other between MP 5 and MP 6. See the discussion below.

4. Mount Albanus was the location for similar triumphs by Quintus Minucius (Livy, *Hist.* 33.23.3) and C. Cicereius (Livy, *Hist.* 42.21.7). The alternate site seems to have been used when triumphs in Rome were denied for political reasons.

*Day 7: Aricia to Rome*

*thriambeuonti*), and through us is revealing the aroma of the knowledge of him in every place" (2 Cor 2:14, trans. Wilson).[5] Little did Paul know (or perhaps he did understand from Jesus's prophetic Olivet Discourse [Matt 24:1–28]) that Jerusalem and its temple would be destroyed in AD 70 and that afterward Jewish captives would similarly be led in triumph into Rome.[6]

For the next 2 mi. (3.2 km), the VA passed southwest of Lake Albano. Country villas could be seen stretching northward up the hill to the rim of the crater overlooking the lake.[7] A few minutes later the group saw on their left a villa owned by Pompey the Great. Today the ruins of the Albanum Pompeii are inside the Villa Doria Park.[8] Among his other notable deeds, in 67 BC this famous general succeeded in clearing the eastern Mediterranean of pirates and then went on to establish Roman hegemony in the Middle East, including Syria and Palestine, by 62 BC. Thus, Pompey had a great impact on Paul's future life, both by bringing Roman rule to the East and by making travel much safer for later travelers like Paul. However, the general also died by the sword, beheaded in 48 BC after losing to Julius Caesar in the civil wars that had rocked Rome a century before Paul's captivity journey. Around 1200 ft. (365 m) past MP 15, another enormous funerary monument rose on the right, which local tradition calls the tomb of Pompey*. However, other sites nearer Rome likewise competed for that honor, so it is uncertain which was his actual

---

    5. Garland (1999, 141–42) explains: "The metaphor refers to the celebration after a major military victory in which the spoils of war, rolling stages presenting battle scenes, and pictures of the cities that were sacked were paraded on chariots through the city of Rome to the Capitoline hill and the Temple of Jupiter. Most relevant for Paul's use of the image is the train of eminent captives who were marched in chains through the streets to their execution at the end of the route." Over 350 triumphs are described in Greco-Roman literature; three examples are Plutarch, *Aemilius Paulus* 32.1–34.8; Appian, *Punic Wars* 9.66; and Horace, *Odes* 4.2.50–52.

    6. For a description of this triumph, see Josephus (*Jewish War* 7.5.3–6). The Arch of Titus, with its depiction of the captives and accoutrements from the temple, was built in Rome in AD 81 by Domitian in honor of his brother.

    7. A century and a half after Paul passed by, Emperor Septimius Severus converted the area into a military camp for *Legio II Parthica*. The main gate*, the outer walls, a cistern, and other remnants remain today. The entrance was located just 165 ft. (50 m) northeast of the VA and 365 ft. (110 m) before reaching MP 15.

    8. For a reconstructed drawing of this villa, see Aranegui and Mar (2009, 53, 54, fig. 15).

tomb. Nevertheless, Paul's party would certainly have known the correct one as they passed it.

## Murder on the Appian Way

From the so-called tomb of Pompey, the party proceeded straight albeit gently downhill for another RM, passing tombs on both sides of the road and with the Albano Hills to the northeast. About 1650 ft. (500 m) after passing MP 14—today by the remains of another large Roman tomb* and just beyond Via Ercolano—a paved road led north into a sanctuary of Bona Dea*, the "Good Goddess." This was located within the estate of Titus Sertius Gallus (Cicero, *For Milo* 31) which extended for a considerable distance along the northeast side of the VA.[9] Bona Dea was the goddess of chastity and fertility and was depicted holding a cornucopia in her right hand; a serpent encircled her left arm while she drank from a cup held in that hand. In Rome she enjoyed a state-sponsored cult on the Aventine Hill and was worshiped with blood sacrifices. Men were prohibited from attending some of her rites. In 62 BC Publius Clodius Pulcher disguised himself as a woman and infiltrated one such nocturnal ritual being held at the house of Julius Caesar, the pontifex maximus at the time. He was discovered, tried, and acquitted thanks only to massive bribes to the jurors (Plutarch, *Caesar* 10; Cicero 28–29).

A decade later this stretch of the VA became infamous for an incident near this sanctuary involving that same Clodius. For years there had been clashes between his retainers and supporters and those of Titus Annius Milo. Clodius was a fiery anti-establishment politician from an ancient patrician family and a supporter of Julius Caesar. Milo, however, was an unscrupulous supporter of Pompey and friend of Cicero. On January 18, 52 BC, Milo, together with his family and bodyguard, set out on the VA from Rome heading for his hometown of Lanuvium (near MP 20). Near the sanctuary of Bona

---

9. The estate is thought to have extended from Via Ercolano to Via Sant Caterina. The Danish Academy in Rome has recently studied the site whose remains are known as the Villa of Clodius and the Villa of Caterina. In the recent summary of their findings, they favor "an identification as a sanctuary of Bona Dea here at the 13th mile on the Via Appia, presumably the same as the *sacrarium* on the property of Sertius Gallus mentioned by Cicero" (Aglietti et al. 2022, 115).

Day 7: Aricia to Rome                                                     147

Dea they passed the retinue of Clodius who was returning to Rome. Insults turned to fighting, and Milo's men wounded Clodius, chasing him back to an inn at Bovillae (at MP 12) where they finished him off.[10]

Knowledge of this ancient incident of road rage spread quickly back to Rome, and the next day Clodius's supporters carried his body into the Curia, the Senate house in the Roman forum, and set it ablaze as his funeral pyre. Days of rioting followed until finally Milo was brought to trial. Although he was defended by Cicero, he was sentenced to permanent exile from Rome. This was but one of the incidents that illustrated the unraveling of the Roman Republic and led first to military takeovers by Julius Caesar and others, and then to the establishment of a single principate by Augustus. The stories of Clodius's indiscretion and his death were undoubtedly recounted to Paul by his companions as they walked past the sanctuary and MP 13* near where the attack took place.

## Bovillae and the Gens Iulia

As they approached MP 12, where the large Roman tomb called Torraccio* can still be seen, the group saw Bovillae on their left.[11] This walled city had declined in importance as its neighbor Rome grew. However, it was the ancestral home of the *gens Iulia*, the family to which Julius Caesar belonged and into which Gaius Octavius, the future emperor Augustus, was adopted (Tacitus, *Ann.* 2.41; 15.23). After Augustus died in Nola east of Naples on August 19, AD 14, senators from surrounding cities and colonies carried his body as far as Bovillae where it lay in state for one month. From Bovillae the Roman equites led the final procession to Augustus's mausoleum in Rome (Suetonius, *Augustus* 100). Paul's friends, who had traveled much farther than Bovillae to accompany Paul back to Rome, must have wondered if this journey might also turn out to be the equivalent

---

10. These events must be reconstructed from numerous ancient accounts including Dio Cassius (*History* 40.48–54), Cicero's *For Milo*, and the mid–first-century-AD commentary on the latter by Asconius. For the complexities, see Ruebel (1979, 231–49). The incident is at the center of Steven Saylor's (1996) historical novel, *A Murder on the Appian Way*.

11. MP 12 was located where the Roman tomb known today as the Torraccio still rises on the east side of the VA/SS7. The Peutinger Map inaccurately shows Bovillae (Bobellas) as being 10 RM (9.2 mi./14.8 km) outside of Rome. The inn of Bovillae where Clodius died was another local landmark.

of a funeral procession. Later in AD 14, the new emperor Tiberius (AD 14–37) chose Bovillae to construct a theater and circus, and to establish a cult center for the priests (*sodales*) of Augustus. The ruins of its circus* have been a favorite subject for artists in recent centuries.[12] It was to Nero, the last of the Julio-Claudian emperors, that Paul had appealed and before whose court he would stand trial.

The road SS7 continues to follow the ancient route for only another 1650 ft. (500 m) after MP 12 before it makes an almost imperceptible shift to the north. The VA, however, continued straight, running beneath the modern structures of Frattocchie along the west side of the Via Appia Nuova. After about 1300 ft. (400 m), its path becomes visible again as the VAA. Here it was intersected at an angle by another road that ran north and northeast (modern SP77b), perhaps toward Tusculum or the recently identified town of Castramoenium (c. 1 mi./1.6 km to the northeast), and south (Via Nettunense/SR207), toward Antium.[13] Some 325 ft. (100 m) farther, the VA was intersected by yet another paved diverticulum that branched at an angle to the east, either to a large country estate or to a town on the north side of Lake Albano, such as Ferentum (modern Marino).[14] While it had no known significance in antiquity, we take special note of it because 165 ft. (50 m) of the road* was discovered in excellent condition in 2014 during the construction of a McDonald's restaurant. The 6.6 ft. (2 m) wide road can now be viewed through a glass floor in the restaurant or accessed via a stairway behind it (fig. 35). Visitors can walk on the well-preserved paving stones and read the informative panels in Italian and English describing the road and its history. This diverticulum was in use from the second century BC to the third century AD, so it would have been in use when Paul passed it.

---

12. For a discussion with illustrations of Bovillae and its monuments, see Liverani and Østergaard (2013). A decade after Paul passed this way, the supporters of Vitellius surrendered to the forces of Vespasian at Bovillae during the Year of the Four Emperors (AD 69; Tacitus, *Histories* 4.46).

13. See Pancotti (2019, 77–86) who convincingly places the town at 41.78287, 12.63052. The VA actually leaves the Via Appia Nuova just before the junction with Via Nettunense Vecchia, which may be where the road from Antium met the VA in antiquity.

14. About 655 ft. (200 m) from the VA and beyond the restaurant, this road would have intersected with or crossed the road leading north (modern SP77b). It is possible that it was built as a shortcut to that road, for travelers heading north.

**Figure 35.** Diverticulum at Bovillae

From this point at the intersection with Via Palaverta, the path of the VA remains walkable all the way to Rome. During the first few miles/kilometers, the ancient paving is visible only occasionally. However, the many tomb remains on either side reassure travelers today that they are on the right path. About 500 ft. (150 m) from the beginning is a large tomb on the right called Torre Secchi*. Although the upper tower was added during the medieval period, its lower section, built on a base 26 ft. (8 m) wide, was there when Paul passed it.[15] A few minutes later, the party passed MP 11*.[16]

## Outskirts of Rome: MP 11–7

The next 4 RM—from MP 11 to MP 7—have lost most of their ancient character.[17] In antiquity every several hundred yards/meters another large tomb appeared like well-spaced sentinels. Smaller ones were found in between. Only a few brick cores remain from these once splendid marble-faced mausoleums. In addition, the area east of the VA is now occupied by Ciampino, Rome's second major airport, as well as by several racetracks, removing much of the ancient ambience. The area to the west, especially after MP 10, is now farmland. Paul's party had a very different experience than modern travelers since they were constantly reminded by the size and splendor of the monuments that they were getting ever nearer the center of the empire. Simultaneously, traffic on the road was also increasing as they neared Rome.

About 2000 ft. (600 m) after passing MP 11, just before Viale della Repubblica, travelers today pass a small excavation on the right labeled *tabernacolo*\* ("little *taberna*"). This has been identified as a roadside shop

---

15. This is some 775 ft. (235 m) before MP 11. We do not know the name of the original occupant. The current name comes from the Jesuit astronomer Angelo Secchi (d. 1878) who followed an earlier Jesuit in using this tower and the tomb of Caecilia Metella as benchmarks in their important geodesic measurements of Italy and the earth's surface.

16. For the monuments in this section, see Quilici (1989a, 53–62); for RM 9 to 13, see also Cavacchioli (2021).

17. For a discussion of the modern attempts to preserve the VA outside of Rome, see van der Boon (2017, 110–23). She includes an interesting photograph of Sophia Loren picnicking beside the road in 1957 (110, fig. 66).

Day 7: Aricia to Rome

that once served travelers. After passing under a modern road and before crossing under railroad tracks, a stretch 325 ft. (100 m) long contains a nicely preserved section of paving and boundary stones delineating the curbs. On the west side of this paving a partially excavated bath complex* can be seen, another amenity for ancient travelers. On the right, 1300 ft. (400 m) beyond the railway, are the ruins of a large late-Republican tomb, today called La Mola* ("millstone").[18] Then on the left is an equally impressive tomb called the Sepolcro di Giovannino*.[19] A few minutes later Paul's group passed MP 10*.[20]

After crossing a small bridge, travelers today encounter another section of paving 500 ft. (150 m) long. At its beginning on the right are remnants of another large tomb* on a square base. The tomb on the left*, 1640 ft. (500 m) farther, dates to the third century AD and is built over a second-century-AD bath complex.[21] Some 1000 ft. (300 m) after crossing Via Capanne di Marino, another huge tomb appears on the left. This tumulus, the same size as Casal Rotondo (see below), is today called Monte di Terra*, and dates to the late Republic.[22] Few other remains are visible today along the final 1640 ft. (500 m) before reaching MP 9*.

A large circular tomb* (not there in Paul's day) looms to the left of the VA near where MP 9 once stood.[23] The fourth-century Bordeaux/

---

18. It is 75 ft. (23 m) in diameter and constructed entirely of concrete, including its original conical top. Bits of its brick facing and decoration can still be seen. The interior of the funerary chamber is shaped like a Greek cross, and it has alternating semicircular and square niches separated by semicolumns.

19. Like most of these tombs, its entrance is on the side away from the road and contains a rectangular funerary chamber.

20. It is about 1450 ft. (440 m) past the Sepolcro di Giovannino and 80 ft. (25 m) before the bridge known today as the Ponte delle Cornacchiole, which spanned the small *Fossa di Fiorano*.

21. Similar to the nearby La Mola tomb, this tomb's interior is also in the shape of a Greek cross. Neither the tomb on the right or the left were there when Paul passed. A third circular tomb, 325 ft. (100 m) farther, also on the west side, is from the Imperial period. Within its rectangular inner chamber, a limestone headrest was found to support the head of the deceased.

22. Its core of cement and basalt was built on a large square base of tufa, and some of its decorative stones still line the road.

23. The tomb, once a domed two-story structure surrounded by a marble colonnade, was constructed in the third century AD. It is traditionally identified as the tomb of the Emperor Gallienus whose tomb stood on his family estate near MP 9. He ruled with his father Valerian from AD 253–260 and then alone from 260–268. While his father is remembered for issuing two decrees that

Jerusalem Itinerary also mentions a *mutatio* called *ad Nonum* that must have stood near here in late antiquity. However, it is uncertain whether the *mutatio* existed in Paul's day since it is not mentioned in the other itineraries. Little else remains between MP 9 and MP 8. A circular tomb* on the left, now in front of a large quarry, is found a quarter way along.[24] On the right about 150 ft. (50 m) past the later Berretta del Prete is another brick tomb* on a high podium that preserves much of its *opus quadratum* façade and central niche. It may well have been there when Julius and his prisoners passed it. An even more significant structure, a substantial Republican-era temple*, came just 150 ft. (50 m) before MP 8. Modern signage and guidebooks often call it the Temple of Hercules, since one of Martial's *Epigrams* (9.64) mentions such a temple in this area built by Domitian. But it is now agreed that these remains belong to a much earlier Republican structure. An inscription found nearby indicates it was dedicated to Silvanus, the god of agriculture, forests, hunting, and boundaries.

Silvanus had no official place in the state religion—no annual festival or state-sponsored temples. Yet he was among the most popular deities for personal worship, especially in Rome itself (Dorcey 1992, 3, 133–40). Some unknown devotees erected this temple in his honor along Rome's great highway to the south. The ruins visible today are part of a four-sided portico where travelers may have been encouraged to rest and snack, and to give an offering to Silvanus for their safe journey, either just starting or now nearing completion. Even though this portico marked the halfway point of the day's journey, Paul and his fellow believers probably found a different place to rest.

When passing MP 8*, Paul's party saw another large tumulus* to their immediate left. Over 65 ft. (20 m) in diameter, it was constructed during the reign of Augustus and decorated with acanthus plants and other flowers. But as with most of these monuments, we no longer know who built

---

formalized the persecution and execution of Christians, Gallienus rescinded the order upon his father's death in 260.

24. About mid-mile is a large domed tomb* on the right. Because of its shape, it is referred to as the Priest's Berretta (Berretta del Prete), but it was not built until three centuries after Paul. This tomb once had a surrounding ambulatory like that at Santa Costanza, and by the tenth century it had become the Church of Santa Maria Dei Genetricis.

it or was interred there.²⁵ Standing 1300 ft. (400 m) beyond on the right is a tomb* dating to the late Republican era. It consisted of a semicircular marble-faced exedra once surmounted by a half-dome with three niches for statues of the deceased.

Just after the VA passes over Rome's current ring road, Raccordo Anulare, some 1150 ft. (350 m) beyond the exedra, the route begins the first of its two small deviations*. It gently veers a few degrees westward for about 800 ft. (250 m) until it was about 130 ft. (40 m) west of the straightaway. Then it gradually turns back northward to rejoin its previous path 800 ft. (250 m) later. Why this deviation was made is unknown. That it was not a post-Roman variation, however, is confirmed by the ruins of an impressive tomb on the right, today called the Tomb of the Vase*, about 450 ft. (135 m) into the deviation. The name comes from a late-first-century-BC Egyptian-style alabaster vase found in its vaulted underground funerary chamber, which also provides an approximate date for the tomb. Just 100 ft. (30 m) past the tomb Paul saw MP 7*.

## Suburbs of the Imperial City: MP 7–3

At MP 7 Tiberius received a frightening portent, according to Suetonius (*Tiberius* 72). He had left his retreat at Capri to return to Rome and came this far when he went to feed his pet snake and found it half eaten by a swarm of ants. A soothsayer then warned him: "Beware the power of the mob." Tiberius immediately reversed course and began his return to Campania, reaching Misenum before dying there on March 16, AD 37.²⁶

In his earlier letter to the Christians in Rome, Paul had asked a rhetorical question about death: "Who will rescue me from this mortal body?" (Rom 7:24, trans. Wilson). Now, as he approached that same city to be put on trial for capital crimes, Paul passed tomb after tomb along the final

---

25. Proceeding another 800 ft. (250 m), another magnificent brick tomb* appears on the left. High above its podium is a niche framed by two columns and surmounted by a pediment. Inside its central chamber are three niches for sarcophagi. Another 1526 ft. (465 m) farther, a beautiful tomb with exedra* can be seen on the right. Its large niche, framed by Corinthian columns, once contained a statue of the deceased. Dating to the mid-second century AD, it too was not yet built when Paul walked past.

26. Suetonius also says that Tiberius saw the walls of Rome from a distance before turning back, something that was hardly possible from MP 7, and an example of the historian's penchant for the picturesque.

miles. Yet he did so without despair, knowing that death could not separate him from "the love of God that is in Christ Jesus our Lord" (Rom 8:39).

Shortly after the deviation ends*, modern travelers pass funerary busts* of three ancient Romans carved into a limestone block that today serves as a bench for passing travelers.[27] This resting place makes a convenient place to view a spur of the Aqua Novus aqueduct 656 ft. (200 m) to the east. This spur, not yet built in Paul's day, brought water to the great Villa of the Quintillii, soon to be discussed.

**Figure 36.** Paving in outskirts of Rome

---

27. Locals have named it the *panchina degli antichi avi* ("bench of the ancient ancestors"). No ruins of the ancient tomb for these three individuals are visible.

Some 656 ft. (200 m) past the bench, Paul saw to his right a large tomb built in honor of C. Atilius Euhodus. This tomb was one of many that demonstrated the peculiar social mobility that occurred within the Roman Empire. A century before Paul passed by, the deceased had been a dealer in pearls (*margaritarius*) with a shop that lay along the Via Sacra in the heart of the Roman Forum. Yet he had started life as a slave and, at some point, became the property of Serranus. That Roman senator later freed him and then probably set him up in business, for a percentage of the profits, of course! The freedman had done so well that he could purchase this choice piece of property along the VA and erect a sizeable tomb. While the tomb has disappeared, the inscription* in which he proudly bears witness both to his past and to his successes has survived. A copy has been placed on the site, reading in translation as follows:[28]

> Stranger, stop and turn your gaze to the small hill on your left; it holds the bones of a poor man—righteous, merciful and loving. Traveler, I beg you not to harm this memorial. Gaius Atilius Euhodus, a freedman of Serranus and pearl-merchant along the Via Sacra, is buried in this tomb. Traveler, farewell!
> According to my last will and testament, it is not permitted to bring in or bury in this tomb anyone except those freedmen to whom I have given and conferred this right by my last will and testament. (*CIL* 1².1212, trans. Thompson)

Also on the right, just 500 ft. (150 m) beyond the inscription, are the remains of one of the larger tombs, dating from the late first century BC. Like the tomb in Albano Laziale, it has also been identified as that of Pompey the Great*. However, its true occupant is unknown. During the twelfth century a signal tower was erected on its ruins, causing it to be named the Torre Selce ("Flint Tower"). When Paul passed, it may well have resembled the magnificent tomb of Caecilia Metella coming a few miles later. After another 575 ft. (175 m) a square brick-faced columbarium comes into view on the left. The *arcosolia*, still visible on its lower level in modern times

---

28. Just northwest of the inscription are the remains of another large tomb (41.81543, 12.56175). Whether the latter was the tomb of Euhodus is unknown.

and mirrored by niches above them, produced the name Tomb of the Six Arcosolia*. Beyond another 200 ft. (60 m) and also on the left is a two-story tomb in the shape of a temple surrounded by a courtyard*. Marble slabs decorated with griffins give a sense of the tomb's original decoration. Several other substantial ruins are still visible in the following 1075 ft. (330 m) before the VA intersects simultaneously with Via di Torricola and Via del Casale Rotondo and passes over a regional railroad line.

Beyond the junction by 328 ft. (100 m), the largest of all the ancient tombs along the VA appears on the right. Known today as Casal Rotondo*, it had a square base measuring 115 ft. (35 m) surmounted by a circular tomb. This area was big enough to hold the substantial eighteenth-century farmhouse, barn, stable, and even olive grove that still sit atop its remains.[29] While carrying out some of the earliest systematic study of the VA in the mid-nineteenth century, Luigi Canina preserved some of the tomb's beautiful architectural fragments in the surrounding walls. Some 330 ft. (100 m) beyond Casal Rotondo Paul passed MP 6*.[30]

The next RM brought an ever-increasing number of impressive monuments in Paul's day. Today the roadsides are dotted only with cement and brick remains of these once impressive tombs, mostly of the Republican period. Behind the tombs on the right for much of this mile, however, is a large villa that had developed in the late Republic. This was taken over in the middle of the second century AD by the well-known Quintilius family, the name by which it is still known, and still later became an imperial estate.[31] Today a small museum houses some of the remains, including an alabaster slab with ΙΧΘΥΣ (*ICHTHYS*) beneath a solar wheel dating to

---

29. On the basis of a fragmentary inscription found nearby and preserved in the nearby wall, it was identified by Canina (1853, 145–56) as the tomb of M. Valerius Messalinus Cotta. However, Quilici (1988, 51–52) and others are dubious, and so the tomb remains officially anonymous.

30. Quilici (1989a, 52) marks his distances from where the replica of MP 1 is erroneously placed and therefore puts MP 6 just southeast ("subito dopo") of Casale Rotondo.

31. Two Quintilius brothers shared the consulship in AD 151. Apparently, they were too prominent, however, and both were killed by Commodus around 182. After that, the emperor took over the estate, and it remained imperial property. Recent excavations have uncovered more of the vast estate, which extended at least 1640 ft. (500 m) to the east. It included palatial living accommodations as well as a circus and a grand nymphaeum supplied with water by a spur of the aqueduct mentioned earlier.

the third to fourth century AD and formerly in the Museo Kircheriano.[32] The villa extended along the VA at least as far as the tomb with square base and pyramid top* located 0.75 mi. (1.2 km) into RM 6. This richly decorated tomb probably contained the remains of some of the Quintilii or their family retainers.[33]

About 250 ft. (75 m) before that tomb and on the opposite side, two circular tumuli lie along the road*.[34] These are often called the Tumuli of the Horatii, connecting them with the story mentioned at the beginning of this chapter. Livy (*Hist.* 1.25.14) wrote that "the graves may still be seen where each soldier fell: two Roman graves in one spot, nearer Alba; those of the three Albans towards Rome, but separated, just as they had fought." Two of these latter were at the fifth mile of the VA, and both tumuli were there when Livy wrote.

About 1000 ft. (300 m) farther north begins the second of the small deviations*. Here the road bends slightly to the east, arcing to a maximum of 35 ft. (10 m) to the right before realigning with the straightaway after 600 ft. (185 m). Some scholars have associated this with the *Fossa Cluilia*, an ancient trench supposedly constructed by Gaius Cluilius, the legendary king of Alba Longa, to mark the border between Rome and Alba Longa. The story continues that the Roman king Tullius Hostilius, however, ignoring the trench, made incursions into the territory of their Latin neighbors raising the specter of war. It was then that the solution of trial by combat between the Horatii and Curiatii took place.

While the ancient accounts are hard to square exactly with the surviving artifacts, it would make sense that the existence of several tumuli at the very place where there is a primitive road deviation might be connected, rightly or wrongly, with this important story of Roman expansion

---

32. The oldest datable use of the Greek word ἰχθῦς (*ichthys*, "fish") as an acronym for "Jesus Christ, Son of God, Savior" is in a hymn in the Sibylline Oracles (8:217); see Collins (1983, 423 n. h2).

33. A 3D restoration of the tomb is shown by de Kleijn, de Hond, and Martinez-Rubi (2016, 27, fig. 3) as part of their digital technology project that aims "to analyse the complex and archaeologically rich area between the fifth and sixth mile of the Via Appia" (2016, 24).

34. These tumuli are immediately across the VA from an access road into the Villa of the Quintilii.

and heroism.³⁵ A third circular tumulus, now with a medieval tower, lies just west of the VA at the beginning of the deviation. It is still known as the Tumulus of the Curiatii*.³⁶ Another round tomb*, but not a tumulus, is found 492 ft. (150 m) farther on the left, just before the deviation ends. Even if these do not date to the Roman strife with the Latins, it is possible that one or more of these monuments were an Augustan "learned reconstruction" to make the ancient legends more vivid (Coarelli 2014, 396).

Milestone 5* stood at the end of the second deviation*, about 100 ft. (30 m) past the last-mentioned tomb. Modern travelers see almost two dozen significant funerary remains between MP 5 and MP 4, many in existence in Paul's day. On the left about 500 ft. (150 m) past MP 5, just to the right or north of the driveway of no. 288a, is the remnant of a cement funerary tower. At its foot is an inscription commemorating three more freedmen* (fig. 37). Although when freed they took the name of their master Lucius Valerius, their tomb inscription still preserves their Semitic names—Baricha, Zabda, and Achiba—which may be Jewish.³⁷ The inscription (*CIL* 6.27959) appears to date to the first century AD, making it likely that these three had first come to Rome as prisoners after the Jewish-Roman War of AD 66–73. Again, we see a sign of social mobility, as the three end up freedmen and wealthy enough to have a memorial and tombstone along the Queen of Roads.

---

35. Leoni and Staderini (1907, 167) wrote that "the tradition is further corroborated by the fact that at this point the road, which runs over flat ground, altogether free from rocks or other obstacles, swerves without any material reason from the straight line it has hitherto followed, and returns to its former direction only after having passed the sepulchre of Curiatius. It is obvious that when Appius Claudius built this road, possibly over the course of the ancient *semita* connecting Rome with Alba, he could have made it straight had he not met with moral or material obstacles. After Casale Rotondo we shall see the Appian Way deviate somewhat to avoid a steep declivity; but what motive can have induced the Censor to make, at this point, a curve which was nowise necessitated by the lie of the ground?"

36. Southeast of this tomb and just across the VA along Via Appia Pignatelli, which lies atop an ancient spur connecting the VA to the Via Latina, are some ruins called Santa Maria Nova. These include a second-century AD water tank and bathing complex, maybe part of the residence for imperial guards stationed to protect the nearby imperial villa of Commodus. A mosaic preserved within the complex pictured a reclining skeleton with the inscription γνῶθι σαυτόν (*gnōthi sauton*, "Know yourself"), a reminder of the ongoing influence of Greek culture and bilingualism well after Paul's day.

37. Ilan (2008, 85; cf. 146, 693), however, writes: "The inscription, containing the names of three freedmen, was considered Jewish because of the names—Baricha, Zabda and Achiba—but all three, although Semitic, need not be understood as Jewish."

# Day 7: Aricia to Rome

**Figure 37.** Inscription of three Jewish (?) freedmen

On the left 1835 ft. (560 m) farther travelers come upon the ruins of two tombs. The first contains a relief of a married couple flanked by two of their children*. The second is decorated with a Gorgon and Erotes*. Both were erected in the first century AD and illustrate the hopes and ideals of the Roman populace. Some 400 ft. (125 m) farther Paul saw a memorial slab with three busts and an inscription (*CIL* 6.2246) on an altar-shaped tomb constructed a half century earlier by a freedman, Gaius Rabirius Hermodorus*.[38] He is shown with his wife Rabiria Demaris, former slaves of C. Rabirius Postumus, who brought them from Egypt. The third occupant of the tomb was Usia Prima, named "priestess" or "devotee" of Isis

---

38. For photographs of the monument and inscription, see https://kb.osu.edu/handle/1811/100838. Their owner may have been the Rabirius whom Cicero defended in 54/53 BC for financial irregularities in Egypt (cf. his *For Rabirius Postumus*). The third bust was altered and the inscription added decades after the original construction. Usia may have either inherited or purchased space in the tomb and then added the inscription and altered the bust to reflect this; see Cupello and Hughes (2010, 3–23).

and pictured with a sistera and patera, implements of worship. This indicates that the Isis cult was enjoying some popularity in Rome about the time of Paul's arrival and is also a reminder of the multireligious nature of the Roman Empire.

On the left 650 ft. (200 m) farther are the reconstructed remains of a tomb that once contained the family of a freedman of Claudius, Tiberius Claudius Secundus Philippianus* (CIL 6.1859). He was buried about the time that Paul passed by, and later was joined by his wife Flavia Irene and their two children, Claudius and Claudia. About 590 ft. (180 m) after passing the tomb of Hilarius Fuscus*, identified by the inscription (CIL 6.19483) accompanying five busts, Paul saw an impressive tomb on the right with a lengthy inscription in Latin verse (CIL 6.24520). This first-century tomb is no longer visible, but the sixteen-line inscription in which Sextus Pompeius Iustus mourns the death of two of his children has been encased in a reconstructed wall*. How unnatural, he laments, that a father should light the funeral pyres of two of his children rather than the reverse. Shortly afterward, modern travelers begin to walk on an almost continuous stretch of ancient pavement stretching for half a kilometer, making this one of the most atmospheric sections to walk today.[39] About 1000 ft. (300 m) along this stretch, Paul's party would have passed MP 4*.

The gauntlet of imposing tombs continued as Julius led his party for the next mile. Some 80 ft. (25 m) beyond MP 4, modern travelers, still walking atop the ancient paving, see a copy of a marble sculptural relief depicting a Hellenistic Greek warrior and his breastplate*. Part of a Republican-era tomb, it may have reminded Paul again of Rome's imperialistic adaptation of Greek culture. Today only a few concrete and brick cores remain here and there along the next 0.6 mi. (1 km), since the roadside becomes increasingly occupied by early modern buildings and modern luxury villas. In the second century AD, a large villa on the west side of the road

---

39. From about 41.84000, 12.53420 to 41.84300, 12.53083. Along this section one passes another early-Imperial circular tomb* on the right, then another reconstruction. The latter has preserved a pediment inscription of the tomb of the freedman M. Servilius Quartus*. Its second and final line, "built with his own money" (*de sua pecunia fecit*), is a phrase seen prominently displayed on numerous Roman inscriptions and emphasizes the individualistic aspect of Roman culture.

Day 7: Aricia to Rome

belonged to the famous Athenian millionaire and philanthropist Herodes Atticus. Some remains of his Greek-themed estate have been found inside the complex now known as Capo di Bove*.

On the right some 1475 ft. (450 m) farther and just 130 ft. (40 m) before MP 3*, Paul came to the second largest and still best-preserved tomb along the entire VA—that built to honor Caecilia Metella*. It consists of a square base surmounted by a circular drum 97 ft. (29.5 m) in diameter and 36 ft. (11 m) high. Portions of its travertine marble façade survive as well as its decorations of bucrania and festoons. Much of the tomb, however, had been covered originally with earth to form a tumulus, similar to the Tomb of Augustus in the Campus Martius.[40] The occupant of this magnificent grave was the daughter of Quintus Caecilius Metellus Creticus, consul in 69 BC and the general who conquered Crete several years later, hence his final honorific name. She was married to Marcus Licinius Crassus, son of the triumvir and millionaire of the same name who was killed in Persia at the battle of Carrhae in 53 BC. The tomb dates to the later first century BC and would surely have merited a brief stop of admiration by Paul's party when they passed it almost a century later. It was a reminder that even the most privileged aristocrats ended in a tomb!

---

40. The original cone-shaped earthen top has since been defaced by the addition of fourteenth-century battlements constructed along with the nearby palazzo and the Church of St. Nicholas (on the opposite side of the VA) by Pope Boniface VIII (r. 1294–1303) and his Caetani family.

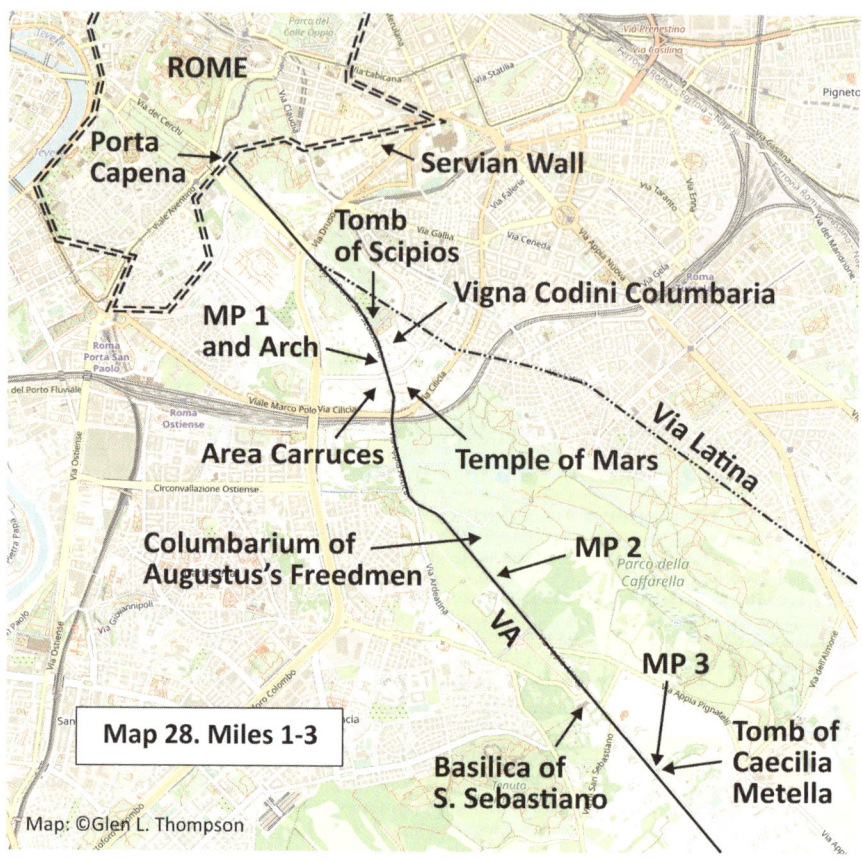

Map 28. Miles 1-3
Map: ©Glen L. Thompson

## RM 2 and 3

Today mile 3 is mainly open countryside on both sides of the VA (map 28). One can assume the road itself was lined with tombs long before Paul passed that way. Behind those, the small farms that had existed for centuries were gradually replaced by large country estates and villas as the Imperial period progressed. Little is known about these during Paul's time, but in the mid-second century much of this area became the estate of the aforementioned Herodes Atticus who expanded his already existing villa and built a nymphaeum and a tomb for his late wife Annia Regilla. By the early fourth century Emperor Maxentius (r. 306–312) expanded the villa yet further to create a magnificent palace. Its ruins survive, most visibly in the circus* as well as the circular tomb for his son Romulus*, both on

Day 7: Aricia to Rome 163

the east side of the VA. Paul's party may instead have seen a small hilltop Greek temple nearby called the Monument of Basilius (Cicero, *Letters to Atticus* 7.9.1), but its exact position has not been identified.

On the west side of the VA, about 1650 ft. (500 m) into MP 3 and just 500 ft. (150 m) northwest of the tomb of Romulus, Paul passed a quarry for pozzolana—that volcanic sand mentioned earlier that was common around Puteoli and used to make concrete. These hollows already contained some columbaria. Several centuries later this area, by then known as *ad catacombas* ("at the hollows"),[41] became the site of underground corridors lined with tombs of Christians, thus giving this type of cemetery the name "catacombs." This one, eventually named after a local martyr named Sebastian who was buried there, would become, at least for a time in the mid-third to mid-fourth centuries, the resting place for the bones of Paul together with those of Peter.[42] The current Basilica of San Sebastiano* was built in the fourth century as a circiform basilica that contained many Christian tombs beneath its floor along with those in its underground tunnels which total some 7.5 mi. (12 km).[43]

Today virtually nothing else is visible from the first century in the remaining 3000 ft. (915 m) to MP 2.[44] In Paul's day, however, several large

---

41. From the Greek κατὰ κύμβας (*kata kymbas*). The majority of Christians in Rome in the first several centuries were Greek-speaking immigrants from the eastern empire and their descendants. The name probably therefore originated within the Christian community.

42. The name *memoria apostolorum* was given to the area where the relics of Peter and Paul appear to have been transferred for safekeeping in AD 258. They remained there until after the persecutions when they were moved back to the churches built in their honor—St. Paul's Outside the Walls on the Via Ostiense and St. Peter's on the Vatican Hill. On the complicated arguments about when and where the bones of Peter and Paul were interred in the first four centuries, see Chadwick (1957) and more recently Eastman (2011, 22–34, 71–116) who deals with the cult of Paul on the VA.

43. This is one of only six known early basilicas, all from the Constantinian period, that take the form of a Roman circus and thus have been given the name *circiform*. They are all found in the suburbs of Rome and served as funerary basilicas. The long central nave with its rounded apse is surrounded by one continuous ambulatory. The end opposite the apse is not perpendicular to the apse walls but is angled just like the *carcares* (starting gate) of a circus. Tombs are found beneath the entire floor of the nave and ambulatory. A bit further along on the east side of VA is another catacomb—Vigna Randanini—that contains exclusively Jewish burials. In addition to Greco-Roman-style wall paintings, it contains images of menorahs, lulavs, and shofars (Brettman et. al. 2017). Although these catacombs are dated from the second to fifth centuries AD, a Jewish community existed in Rome from about 150 BC.

44. Quilici (1989a, 36) mentions a plaque placed at VAA 103 to mark the location of MP 2. This seems to be the now-faded *tabula ansata* at 41.86152, 12.51003. Unfortunately, this was erected by measuring from the incorrectly located copy of MP 1 and thus is off by some 460 ft. (140 m). See below.

columbaria occupied the area just before and after MP 2. One, known as the *Monumentum Volusiorum\**, may have contained some three hundred slaves and freedmen of the prominent Volusius Saturninus family. Quintus Volusius Saturninus was *consul ordinarius* in AD 56. The facility was in use from AD 20 on, so it was active when Paul passed. Located east of the VA about 1100 ft. (335 m) south of MP 2, the columbarium has been incorporated into the group of buildings that currently stand at VAA 109 (Treggiari 1975, 393–401; Quilici 1989a, 36; cf. Duinker 2015, 103). Two others on the east side are of particular interest. In the early eighteenth century, ruins of one columbarium\*, about 250 ft. (75 m) before MP 2, were found with a large number of burials and inscriptions. These enabled its identification as the resting place of many freed slaves who had served Augustus's wife, Livia. Although it has now completely disappeared, it apparently contained as many as sixteen hundred funerary urns. The more than 375 inscriptions mention some 670 occupants. About 725 ft. (220 m) after passing MP 2\*, Paul's group saw an even larger columbarium\* containing freed slaves of Augustus himself. Until recently it was incorporated into a restaurant. Some three thousand cinerary urns are estimated to have lined the walls from floor to ceiling in its three adjoining vaulted chambers (Spera and Mineo 2004, 94–95). Now open to the air, some of its interior can be seen in Google Maps satellite view.

Somewhere along RM 2, Paul perhaps saw on the left a small shrine (*fanum*) and altar to Rediculus, the god of travelers.[45] Outbound Romans may have stopped to say a prayer for protection on their journey, and those returning stopped to give a libation or prayer of thanks for their safe return. Ancient travelers also erected votive altars to enlist divine assistance for their journeys. One such altar was erected by Titus Albanius Principianus in honor of the imperial household (*CIL* 6.830). On the right side above the reclining figure of Fortuna is inscribed *salvos ire*, wishing a safe outbound journey. On the left side above a sitting female figure, possibly a personification of the VA, is inscribed *salvos venire*, wishing a safe return (fig. 38). Another dedication similarly wishes that the deity

---

45. Pliny the Elder (*Nat.* 10.60.122) is one of the few references to this shrine and confirms its existence during the reign of Tiberius. Its exact spot has never been determined. A striking temple-shaped tomb in nearby Caffarella Park has for several centuries been called the Temple of Rediculus, but it is a second-century tomb, perhaps that of Annia Regilla, the wife of Herodes Atticus.

Day 7: Aricia to Rome

Caelestis would provide a safe round trip and shows two sets of feet, those on the right outbound and those on the left inbound.[46]

**Figure 38.** Votive offerings of travelers

---

46. These travel votives are displayed in the inscription gallery of the Capitoline Museum; see Velestino (2015, 70–71).

By Paul's day, Roman writers had begun to incorrectly identify the site of that temple as the place where Hannibal stopped his advance on Rome in 211 BC and then turned his army away, giving Rediculus credit. Centuries later a Christian church was erected within a few hundred meters of that shrine on the basis of a somewhat parallel story. This time, however, it was someone leaving Rome who turned around to return to his death. The account of Peter's return after an appearance of Jesus asking him, *Quo vadis*? ("Where are you going?"), is still commemorated in the seventeenth-century Church of Domine Quo Vadis* found on the right side of the VA about 2050 ft. (625 m) past MP 2.[47] Inside the church is a pair of footprints in marble, held to be those of Jesus or Peter. They are in fact a copy of an ancient stone now in the basilica at the San Sebastian catacombs. It has been suggested that these footprints were originally an *ex voto* offering presented by a Roman traveler to Rediculus at his nearby shrine.[48]

About 600 ft. (180 m) before the Quo Vadis church, the long straight stretch of the VA ended*.[49] An early Roman road exited the city from the Porta Capena 1.2 mi. (2 km) to the northwest, and then meandered slightly over the next 1.6 mi. (2.5 km) to reach this point. Appius Claudius's engineers incorporated this earlier road as the first 1.4 RM (1.5 mi./2.4 km) of the new VA. From this point they then began the new "straightened" roadbed for the VA. It now headed southeastward to Tarracina in a straight line for the next 56.88 RM (52.3 mi./84.1 km), apart from the few exceptions noted above.

Paul and his party continued on the gentle arc of the older road westward just past Quo Vadis church to where the ancient and modern Via Ardeatina* fed traffic into the VA from the south. The VA then turned more northward again toward the city. After the junction on the west side

---

47. The church is also called Santa Maria in Palmis or Santa Maria delle Piante.

48. The suggestion of Quilici (1989a, 34–35), without citing evidence, is that the shrine of Rediculus was in the field directly across the VA from the church. On the false association with Hannibal who would have arrived in Rome along the Via Latina instead, see Meyer (1915, 151–54).

49. This is about 80 ft. (25 m) south of the small circular Chapel of Reginald Pole.

of the VA, a medieval tower still sits atop the ruins of another once-magnificent tomb built several decades after Paul passed the spot.[50] On the east side of the VA at numbers 43–45 VAA, 165 ft. (50 m) beyond the tomb of Priscilla, an archaic fourth-century-BC temple was discovered in the 1970s. Recent research suggests that this may have been the Temple of Mars Gradivus* (*Aedes Martis*; Dubbini 2016, 327–47).[51] It measured 88 × 52 ft. (27 × 16 m) and had two *cellae*. Between the tomb of Priscilla and the Aurelian Wall, several other locations on the east side of the VA have also been proposed as the location for the temple—beneath the current overpasses for the railway and the Via Cilicia*[52] or on the hill just southeast of the Porta San Sebastiano and the Aurelian Wall* (Richardson 1992, 414). Entering into the debate are sources which also mention a *clivus Martis* ("hill of Mars"), usually interpreted to mean that either the temple was on a rise or hill or that the VA went up a hill as it approached the turnoff to the sanctuary. Its location remains a matter of debate and speculation.

The VA from the Porta Capena to the temple of Mars was the first section to be paved in 295 BC and repaved again in 189 BC (Livy, *Hist.* 10.23.12, 38.28.3). Numerous references in ancient sources make it clear that the

---

50. Here Titus Flavius Abascantius, an important and powerful freedman, Emperor Domitian's *ab epistulis* until around AD 95, built a beautiful house-tomb* for his pre-deceased wife Priscilla. The poet Statius (d. AD 96) was a friend of Abascantius, and their wives were good friends as well. When Priscilla died prematurely, Statius (*Silvae* 5.1) penned an entire elegiac poem for her. From this we learn that Abascantius could not bear to cremate Priscilla but instead, after a magnificent funeral procession, had her body laid in an ornate sarcophagus surrounded by statues of virtuous heroines of legend. It has been suggested that this inhumation made headlines in Rome and began a new fashion that grew to be the common practice among the upper classes in second-century Rome. Maglio (2016, 339–61) explores the location of a tavern called Acquataccio at or near the tomb.

51. The land has recently been purchased by the Italian government, and so further excavations may settle the question in coming years. Literary sources clearly state that such a temple existed outside Porta Capena from 388 BC (Livy, *Hist.* 6.5.7). Appian (*Civil Wars* 3.41) says that Octavian was camped there 15 stades (1.73 mi./2.78 km) from the city. The proposed location is 1.4 mi. (2.25 km) from Porta Capena. An inscription (*ILS* $2^2$.7213) with regulations for a *collegia* of Aesculapius and Hygia makes clear that it was located "between the first and second mileposts, on the left when exiting the city" (*via Appia ad Martis intra milliarium I et II ab urbe euntibus parte laeva*).

52. Known as the Area Archaeologica di Via Cilicia, excavations have uncovered tombs from the Republican era and later, buildings converted to *tavernae*, and some *ex votos* that might favor a religious site being nearby (see https://sovraintendenzaroma.it/i_luoghi/roma_antica/aree_archeologiche /area_archeologica_di_via_cilicia).

Mars temple was the most important site along the second mile of the VA. It was used as the point of reference for other properties, such as the Garden of Terence, a property of some twenty *iugera* that belonged to the comic poet of that name (Suetonius, *Life of Terence* 5), and the Garden of Crassipes, the second husband of Cicero's daughter Tullia (Cicero, *Letters to Quintus* 3.7.1). Perhaps Paul caught a glimpse of these between the tombs lining the road.

About 650 ft. (200 m) after passing the Tomb of Priscilla, Paul's party crossed the Almo (modern Almone) River* where the "great Appia begins and Cybele lays aside her grief in Italian Almo" (Statius, *Silvae* 5.1.222–24). This short but sacred tributary flowed between the Via Latina and the VA before emptying into the Tiber River. In 204 BC during the Second Punic War a prophecy by the Sibylline Oracle directed the Romans to send a delegation to the Galatian city of Pessinus. They were to bring back the cult stone of Cybele, the Phrygian mother goddess, believed to have fallen from heaven. The ship carrying the stone ran aground at the confluence of the Tiber and the Almo and could resume its trip only after a purification ceremony was performed. In 191 BC a magnificent temple in honor of the Magna Mater (Great Mother) and repository for the stone was erected on the Palatine Hill.[53] Thereafter, a festival of *lavatio* (washing) occurred every March 27. A sacred procession wended its way with the stone from the Palatine through the Porta Capena to give it a ceremonial washing in the Almo.[54] Paul had spent much time in Galatia during three of his journeys, so he was undoubtedly familiar with the legend of the black stone of Cybele and its removal to Rome.[55] But for him sacred stones, particularly stones fallen from heaven, had no spiritual significance (17:29; 19:35).

---

53. Various Latin authors recount the story; see Livy, *Hist.* 19.15; 36.35; Ovid, *Fasti* 4.259; and Varro, *On the Latin Language* 6.15.

54. For a discussion of the geography and myths regarding the river, see Tallini et al. (2013, 727–31). Ovid (*Fasti* 4.335–342) records that the ceremony took place where the Almo joined the Tiber. Richardson (1992, 243), however, believes the washing took place closer to the VA than to the Tiber.

55. Whether Paul visited Pessinus in north Galatia is unlikely, though this is disputed; see Wilson (2019a, 483–92).

Day 7: Aricia to Rome

Rather it was *the* Stone—Jesus—rejected by the builders, who was now the chief cornerstone of the new faith he was proclaiming (Luke 20:17).

Although few details are known about the final stretch of RM 2, it must have been crowded with tombs, though perhaps not to the extent imagined in Piranesi's famous view where the Via Ardeatina diverged from the VA just south of the tomb of Priscilla.[56] The hubbub of traffic would be constant day and night as pedestrians, horsemen, and carts merged while streaming in and out of the city.

The present Porta San Sebastiano* must have been the approximate site of the *Area Carruces*, listed as being in the city's *Regio I* in the regionary catalogues. Here travelers left their horse-drawn vehicles for litters since vehicular traffic was regulated within the city. Connected with it was the *Schola Carrucariorum*, the headquarters of the transportation guilds (*Digest* 19.2.13). Even though the Aurelian Wall was two centuries in the future, Augustus had divided the city of Rome into fourteen administrative *regiones*, and *Regio I* appears to have extended along the VA to about this point, even though this was well outside the older Servian wall. Therefore, urban traffic regulations may also have been enforced beginning here.

---

56. Used as a frontispiece to Piranesi's (1757) second volume of *Le antichita Romane*, this image is widely available on the internet, including at https://artsandculture.google.com/asset/frontispiece-ancient-intersection-of-the-via-appia-and-via-ardeatina/xgHkQmnfxs_J4w.

**Figure 39.** Replica of MP 1 (left) and original on the Campidoglio (right)

## The Final Mile

Paul's party now passed the final milestone, MP 1*. The milestone that stood there since the last quarter of the first century AD was discovered in 1584 and soon after was transferred to the center of Rome. Placed atop the Campidoglio, it can still be admired there today (fig. 39).⁵⁷ It was either not in situ when

---

57. It has inscriptions from Vespasian (AD 76) and Nerva (AD 97); *CIL* 10.6812–6813 (= *ILS* 5819).

*Day 7: Aricia to Rome*

discovered, or else its find location was not accurately recorded, for in 1905 a copy* was mistakenly placed 445 ft. (135 m) farther out on the VA where it remains today. This still causes confusion in many guidebooks![58] Its true location would be inside the still-standing Aurelian city wall from the third century AD and just outside the so-called Arch of Drusus, which is actually a later arch carrying an aqueduct rather than being a memorial arch (fig. 40).

**Figure 40.** So-called "Arch of Drusus," site of MP 1

---

58. The correct placement of the first milestone *inside* the Aurelian Wall was noted already a century ago by Lanciani (1907, 11) who called for the copy's removal to avoid confusion. His advice and his warning were ignored, and so the copy is still assumed to mark the proper location. Dessau (1882, 125–26) thinks that Fabretti made the initial mistake by equating the milestone's discovery with the contemporaneous discovery of the *Martis clivum* inscription, which may have come from a vineyard near the site of today's copy.

By the early-Imperial period the area on both sides of the VA was quite crowded with tombs, especially the next 0.5 RM before its junction with the Via Latina. The long narrow triangular area between the VA and the Via Latina to the east provides wonderful examples of family tombs and columbaria. Behind the high walls along the right side of the VA for the first 656 ft. (200 m) past the Arch of Drusus—an area once known as the Vigna Codini—three substantial columbaria were discovered between 1840 and 1852. In antiquity the wall was not present, for the tombs were meant to be accessible, seen, and admired by passersby. Steep staircases provided access to the interior of each columbarium.[59] The first and southernmost of the surviving columbaria,* approximately 200 ft. (60 m) to the right of the VA and perhaps hidden behind other tombs, held about 500 burials mostly from the reign of Tiberius (fig. 41).[60] The second columbarium*, built slightly earlier than the previous one, held some six hundred burials in three hundred niches (*loculi*); it lay about 130 ft. (40 m) from the VA.[61] The third columbarium*, a bit farther north and only 66 ft. (20 m) from the VA, had larger niches capable of holding up to six urns each, with a total of some nine hundred burials for the age of Tiberius, including imperial slaves and freedmen.[62]

---

59. Concise summaries and good photographs of these and other Roman columbaria can be found in Duinker (2015, passim).

60. The rectangular brick building measures 16.5 × 23 ft. (5 × 7 m) and has a floor now 20 ft. (6 m) below ground and a vaulted ceiling supported by a central brick pier. Arranged in nine rows from the floor to its ceiling 25 ft. (7.5 m) high, semicircular niches (*loculi*) for cinerary urns fill every wall and all sides of the central pier. Those interred represented a wide variety of individuals and social classes.

61. The second columbarium had a structure similar to the first, measuring 16 × 20 ft. (5 × 6 m) and faced in *opus reticulatum*. Again, nine rows of *loculi* are found totaling about three hundred, but with two urns in each. The earliest burials date to the late Augustan period. The surviving inscriptions mention a midwife, members of a guild of florists and wreath-makers, and a number of musicians in a *collegia symphoniacii* (CIL 6.4458, 6.4414, and 6.4416 respectively). Imperial freedmen were among those who funded the building of this columbarium and were then buried in it.

62. The third columbarium consisted of three 26 × 5 ft. (8 × 1.5 m) oblong rectangles, joined into a U-shape around a small garden. Here the niches, also rectangular, are arranged in seven rows. The wall space in between had marble facing and painted decoration. Only about 150 name plates survive but these include those of imperial slaves and freedmen. A few inhumations were also discovered, indicating that there were new arrivals yet in the second century.

# Day 7: Aricia to Rome

**Figure 41.** Southernmost Columbarium in Vigna Codini

This area of RM 1 was also a burial spot for the rich and famous of Rome's aristocratic families. A century before Paul passed by, Cicero (*Tusculan Disputations* 1.7) wrote: "When you come out of the Porta Capena, you see the tombs of Calatinus, the Scipios, the Servilii, the Metelli." While most have not left a trace, one is still known. About 395 ft. (120 m) past the U-shaped columbarium of Vigna Codini, Paul came to a smaller sideroad or path to the right. Just around the corner and facing the city, that is, in full view of all outbound travelers, was the mausoleum of one of Rome's most distinguished families, the Scipios*. About 280 BC, just a few years after the VA was constructed, the family, who may already have owned a villa here, carved a tomb into the rocky hillside for Lucius Cornelius Scipio Barbatus, consul of 298 BC.[63] Scipio also served as censor and was an important general in Rome's defeat of its neighbors in the Third Samnite War (298–290 BC). This then became a family tomb, eventually containing some thirty members of the family over the next century or so, including another L. Cornelius Scipio, the son of Barbatus and consul in 259. The original tomb complex was given its monumental façade and entrance in the mid-second century BC. Looking down on passing travelers were three life-size statues of heroic family members. Publius Cornelius Scipio Africanus, consul in 205, and his brother Lucius Cornelius Scipio Asiaticus, consul in 190, were probably two of them (Livy, *Hist.* 38.56.2–4).[64] When the tomb ran out of space, a side chamber was hollowed out of the tufa for use by later family members. By Paul's days the Scipio family had died out, but the related Cornelius Lentulus family continued to use the tomb into the early first century AD. Additional funerary structures occupied the 65 ft. (20 m) or so between the Scipio mausoleum and the VA, all associated with the Scipios. One is an early-Imperial columbarium containing over 450 niches.[65]

After passing another 1650 ft. (500 m) of tombs lining the VA, Paul's party came to another major road junction. Just 3 RM or so after Paul had left Capua, and shortly after crossing the great bridge of the Volturnum River at Casilinum, the Via Latina had separated from the VA and headed north to Rome. Here, just 3000 ft. (700 m) from the Porta Capena, after running inland to the capital via the mountains, the Via Latina again merged with the VA.[66]

---

63. Volpe (2014, 182–85), on the basis of the most recent excavation, has conjectured that the Scipios built the tomb on the property of a villa they owned here.

64. While this reconstruction of Coarelli (1988, 13) seems to have gained some favor, see the suggested improvements by Richardson (1992, 360) and the reconstruction of Volpe (2014, 182–85).

65. At the other end of the Parco degli Scipioni on the Via Latina is the well-preserved smaller columbarium of Pomponius Hylas. Hewson (2020, 75) notes that nearby is "one more saintly episode of legend running alongside the Via Appia." A chapel called San Giovanni in Oleo ("St. John in Oil") commemorates where the apostle John was allegedly immersed in a vat of boiling oil in AD 92 by Domitian. According to this tradition mentioned by Tertullian (*Prescription against the Heretics* 36) and Jerome (*Against Jovian*, 1.26), John emerged unharmed and was then exiled by the emperor to Patmos where he wrote the book of Revelation. Frescoes on the walls painted by Lazzaro Baldi (17th century) depict scenes from John's persecution and later exile to the island.

66. Richardson (1992, 416) gives the distance as 830 m (2723 ft.) from Porta Capena, basing this on the incorrect calculations of Ashby (1907, 13). The latter also gives the distance for the Via

## Day 7: Aricia to Rome

Beyond the junction the road passed beneath an ornate monumental marble arch* which in 9 BC had been erected by senatorial decree in honor of Drusus the Elder.[67] No longer extant, it was erected in memory of Nero Claudius Drusus, the stepson of the first emperor Augustus, brother of the second emperor Tiberius, and father of the fourth emperor Claudius. He was granted posthumously the hereditary name of Germanicus for his victories over the northern barbarians between 12 and 9 BC. Suetonius (*Claudius* 3) confirms that the arch, decorated with military trophies, was erected for this popular general along the VA.[68] As he passed through the arch, Paul may have thought not only about Rome's military might but also how the expansion of Rome's borders might also allow the good news of Jesus to be carried to new nations. Who would be the future Christian "Germanicus" who would bring the conquering gospel to far-off lands, indeed to the ends of the earth (1:8)?

Today travelers, following these final 2300 ft. (700 m) of the VA, walk the first half in the shadow of the immense ruins of the Baths of Caracalla west of the VA. These, however, were not yet built in Paul's day, and instead a combination of businesses and residences then occupied the area. To the east was located the *Mutatorium Caesaris*, though it is uncertain whether it had been formally organized by Paul's day. Known from the regionary catalogues and shown on the *Forma Urbis Romae*—the gigantic marble map of Rome measuring 60 × 42 ft. (18 × 13 m) and created during the principate of Septimius Severus (AD 203–211)—this was an open area northeast of the VA.[69] As with the *Area Carruces*, the *Mutatorium*

---

Latina from the junction to the Porta Latina as 500 m instead of nearly 600. Ashby's lengthy article, however, is still one of the most complete on the Via Latina in general.

67. The so-called Arch of Drusus by Porta San Sebastiano, actually built in the third century AD, was mistakenly identified as the one that actually stood here.

68. Its ancient position is not certain but seems to have been just north of the junction with the Via Latina since the side road that runs to the northeast here toward Porta Metrona is thought to have been the Vicus Drusianus. Current maps of the ancient city, such as the *Roma Urbs Imperatorum Aetate* of Scagnetti and Grande (1986), show the Vicus Drusianus in this location; the modern street is Via Druso. Richardson (1992, 423) does not disagree but notes that the evidence leaves room for uncertainty. The inscription *CIL* 6.975 (= *ILS* 6073) confirms there was an ancient Vicus Drusianus and that it was part of *Regio I*.

69. The VA seems to have run straight from the junction with the Via Latina to the Porta Capena. It passed 30–65 ft. (10–20 m) in front of today's Basilica dei Santi Nereo e Achileo. The *Mutatorium* was to the east beneath the basilica or monastery of San Sisto Vecchio. It is pictured

("changing place") was also a place for travelers to change to or from the litters used as urban transportation to the carriages used for travel outside the city. As its name suggests, however, this area was for the use of imperial officials. The marble plan indicates that it was a slightly skewed rectangular building with twelve interior columns and itself surrounded by insulae with shops and residences.

An adjoining fragment of the marble plan shows an area on the west side of the VA marked as the *Area Radicaria*, beyond the row of small shops that lined the main road. It consisted of a row of temples and dedications. This may also have contained a vegetable market if the name *radicaria* comes from *radix* ("root" or "radish"). The regionary catalogues speak of two more market areas outside the Porta Capena—*Area Pannaria* on the east side of the VA in *Regio I* and *Campus Lanatarius* or *Lanarius* on the west side in *Regio XII*.[70] These were probably open-air markets flanking the VA, the former specializing in cloth and the latter in wool.[71] As Amanda Claridge (1998, 319) observes, "its endless stream of travellers submitted to a constant barrage of street-side advertisements." Fish markets and stables were also found outside the Porta Capena, so the last couple hundred yards/meters were filled with people, smells, and noise!

Along this same stretch Paul saw the Caelian Hill sloping up on his right behind the shops and markets. Through the trees Paul may have glimpsed the Temple of Honos and Virtus (Honor and Virtue) gleaming in the sunlight—that to Honos built by a Q. Fabius Maximus, either around 300 or 234 BC, and a second cella for Virtus added by M. Claudius Marcellus in 208 BC. The latter did so against the Senate's wishes. Perhaps they saw it as an act of hubris, since the tombs of the Marcelli stood right

---

on one of the surviving fragments of the *Forma Urbis Roma*, Carettoni plate 15, Slab # XI-6. The regionary catalogues also mention an *Ara* or *Area Splenis* that may have been in this area (the latter is on Scagnetti and Grande's [1986] map, *Roma Urbs Imperatorum Aetate*). However, nothing else is known of it; see Richardson's (1992, 37, 366) discussion of "Area Splenis" and "Splenis, Ara." For the *Forma Urbis* with pictures of all surviving fragments, see the Stanford Digital Forma Urbis Project at https://formaurbis.stanford.edu/.

70. While *Regio I* extended on both sides of the VA in the area south of the Arch of Drusus, the first 1640 ft. (500 m) outside the Porta Capena, the area to its southwest, was part of *Regio XII*, while the area on the northeast side remained *Regio I*.

71. On these see Richardson's (1992, 32–33, 65) discussion of "Area Pannaria," "Area Radicaria," and "Campus Lanatarius." Their exact locations are unknown.

## Day 7: Aricia to Rome

next to the new temple, with statues of three generations of consuls on its façade (Coarelli 2014, 367)! Marcellus filled the new temple with famous works of art that he had taken as spoils when he captured Syracuse in 212 BC (Livy, *Hist.* 25.40.1–3). It also contained an altar to Fortuna Redux which was added by the Senate in 19 BC to commemorate the return of Augustus from the East via Brundisium and the VA.[72] It was from this temple that new proconsuls were sent off to their provinces and welcomed home again. Rome's domination of the Greek East was on full display.

Now Paul's party saw Porta Capena* rising before them, the spot from which the VA's mileage was measured.[73] It pierced the old wall that surrounded Rome and was attributed to King Servius Tullius (Livy, *Hist.* 1.44.3). In reality the wall had been constructed after the Gauls had sacked the city in the fourth century BC. It crossed the valley from the lower peak of the Aventine Hill (Aventine Minor) on the west to the Caelian Hill on the east. For several centuries an aqueduct had been carrying water across its top, probably to the Aventine. By the first century it was old and leaky, for Martial (*Epigrams* 3.47), writing twenty years after Paul's visit, mentions Porta Capena "raining big drops" on those passing beneath its arches.[74] Today only a small remnant of a single pylon in concrete and brick remains from the once grandiose gate and aqueduct. Even this close to the gate, however, some tombs were still to be found. A tomb inscription for a corn merchant, Lucius Ampudius Philomusus, was found close by, reminiscent of the large baker's tomb still standing outside Porta Maggiore today—final evidence of the prosperous and confident entrepreneurial class.[75]

---

72. "In honor of my return, the Senate consecrated an altar to Fortuna Redux at the Porta Capena, near the temple of Honos and Virtus; they ordered the pontiffs and the Vestal virgins to perform a yearly sacrifice there on the anniversary of the day I returned to the city from Syria, in the consulship of Q. Lucretius and M. Vinicius [October 12, 19 BC]. That day was named the *Augustalia* after my cognomen" (*Res Gestae Divi Augusti* 11, trans. Thompson; cf. Cooley 2009, 151–52).

73. Around 20 BC Augustus placed a Golden Milestone (*Miliarium Aureum*) at the western end of the Forum Romanum as a symbol that Rome was the center of the empire's road system (Cassius Dio 54.8.4; cf. Keppie 1991, 60). However, the actual mileage, as reflected on the milestones long in place, was not measured from the Golden Milestone, as is often mistakenly assumed.

74. In a note to Martial's epigram, Shackleton Bailey (1993, 221) postulates that this was a branch of the Aqua Marcia, as does Quilici (1989a, 21). Richardson (1992, 301) thinks that it was more likely a part of the early Anio Vetus.

75. For the grain merchant inscription, see: https://www.britishmuseum.org/collection/object/G_1920-0220-1; for the baker's tomb see Claridge (1998, 359–61).

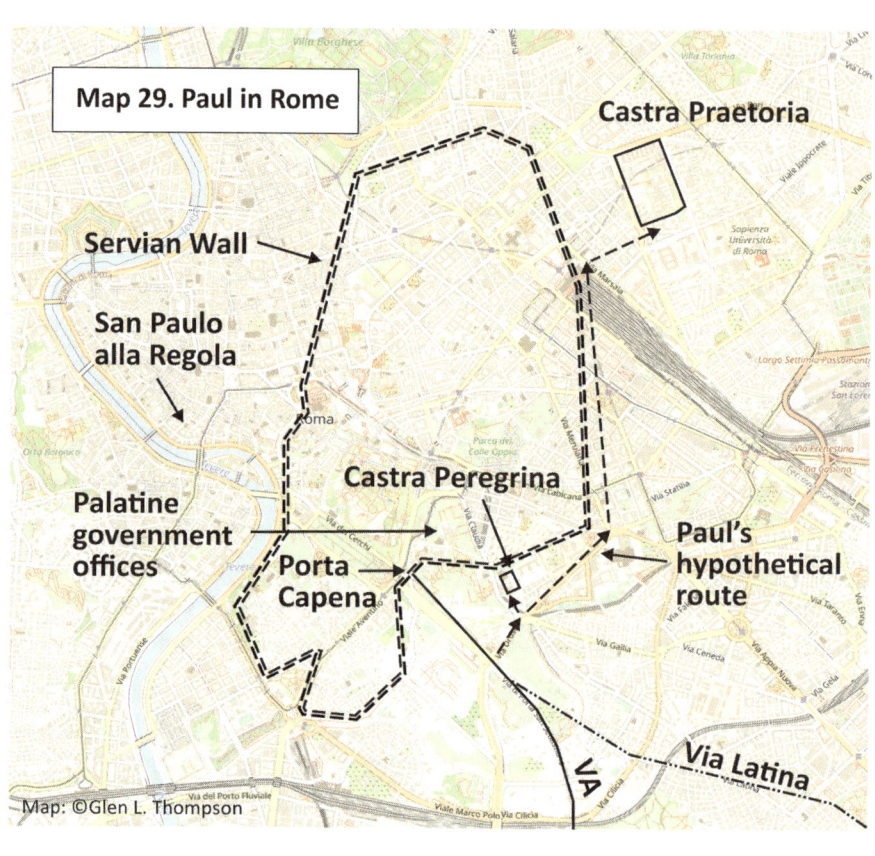

CONCLUSION

# Paul in Rome

Paul's party perhaps passed beneath Porta Capena about mid-day after their walk of 16 RM (15.1 mi./24.3 km) from Aricia (map 29). Now, if not earlier, his escort of Roman Christians dispersed to their individual homes. Julius had to conclude his duties by delivering the prisoners to the proper authorities. But where did this take place and to whom were they handed over? The Greek text is strangely silent regarding Paul's remand upon arriving in Rome. A clause added to 28:16 became widespread in the Byzantine text tradition: the centurion "handed the prisoners over to the στρατοπεδάρχης [*stratopedarchēs*, 'military commander']."[1] But who is meant? There are two possibilities. One is that Paul was handed over directly to the praetorian prefect, and thus the centurion would take him another 1.8 mi. (3 km) to the praetorian camp (Castra Praetoria; Richmond 1927, 12–14).[2] The other is that he was taken instead to the Castra Peregrina on the Caelian Hill near the Church of St. Stefano Rotondo, and there handed over to the *princeps peregrinorum* or *praefectus peregrinorum* of that camp, that is, to the commander of the foreign troops stationed at least temporarily in Rome.

---

1. Lightfoot (1873, 7–8) thinks the statement "probably contains an authentic tradition, even if it was not part of the original text." Metzger (1975, 501) notes that this expansion lies behind the King James (also New King James) translation as "captain of the guard."

2. See also Richardson's (1992, 78–79) discussion of the "Castra Praetoria" (Castra Praetorium, *CIL* 15.7239b, c).

## Remand in Rome

If Paul was taken to the Castra Peregrina, Julius's party may never have walked the final 0.75 RM to Porta Capena. Instead, the group may have turned north just after the junction with the Via Latina, today near San Sisto Vecchio, along the Vicus Drusianus, modern Via Druso, for 1300 ft. (400 m). They then would turn left onto the Vicus Cyclopis, today's Via della Navicella, arriving at the *castra* some 650 ft. (200 m) later.[3]

The Castra Peregrina* is where "foreign," that is, provincial, soldiers were housed when in Rome. This included the *frumentarii* whose original duties were to ensure an adequate grain supply for the city as well as for the legionary camps. As a result, some were attached to legions and others to provincial officials. When so assigned, they could be used as military couriers and escorts for prisoners. Although the chronology of their development is somewhat sketchy, it is possible that Julius, the centurion accompanying Paul, was a *frumentarius* and thus delivered his charge to the Castra Peregrina. There is also uncertainty about when the camp on the Caelian Hill was built, but early twentieth-century excavations beneath what is now called the Ospedale Britannico have suggested a presence during the first century (Richardson 1992, 78; Baillie Reynolds and Ashby 1923, 152–67). Several stone ships, like the one displayed in the nearby fountain, were found in the excavations at the site of the *castra*. Thus, Paul's journey may have ended a mere 1640 ft. (500 m) after leaving the VA.[4] Interestingly, Codex Gigas, the only manuscript to provide the Old Latin translation of 28:16, has the same reading as the Byzantine text, and στρατοπεδάρχης

---

3. The Servian Wall passes over the top of the Caelian Hill, but its exact route remains a matter of speculation. The *castra* might logically have been just outside the wall near the Porta Caelimontana, which Richardson (1992, 300–301) in his discussion of the "Porta Caelimontana" places at the Arco di Dolabella e Silano.

4. This identification seems to have originated with Mommsen and von Harnack (1895, 491–503). (Harnack wrote pages 481–95a and Mommsen pages 495b–501). Their views were quickly adopted and spread by Ramsay (1895, 315, 347–49), Rendall (1897, 340–41), and Knowling (1903, 516). But it was opposed by Zahn (1897, 389) who pointed out that there is no clear evidence for the use of the title *princeps peregrinorum* before Septimius Severus, and that we have evidence that prisoners were sent from the provinces and committed to the care of the *praefectus praetorio*. For the latter, see Trajan's letter to Pliny the Younger (*Epistles* 10.57), with reference to another accused man who had appealed: *vinctus mitti ad praefectos praetorii mei debet* ("I would have sent him in chains to my praetorian prefects [*praefectos praetorii*]").

Conclusion: *Paul in Rome* 181

(*stratopedarchēs*) is rendered as *princeps peregrinorum*, not as *praefectus castrorum* ("camp prefect"), as might be expected.[5]

**Figure 42.** Castra Praetoria

Even if this were Paul's first stop, he would later be taken to the Castra Praetoria*, or Praetorium, up the Esquiline Hill past the modern Termini train station. The neighborhood is still called Castra Pretorio today. Here in AD 23 Tiberius's praetorian prefect, Sejanus, built a new barracks for the urban cohorts and the nine praetorian cohorts (Tacitus, *Ann.* 4.1–2). Large sections of the exterior walls of the camp measuring 1450 × 1250 ft. (440 × 380 m) are still visible since three of its sides were later incorporated into the Aurelian Wall (fig. 42). If Paul was taken to the praetorian

---

5. Stockholm, Kungliga Biblioteket, A. 148, fol. 273r. *"centurio tradidit custodias principi peregrinorum* ("the centurion handed over the prisoners to the *princeps peregrinorum*"). This addition seems to have been the catalyst for Mommsen and von Harnack's (1895) article and arguments (see note 4 above). Sherwin-White (1963, 108–10) argues against the identification as either the prefect of the praetorian guard or the *princeps peregrinorum*, opting instead for the *princeps castrorum*.

camp directly, there were two possible routes. Eckhard Schnabel (2019, 409) describes the first:

> Assuming that Paul was taken to the Praetorian Prefect, Paul would have been taken through the center of the city from the *Porta Capena* to the so-called *Porta Clausa* and to the barracks of the Praetorian Guard (*Castra Praetoria*) located just outside the city walls on the northeast side of the city—past the east side of the Circus Maximus, Nero's Colossus on the east side of the Temple of Rome and Venus, and via the *Vicus Sandalarius* and the *Vicus Collis Viminalis*.

From the Arch of Drusus, the junction with the Via Latina, the distance would be about 2.6 mi. (4.2 km).[6]

However, if the party was heading directly to the praetorian camp, they may have taken the Vicus Drusianus from the Arch of Drusus up the Caelian Hill. However then, instead of turning, they would continue onto the Via Merulana around the eastern side of the Oppian Hill. This connected to the road running along the outside of the Servian Wall to the Porta Viminalis, then turned toward the *castra*. Such a route was not only considerably shorter (2.3 mi./3.7 km) but also less crowded, allowing Julius and his soldiers to stay outside the walls the entire time. It was Julius who would determine whether the group took the scenic "business route" through the city or the "bypass" around it.

Lightfoot and others suggest that Paul actually appeared before Sextus Afranius Burrus, the praetorian prefect from AD 50 until his death in early 62 (Lightfoot 1873, 8; cf. Schnabel 2019, 409). He was a friend of Seneca the Younger, a Stoic philosopher, and the former tutor to the young Nero, although after 59 he lost his influence. In his position as prefect, Burrus served as instructor in criminal trials.[7] No matter which camp Paul was in,

---

6. The party would have actually left the city proper through the Porta Viminalis in the Servian Wall before arriving at the Castra Praetoria outside the wall. The Porta Clausa/Chiusa near the castra was in the later Aurelian Wall.

7. Since Tiberius's reign, the praetorian prefect led the prosecution in cases of lese majesty and high treason; see the discussion of Lendering (2018) about the praetorian prefect. It is an interesting

however, at this initial stage he was merely handed over to the duty officer. If at the Castra Peregrina, he would soon afterward be transferred to the praetorian camp, probably using one of the two routes described above. He would then be housed temporarily at the camp awaiting arraignment with a decision on the terms of his pretrial confinement. Paul would also have to make arrangements for his own accommodations until trial. This may all have taken a week or more.[8] Perhaps it was during this period that Paul and his message became known "throughout the whole praetorian guard" (ἐν ὅλῳ τῷ πραιτωρίῳ, *en holō tō praitōriō*; Phil 1:13), thus working for "the advancement of the gospel" (Phil 1:12).

After his initial arraignment, Paul was accorded what was considered a relatively mild form of detention, the *custodia militaris* ("military custody"; Digest 48.3.1).[9] He was kept under house arrest with his right wrist chained to the left wrist of a praetorian guardsman, thus restricting his movement.[10] Paul must have been given a positive report by the centurion, which may have influenced the apostle's conditions as he awaited trial. Perhaps the chain was only imposed when he left his dwelling.

## Residence for Two Years

After temporary housing at the camp, Paul was probably expected to arrange for his own lodging at a nearby inn (*hospitium*/ξενία, *xenia*) for which he would pay by the day.[11] This is exactly the terminology found in

---

coincidence that Burrus served as procurator of the province of Galatia at the time of Paul's first journey there. During that time might Burrus have met Paul, or at least heard of him? If so, Paul perhaps requested to meet Burrus and present his case personally before the prefect. For Burrus in Galatia, see Wilson (2018a, 342).

8. Parisi (1959, 130), without providing evidence, says that for ten days the prisoner would have to remain at the praetorian camp "available for the preliminary investigation which aimed at ascertaining the validity of his appeal to Caesar." He also states that *praetorion* is never used in a local sense unless *castra* is attached to it (63).

9. Walker (2008, 189) calls this *libera custodia*, the term used by Bede (*Epistulae* 10).

10. Seneca (*Letters* 5.7): *eadem catena et custodiam et militem copulat* ("the same chain fastens the prisoner and the soldier who guards him"). This has been compared to the imprisonment of Herod Agrippa in Rome, first in the camp and afterward, on the accession of Gaius, in a house of his own, although still under military custody (Josephus, *Antiquities* 18.6.5).

11. Freier (1980, 27) says that such a lodging house could also be called *deversoria, stabulum, taberna, synoecium,* or *caupona*.

28:23. At such an inn he had his preliminary meetings with local Jewish leaders. But when it became apparent that there might be a significant delay in the proceedings against him, he moved into a longer-term rental (μίσθωμα [*misthōma*]/Lat. *conducto*; 28:30). Roman legal documents allow us to get a glimpse into the rental property market in first-century Rome. Contracts were usually signed initially for one year, with agreements made in May with a move-in date set for July 1. Bruce Freier (1980, 3, 34–37) speaks of Rome having "sturdy four- and five-story apartment blocks (*insulae*), constructed primarily in brick and concrete" and with "a high density of settlement."[12] An outside staircase would often lead to the rental units, which typically were not on street level, but were rather upper story rooms (*cenacula*; Wallace-Hadrill 1994, 110; cf. Wilson 2020a, 237–40). Thus, if Paul arrived in Rome in early April, he may have stayed in a *hospitium* for some weeks, unless he could find an unoccupied property that allowed him to move in earlier. The local Christians undoubtedly helped in the search and other arrangements. However, regarding payment, he remained in "his own" (ἐν ἰδίῳ, *en idiō*) rental, that is, Paul paid for it. Once again Paul appears in Acts as an individual with access to money (cf. 24:26).[13] The terms of his custody prevented him from living as the guest of a local Christian. The text also states that he remained for "two full years" (διετίαν ὅλην, *dietian holēn*; 28:30), perhaps reflecting that Paul remained in the rented space even after his acquittal until the contract expired.

The location of Paul's rental unit has evoked much speculation over the centuries. A questionable medieval account caused some to put Paul's lodging on the site of the Church of Santa Maria in Via Lata* in the

---

12. Jerome (*Commentary on Philemon*), however, argued for a ground-floor apartment: "It was necessary that the house ... was on the ground floor rather than on a higher level. For this reason, I think that he stayed in Rome for two years in a house rented for this purpose. Such a dwelling could not be small, as I believe, for a swarm of Jews came to it daily" (trans. Thompson; cf. Parisi 1959, 198).

13. If the letter to the Philippians was written during this two-year period, the church there was apparently the only congregation from whom Paul would receive offerings. Perhaps the gift from the Philippian church helped with the rental costs (Phil 4:15–19). For more on their gifts, see Fee (1995, 439–54).

Campus Martius.¹⁴ However, this entire area was covered by the Saepta Julia until the seventh century. Planned by Julius Caesar, it consisted of a huge quadraporticus measuring 1000 × 400 ft. (310 × 120 m) that was used for voting, gladiatorial games, and other public events. No private house could have existed there (Richardson 1992, 340–41). Others have suggested that Paul resided at the third mile of the VA known as *ad Catacombas*, and that this gave rise to the pilgrimage site there, even housing the bones of Peter and Paul during parts of the third century.¹⁵ The fourth-century poem of Damasus figuratively speaks of Peter and Paul living (*habitasse*) there. This simply means that their remains/tombs were there at the time Damasus wrote, and every other early reference speaks of this only as a place where their deaths were memorialized.¹⁶

Giovanni Parisi (1959, 57) points out that it was necessary for Paul as a prisoner "to fix his residence near the center of public affairs and not far from the courts and offices of the relevant authorities." He may have had frequent appearances before officials and a regular change of guard. This led Orazio Marucchi (1903, 159) to postulate that his residence was somewhere near the praetorian camp, connecting this also to Philippians 1:13. However, Theodore Mommsen (Mommsen and Harnack 1895, 498 n. 1) pointed out that the actual trial would be held before a praetorian council composed of the praetorian prefect and his assistants as well as the public. He too links it with the verse in Philippians.¹⁷ Karl Wieseler thought Paul resided in a military barracks on the Palatine, since Drusus and Agrippa were imprisoned there.¹⁸ But Paul was not a Roman aristocratic political prisoner. It is plausible, however, that the actual court proceedings involving Paul did take place on the Palatine.

---

14. Parisi (1959, 23–36) lays out the evidence and then refutes it.

15. According to Parisi (1959, 39–41), this view began in 1900 with the archaeologist Gian Francesco Gamurrini and was continued by Joseph Wilpert and Rodolfo Lanciani.

16. See p. 163, note 42 above on the *memoria apostolorum*.

17. Mommsen (Mommsen and Harnack 1895, 498 n. 1) further argues that the "whole" praetorium refers to a praetorian council made up of the prefect and his assistants.

18. Wieseler (1848, 403–5, n. 3) cited by Parisi (1959, 69).

The prisoner had the right to select any rented house where he could be supervised by his guard. Paul's choice of location would be influenced by his usual considerations, namely, ease of communication with his countrymen, fellow believers, and evangelistic prospects. The focal point of the Jewish community during this period was apparently Trastevere, site of the Synagogue of the Hebrews (Philo, *Embassy to Gaius*, 155–157). Whether or not the local Jewish leaders were formally involved in Paul's trial, Luke certainly makes it clear that Paul felt it important to present his case informally to them. Peter Lampe has further pointed out that one of the earliest Christian communities was also in that area.[19] There was also ease of access between there and the Palatine complex, the probable site for his hearings.

Thus, Trastevere, or the area between it and the Palatine, were likely locations for Paul's abode. The Greek and Latin texts of the second-century Acta Pauli say that Paul rented "a granary (*horreum*) outside Rome" (Lipsius 1891, 104–5).[20] The detail that Paul's residence was "outside the city" (ἔξω τῆς παρεμβολῆς [*eksō tēn parembolēs*]/Lat. *extra urbem*) is also found in a variant reading on 28:16 in several Greek minuscules.[21] The remains of such *horrea* can still be seen in Ostia, and numerous ones were found on the banks of the Tiber near Rome. Thus, the earliest local traditions seem to point to a location outside the *pomerium* (sacred boundary)

---

19. Lampe (2003, esp. 19–47) identifies the earliest Christian communities as being in the Trastevere neighborhood, the area between the Porta Capena and the Almone River along both sides of the VA, the area of the Aventine and Lesser Aventine, and the area of the Campus Martius on both sides of the Via Flaminia—all "suburban" areas outside the pomerium.

20. This work is dated by its mention by Tertullian (*De Baptismo* 17.5). Note that one Greek version of the Passio Petri et Pauli mentions Paul in Puteoli, Baiae, Tres Tabernas, and Tarracina, Forum Apii, and Aricia (Lipsius 1891, 183–87). Parisi (1959, 180) further states that the Passio Petri et Pauli has Paul lodging in a *hospitium* located in the area of Arenula near the Tiber Island, and preaching in a grain warehouse at the Porta Ostiense, *horreaum extra urbem*. That reference cannot be confirmed.

21. Although Acts uses παρεμβολή (*parembolē*) frequently for an army barracks, here the meaning (as the Latin shows) must be city. The author may have been thinking of Hebrews 13:11–12 where the burning of the sin offering "outside the camp" is said to foreshadow Jesus's death outside the city of Jerusalem. The Greek manuscripts are listed in Swanson (1998, 486); cf. Metzger (1975, 501). Parisi (1959, 72) refers to L and P. However, he wrongly adds the "fifth-century Codex Washingtoniensis," which does not contain Acts.

Conclusion: Paul in Rome

and at or near a *horreum*. One site that fits this description is the Church of San Paolo alla Regola* along the ancient Vicus Aescletus ("Beech Street").[22]

San Paolo alla Regola is dedicated to Paul's conversion, not his martyrdom, and located on top of and/or adjacent to several *horrea* along the Tiber.[23] Although in *Regio IX* (Circus Flaminius) of Augustus's fourteen *regiones*, it was technically "outside the city" because it was outside the Servian Wall. At the same time, it is located in a most advantageous location between the Jewish community and the Palatine offices. While the current eighteenth-century Baroque church claims to be situated on the site of an early fourth-century foundation, the first credible reference to this church and monastic complex is from the mid-twelfth century. Of all the proposed sites, this has the strongest possibility of being at or near the location of Paul's two-year residence.

The book of Acts ends on a triumphant note, or "paradoxically triumphant" as Ryan Schellenberg (2011, 159) observes: "triumphant because 'the Word' is proclaimed in the heart of the empire, paradoxical because Paul arrives as a prisoner." For two years Paul welcomed anyone, both Jew and gentile, to his rented house. There he proclaimed the kingdom of God and taught about Jesus Christ (28:30–31).[24] If Paul's letter to the Philippians is dated to this first imprisonment, his message reached not only the entire praetorian guard (Phil 1:13) but also the household of Caesar (ἐκ τῆς Καίσαρος οἰκίας, *ek tēs Kaisaros oikias*; Phil 4:22).[25] Despite confinement and possible manacles, Paul remained free in spirit. This

---

22. On the ancient street name, see Forbes (1897, 36–38).

23. "Regola" seems to be a corruption of the Latin *renula* ("fine sand"). The area is called *Arenula* for the same reason. One such *horrea*, excavated in the past half century, can be visited underground just a few doors from San Paolo. It has been dated to the Flavian period.

24. Knox (1948, 59 n. 1) is likely correct when he observes that the ending of Acts presupposes a sequel: "It is of course quite possible that the third part was never begun, but it seems unthinkable that it was never intended."

25. For Rome as the likely provenance of Philippians and its dating between AD 60–62, see Fee (1995, 34–37). "Household of Caesar" (*familia Caesaris*) was a common expression that included not merely the members of the imperial family but all the slaves, freedmen, and other retainers working for or belonging to it.

attitude is evident in Luke's four closing words that describe him living in Rome "with great boldness, unhindered" (28:31).[26]

His imprisonment did not eventuate in his death, for he was apparently released and perhaps journeyed to Spain to fulfill his contemplated ministry there (Rom 15:24, 28).[27] A reconstruction of his Prison Letters suggests Paul later returned to Asia where he was arrested in Troas (2 Tim 1:15; 4:13–14, 20) and returned to Rome for a second trial (2 Tim 4:16–17).[28] However, on this occasion Paul was not destined for release. According to the earliest traditions, he was caught up in Nero's persecution of Christians after the fire in Rome in AD 64, beheaded at the site of the Church of Tre Fontane, and buried at the location of the Church of St. Paul Outside the Walls.[29] However, the details of Paul's final years go beyond the scope of this volume. Paul's arrival in Rome provides the climax for the book of Acts. The great apostle, whose travels dominate the second half of the book, is seen preaching his message in the imperial capital in chains but unhindered. Just as all roads were said to lead to Rome, so from there his message now spreads along those same roads "to the ends of the earth" (1:8).

---

26. For the theme of hindrance related to Paul's Roman mission, see Wilson (2021, 2–4).

27. Kilgallen (2007, 254) speculates that Luke did not include this subsequent ministry because Theophilus (1:1–2) lived in Rome and so ending Acts in Rome was to "show Theophilus how Christianity came to his church."

28. For a historical reconstruction of this period, see Mounce (2000, liv–lxiv).

29. Paul's burial site has much earlier testimony than the site of his beheading. Some have suggested that putting the execution at Tre Fontane and the burial at St. Paul's Outside the Walls was a way of reconciling two different traditions about the apostle's death. See the extensive study of Eastman (2011, esp. 15–69).

APPENDIX 1

# Paul's Land Journey in Bible Atlases

The maps in Bible atlases depict Paul's land journey from Puteoli to Rome in a very imprecise manner. The line of the route in *The Sacred Bridge* (Rainey and Notley 2006, 248) shows a sea crossing from Cumae to the Forum of Appius, which is depicted on the coast, as is Three Taverns.[1] The route onward into Rome is also shown as along the coast. The *Zondervan Atlas of the Bible* (Rasmussen 2010, 233) shows a similar sea crossing; however, the two sites are correctly depicted as inland. The *New Moody Atlas of the Bible* (Beitzel 2009, 265, map 113) shows a somewhat inland route north from Puteoli, where a road never existed, but the Forum of Appius and Three Taverns are strangely situated on the coast where Formia and Gaeta are located. The *Historical Atlas of the Bible* (Barnes 2010, 292) provides a dot for Capua, but the route bypasses it and stays nearer the coast. Neither the Forum of Appius nor Three Taverns is shown. The *ESV Bible Atlas* (Currid and Barrett 2020, 249, map 12–23) depicts Paul taking the coastal route from Puteoli on his way to Rome. The *IVP Atlas* (Lawrence 2006, 162) shows the coastal route but more accurately depicts the Forum of Appius and Three Taverns geographically in their relationship with Rome. The *HarperCollins Atlas* (Pritchard 2010, 166) misplaces Puteoli, marking it where Sinuessa is located, and both the Forum of Appius and Three Taverns are omitted. The *Lexham Geographic Commentary*

---

1. The *Discovery House Bible Atlas* (Beck 2015, 307, map 11.8) similarly shows the two sites on the coast with a curving line drawn from Puteoli to them. The *Kregel Atlas* (Dowley 2004, 87) omits the two sites and shows only an imprecise line curving between Puteoli and Rome. Although including the two sites, the line of the route in the *MacMillan Bible Atlas* (Aharoni and Avi-Yonah 1997, 253) is very imprecise. The *Oxford Bible Atlas* (Curtis 2009, 168–69) fails to even show Paul's captivity journey.

on *Acts through Revelation* (Laney 2019, 426) provides the most precise depiction, showing an inland route to the Via Appia, although Capua is not depicted. Hopefully the maps in our volume will help editors of future Bible atlases produce more accurate depictions of Paul's route in Italy.

Appendix 2

# Bypass at Tarracina

Dora Jane Hamblin and Mary Jane Grunsfeld (1974, 103–5), among others, have claimed that the VA rose almost 1000 ft. over Mount Sant'Angelo to Tarracina. They further suggest that Trajan's cut at Pesco Montano, while shortening the distance by only one mile, saved half a day in walking time. Google Earth Pro indicates that the road only rises to around 500 ft. (152 m) above sea level above the Piazza Palatina and that the distance between the routes is virtually the same.

Map modeling in Google Earth allows us to plot the alternative routes, calculate the rate of ascent, and determine the time needed to walk the upper road compared to the coastal road. We have previously used this map software to calculate data regarding the walking time between Troas and Assos (Thompson and Wilson 2016, 280–81) and between Perga and Pisidian Antioch (Wilson 2018b, 19–26). The 3D modeling of the two routes at Tarracina is depicted below using Naismith's rule (see fig. 43).[1]

---

1. For a discussion, see "Naismith's Rule" on Wikipedia: https://en.wikipedia.org/wiki/Naismith%27s_rule.

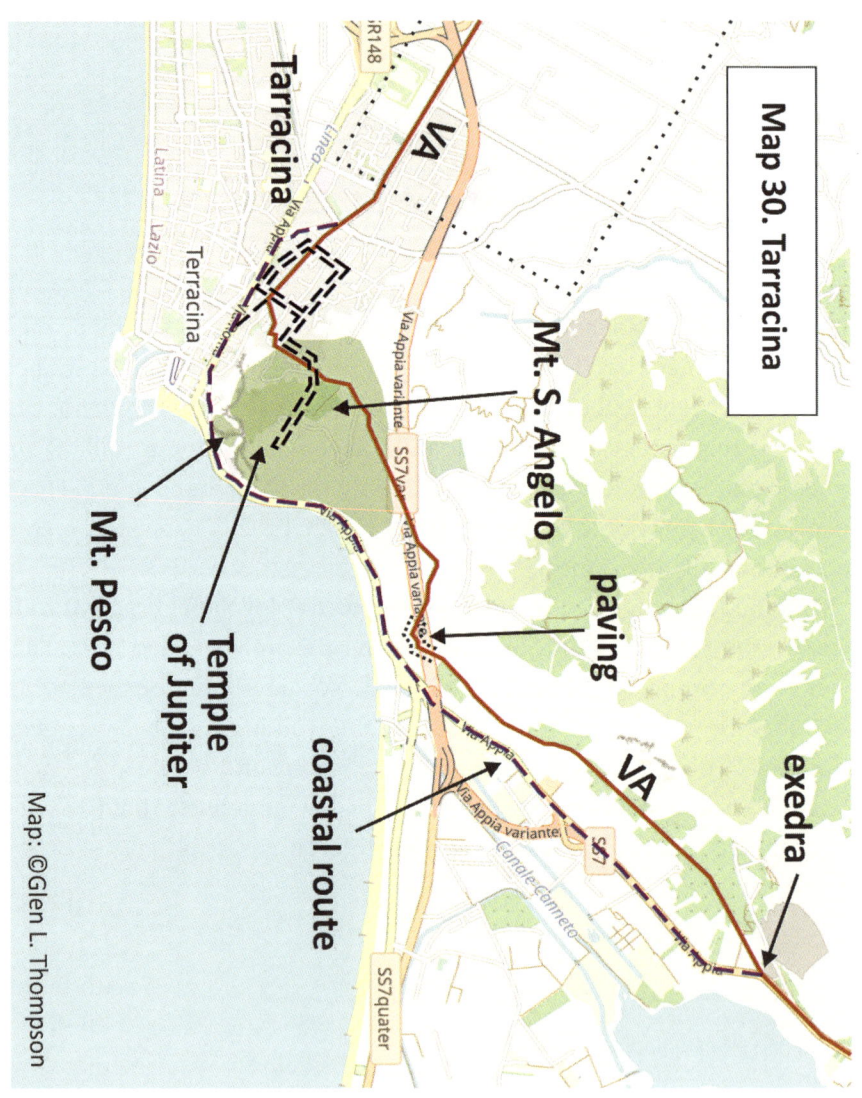

Map 30. Tarracina

*Appendix 2: Bypass at Tarracina* 193

| | Distance Points (mi./km) | Elevation (ft./m) | Change + or − (ft.) | Time (min.) |
|---|---|---|---|---|
| **Upper Route** | | | | |
| exedra up hill | 0-0.67/0-1.08 | 44-110/13.4-33.5 | +65/20 | 16 (14 + 2) |
| up hill | 0.67-1.5/1.08-2.41 | 110-270/33.5-82.3 | +160/49 | 22 (17 + 5) |
| to top of hill | 1.5-2.2/2.4-3.5 | 270-500/82.3-152.4 | +230/70 | 21 (14 + 7) |
| down into saddle | 2.2-2.6/3.5-4.2 | 500-400/152.4-121.9 | -100/30.5 | 8 |
| up over saddle | 2.6-2.95/4.2-4.75 | 400-495/121.9-150.9 | +95/29 | 10 (7 + 3) |
| down hill to forum | 2.95-3.75/4.75-6.04 | 495-135/150.9-41.1 | -360/110 | 16 |
| level thro' city center | 3.75-3.85/6.04-6.2 | 135/41.1 | – | 2 |
| to Quatro Lampioni | 3.85-4.15/6.2-6.68 | 135-27/41.1-8.2 | -108/33 | 6 |
| | **4.15 mi./6.68 km** | | | **101 min.** |
| **Coastal Route** | | | | |
| exedra to near coast | 0-1.0/0-1.6 | 44-20/13.4-6.1 | -24/7.3 | 20 |
| along coast | 1.0-4.1/1.6-6.6 | 20-15/6.1-4.6 | -5/1.5 | 62 |
| up to Quatro Lampioni | 4.1-4.25/6.6-6.84 | 15-27/4.6-8.2 | +12/3.6 | 3 |
| | **4.25 mi./6.84 km** | | | **85 min.** |

**Figure 43.** Comparison of distances for the two routes of the VA at Tarracina

As the calculations show, the time saved walking the coastal route is only a quarter hour or so, although the road through the forum may have necessitated a slower pace for that short stretch. However, the flatter seaside route would certainly have been much easier and quicker for carriages and wagons and the animals that pulled them.

Figure 44 shows the routes from where they part in the east (the exedra) to the point where they reunite near the current Piazza Quattro Lampioni. Since the ancient path is now at places covered with buildings and this has skewed the ancient path's elevation (the red line), we have "smoothed" it (the blue line) to more accurately approximate the ancient road.

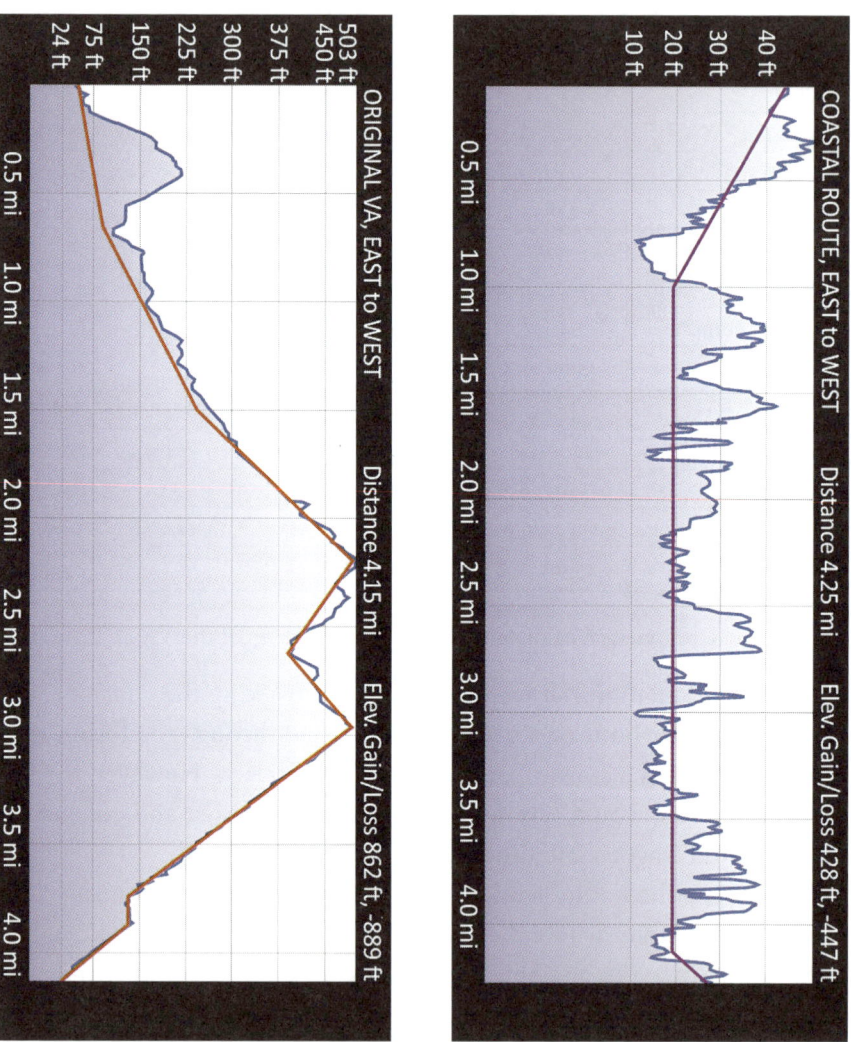

**Figure 44.** Comparison of the elevation for the two routes of the VA at Tarracina

Appendix 3

# *Mansiones* and *Stationes*

Ancient travelers had a variety of needs as they walked or rode along the Roman roads—food, water, shelter for the night or during storms, livestock care, and the like. Upper class Romans would most often overnight at the estates of their friends and acquaintances (Horace, Satires 1.5.38, 71), but the common traveler did not have that option, although some rural farms (*villae*) did take in lodgers. Instead, the main roads had a variety of options along the way with sources mentioning three types in particular—*mansio*, *statio*, and *mutatio*.

*Mansio* (plural *mansiones*) were often established at the same time as the roads. They were constructed a day's journey apart and offered a safe place "to stay" (Lat. *manere*) overnight. Their exact placement was often at road intersections, on river ports, or near sources of water.

*Statio* (plural *stationes*) may have originated as military outposts that guarded stretches of roads. They also became places for imperial officials to obtain fresh horses, so they were more numerous, being found every 5 to 10 RM. Soon, however, the word became associated more generally with stopping places for travelers and was often used interchangeably with *mansiones*. Over time the word *mutatio, mutationes* ("changing places") also came into use as an equivalent term (Kolb 2016, 4–5).

The *mansiones* and *stationes* were not uniform in size or in their amenities but varied in keeping with their locality and the number of travelers that passed by. The *mansio* would have a courtyard where horses and other pack animals could be safely fed and sheltered, a dining and tavern area, and sleeping facilities. Many would have a separate bath complex since regular bathing was a cultural habit among the Romans. Gambling and prostitution (Horace, *Satires* 1.5.82–85) were likely among the features of many *mansiones*. A funerary epitaph from Isernia, Italy, was erected by a former slave and innkeeper named Calidius Eroticus for himself and his wife Fannias Voluptas. Depicted is a guest with his horse paying the innkeeper with the charges mentioned in the inscription: a sextarius of wine and bread for one *as*; relish, two *asses*; a girl, eight *asses*; hay for the mule, two *asses*.[1] Guests have also left a variety of pictorial or textual graffiti inscribed on the walls. In a marble frieze depicting the arrival of a *carpentum* ("carriage") at a *mansio*, the driver sits in front of two passengers. In front of the horses, a servant pays a woman, perhaps the wife of the proprietor, while the latter oversees the transaction from a window.[2]

Clients frequently complained about fleas and bedbugs, bad smells from the kitchen and toilets, overcrowding (with persons having to share the same bed), and the constant din of arrivals and departures at all hours of the day or night. In this vein Horace (*Epistle* 1.11.1, trans. Martin) quipped: "But surely, friend, the man who gains an inn / besplashed with mud, and soaking to the skin / when on his way from Capua to Rome / will not desire to make that inn his home."

Only a comparatively few of these rest stops have survived and received archaeological attention. A *mansio* in Chelmsford, UK, has been visually reconstructed, thus giving an idea what such a building looked like (fig. 45).

---

1. Mary Beard (2015) calls this one of her favorite Roman inscriptions and translates their names as "Mr. Hot Sex" and "Mrs. Gorgeous." The stone is now in the Louvre Museum. The couple is remembered by the names of red and white wines produced by a local winery, Campo Valeri.

2. The frieze, now in Rome's Museum of Roman Civilization, can be seen at: https://www.agefotostock.com/age/en/Stock-Images/Rights-Managed/DAE-10327264.

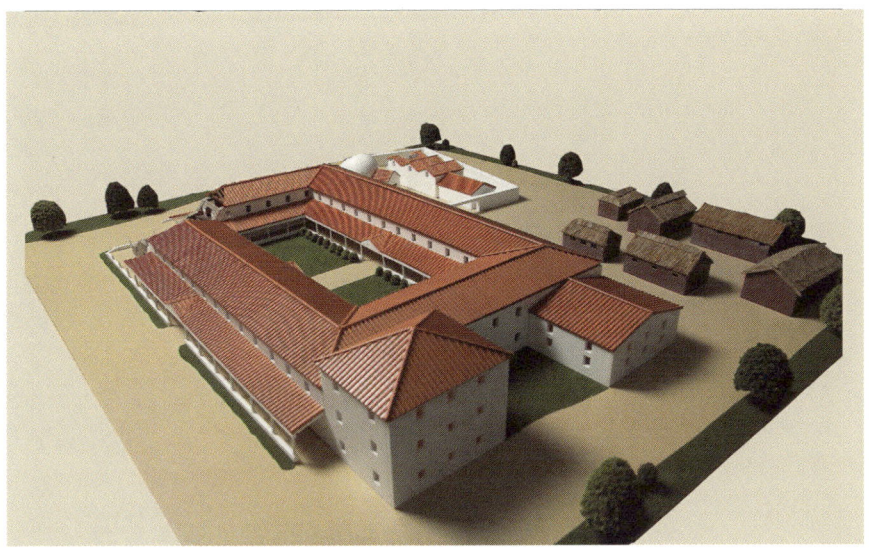

**Figure 45.** Reconstruction of the Chelmsford *mansio*

# APPENDIX 4

# GPS Coordinates for Places Mentioned

The chart below gives all the coordinates marked in the text with an asterisk. They are listed in order from Puteoli to Rome, as Paul would have passed them. When a feature (such as extant paving) extends for some length, coordinates are given for its beginning and end, calculated in the direction Paul was traveling. The road column gives the location on the road in front of the item mentioned. The object column gives locations for the objects themselves. The GPS location, given in decimal form, is limited to five places, and should be accurate to within a few meters. Readings that are described as "approx(imate)" are either (1) locations the authors have not visually seen on the ground or via Google Satellite or Street View imagery, (2) locations we have not been able to confirm through reliable third parties, or (3) are based on our calculations from other known sites and/or ancient descriptions. The appendix can be downloaded at https://lexhampress.com/appianway.

| Page | | Road | Object |
|---|---|---|---|
| **Introduction** | | | |
| **Puteoli** | | | |
| 15 | Harbor mole | | 40.82200, 14.11668 |
| 20 | Civic temple (Augusteum?) | | 40.82129, 14.12055 |
| 21 | Macellum | | 40.82617, 14.12057 |
| 21 | Stadium | | 40.83285, 14.11215 |
| 21 | Republican amphitheater | | 40.82608, 14.12829 |
| 21 | Flavian amphitheater | | 40.82596, 14.12524 |
| 22 | Taberna 5 on Via G. Pergolesi | | 40.82967, 14.12045 |

| Day 1 | | | | |
|---|---|---|---|---|
| **VCC** | | | | |
| | 35 | Puteoli city gate | 40.83064, 14.12013 | 40.83066, 14.12016 |
| | 35 | *Statio* (of the Tyrians?) | | 40.83083, 14.11884 |
| | 36 | The Via Celle tombs | 40.83248, 14.12129<br>40.83306, 14.12248 | |
| | 38 | Ancient pavement on Via Celle | 40.83333, 14.12218<br>40.83627, 14.11985 | |
| | 38 | Via S. Vito tombs | 40.84484, 14.11908<br>40.84624, 14.11971 | |
| | 38 | Villa Elvira Christian tomb | | 40.84600, 14.11894 |
| | 38 | Large circular tomb at end of Via S. Vito | | 40.84660, 14.11975 |
| | 38n22 | First Roman ruin after joining modern VC | | 40.85186, 14.11910 |
| | 39 | Suburban villa of *gens Bovi* | | 40.85374, 14.12000 |
| | 40 | Cut at Montagna Spaccata | 40.86732, 14.12463<br>40.86905, 14.12422 | |
| | 41 | Ad Quarto *mansio* | 40.87721, 14.12428 | 40.87721, 14.12428 |
| | 41 | Bridge and diverticulum by the *mansio* | | 40.87734, 14.12478 |
| | 43 | Cupa Orlando | 40.89437, 14.13867<br>40.90014, 14.14585 | |
| | 44 | VCC in Qualiano | 40.91905, 14.15421 | |
| | 45 | VCC at S. Lorenzo ad Septimum | 40.98570, 14.19930 | |
| | 48 | VCC junction with Naples road | 41.07054, 14.25806 | |
| | 48 | South gate of Capua | 41.07449, 14.26035 | |
| | 48 | VCC intersects with VA in center of Capua | 41.08183, 14.26004 | |
| **Capua** | | | | |
| | 50 | Republican amphitheater | | 41.08460, 14.24998 |
| | 51 | Imperial amphitheater | | 41.08598, 14.25017 |
| | 51 | Mithraeum | | 41.08006, 14.25219 |
| | 51 | Temple of Diana Tifatina | | 41.11824, 14.26060 |
| | 52 | Carceri Vecchie | | 41.08090, 14.27225 |
| | 52 | Conocchia | | 41.07778, 14.27853 |

*Appendix 4: GPS Coordinates for Places Mentioned* 201

| Day 2 | | | |
|---|---|---|---|
| **VA** | | | |
| 55 | Capua's Porta Romana | 41.08228, 14.25104 | |
| 55 | Arch of "Hadrian" in Capua | 41.08400, 14.24768 | |
| 55 | VA enters Casilinum from east | 41.10622, 14.21396 | |
| 57 | Casilinum bridge | 41.10935, 14.20928 | |
| 57 | Approx. intersection of VA and Via Latina | 41.11107, 14.20425 | |
| 63n8 | MP 126 (approx.) | 41.10997, 14.16522 | |
| 63 | *Ad Octavum* and MP 124 (approx.) | 41.11595, 14.12970 | |
| 63 | *Ad Nonum* and MP 123 (approx.) | 41.11656, 14.11387 | |
| 64 | Urbana and MP 119 (approx.) | 41.11921, 14.04642 | 41.12247, 14.04468 |
| 66 | *Pons Campanus* and MP 115 (approx.) | 41.13430, 13.96720 | 41.13401, 13.97109 |
| 67 | Torre Ballerino | 41.12971, 13.93736 | 41.12992, 13.93736 |
| 67 | *Mansio* at Mondragone cemetery | | 41.12285, 13.91257 |
| 68 | VA paving at Mondragone cemetery | 41.12258, 13.91223 41.12255, 13.91126 | |
| 69 | MP 108/Aquae Sinuessa | 41.14078, 13.85586 | |
| 71 | VA paving just south of Sinuessa | 41.14872, 13.84978 41.14980, 13.84894 | |
| **Sinuessa** | | | |
| 72 | Amphitheater (approx.) | | 41.15596, 13.84941 |
| 72 | Diverticulum to coast, south of Sinuessa city wall | | 41.15282, 13.84640 |
| 72 | South gate of Sinuessa (approx.) | 41.15292, 13.84666 | |
| **Day 3** | | | |
| 75 | North gate of Sinuessa (approx.) | 41.15561, 13.84689 | |
| **Minturnae** | | | |
| 77 | Pons Teretina over the Liris River | 41.24120, 13.77117 | |
| 79 | Theater | | 41.24243, 13.76846 |
| 79 | Capitolium | | 41.24202, 13.76811 |
| 79 | Temple of Augustus | | 41.24198, 13.76833 |
| 79 | Imperial forum | | 41.24172, 13.76798 |

| | | | |
|---|---|---|---|
| 79 | Macellum | | 41.24187, 13.76714 |
| 79 | Amphitheater | | 41.24174, 13.76394 |
| 79 | Porta Gemina (western gate) | 41.24310, 13.76392 | |
| 79 | Aqueduct | | 41.24368, 13.76331 |
| 79 | Hill of Gianola (Scauri) ? | | 41.25234, 13.68623 |
| 80 | Sepolcro Romano (Scauri) | 41.26195, 13.63802 | |
| **Formiae** | | | |
| 80 | Torre di Mola | | 41.25894, 13.61396 |
| 82 | Amphitheater | | 41.25812, 13.60755 |
| 83 | *Titulus pictus* on the Via Mamurra | | 41.25506, 13.60179 |
| 83 | Theater | | 41.25501, 13.60025 |
| 83 | Torre di Castellone | | 41.25628, 13.59981 |
| 83 | Roman cistern | | 41.25557, 13.60118 |
| 83 | Fountain of San Remigio | 41.25279, 13.59278 | 41.25279, 13.59278 |
| 83 | Tomb of "Vitruvius" | 41.25233, 13.59081 | 41.25245, 13.59077 |
| 84 | "Cicero's" tomb | 41.25186, 13.57867 | 41.25157, 13.57867 |
| 87 | Milestone 85 south of Itri | 41.26510, 13.55171 | |
| 87 | Milestone 84 east of Itri train station | 41.27289, 13.54505 | |
| **Itri** | | | |
| 88 | Ponte San Gennaro in Itri | 41.290, 13.535 | |
| 89 | VA paving in Itri | 41.29014, 13.52258<br>41.29021, 13.52176 | |
| **Day 4** | | | |
| 91 | Ancient paving in Gola di S. Andrea gorge | 41.30802, 13.49377 | |
| 92 | Rest station in San Andrea Valley? | | 41.31.435, 13.48647 |
| 92 | Temple of Apollo | | 41.31388, 13.48770 |
| 94 | Bridge at northwestern end of S. Andrea | 41.31758, 13.48056 | |
| 94 | Reticulated wall south of Fundi | 41.34962, 13.43932<br>41.35098, 13.43735 | |
| **Fundi** | | | |
| 96 | Porta Capuana/southeastern gate of Fundi | 41.35775, 13.42884 | |

## Appendix 4: GPS Coordinates for Places Mentioned

| | | | |
|---|---|---|---|
| 96 | Porta Romana/northwestern city gate | 41.25985, 13.42520 | |
| 96 | "Bypass" south of the city | 41.35553, 13.42951<br>41.35973, 13.42174 | |
| 97 | Forum of Fundi | | 41.35918, 13.42714 |
| 97 | VA bridge over Aqua Chiara canal | 41.35907, 13.41826 | |
| 97 | Tomb of Q. Gavius Nauta | | 41.35879, 13.41611 |
| 98 | MP 71 in cathedral of San Biagio | 41.35296, 13.35222 | |
| 98 | Portella | 41.34436, 13.33761 | |
| 98 | Wall remains on north side of VA | | 41.33689, 13.32902 |
| 98 | Tomb of Sestus Julius Frontinus | 41.33452, 13.32144 | 41.33469, 13.32133 |
| 99 | Tomb at Torre dell'Epitaffio | 41.33062, 13.31000 | 41.33069, 13.30990 |
| 99 | Exedra east of Tarracina where VA splits | 41.31905, 13.30094 | |
| **Tarracina** | | | |
| 102 | Cut on rock face of Pisco Montano | 41.28794, 13.25945 | |
| 103 | Piazza Palatina | 41.29916, 13.27474 | |
| 104 | Temple of Jupiter Anxur | | 41.29083, 13.26011 |
| 104 | Northeast gate of Tarracina (approx.) | 41.29315, 13.25432 | |
| 105 | *Arco quadrifronte* | 41.29148, 13.24941 | |
| 105 | theater | | 41.29212, 13.24930 |
| 105 | VA in Villa Salvini | 41.28804, 13.25605 | |
| 106 | Forum | 41.29185, 13.24880 | |
| 106 | VA in the forum | 41.29181, 13.24890 | |
| 107 | Temple of Rome and Augustus (cathedral?) | | 41.29191, 13.24846 |
| 107 | Capitolium | | 41.29216, 13.24863 |
| 107 | Theater | | 41.29212, 13.24928 |
| **Day 5** | | | |
| 109 | Northwest gate of Tarracina | 41.29300, 13.24692 | |
| 109 | Current location of Porta Romana | 41.29427, 13.24499 | |
| 109 | VA junction (Quatro lampioni) | 41.29522, 13.24397 | |
| 110 | Feronia Spring | | 41.31134, 13.19970 |

| | | | |
|---|---|---|---|
| 111 | Roman bridge over Fossa dell'Acqua Traversa | 41.31372, 13.19764 | |
| 111 | Ponte Alto | 41.31500, 13.19330 | |
| 111 | South end of the canal and "straightaway" to Aricia | 41.31547, 13.19170 | |
| 115 | Bridge near Ponte Maggiore | 41.32681, 13.17722 | |
| 117 | Ad Medias | 41.38531, 13.10237 | |
| 117 | Tomb of Clessipus Geganius | | 41.38620, 13.10156 |
| **Forum Appii** | | | |
| 121 | MP 43 in situ at Forum Appii | 41.46493, 13.00011 | |
| 119 | Forum Appii bridge | 41.46672, 12.99778 | |
| 119 | Forum Appii *mansio* (approx.) | | 41.46760, 12.99695 |
| **Day 6** | | | |
| 125 | Bridge at Tripontium | 41.50346, 12.95045 | |
| 125 | Two milestones at Torre Tre Ponte (no mile nos.) | 41.50781, 12.94500<br>41.50810, 12.94458 | |
| **Tres Tabernae** | | | |
| 128 | Diverticulum from VA to *mansio*? | 41.56184, 12.87495 | 41.56160, 12.87436 |
| 128 | *Mansio* | 41.56201, 12.87473 | 41.56166, 12.87417 |
| 128 | Outbuildings/baths with mosaic floors | | 41.56240, 12.87371 |
| 129 | Monumental tomb north of Tres Tabernae | | 41.57667, 12.85597 |
| 129 | Church of San Giacomo Apostolo | | 41.61490, 12.80605 |
| 131 | Ancient paving at Scuola Sole Luna | 41.64327, 12.76873 | |
| 131 | Ancient paving south of Via Soleluna | 41.64565, 12.76581 | |
| 131 | Bridge over Fossa di Civitana | 41.65118, 12.75851 | |
| 132 | Bridge over Fossa de Mele | 41.65822, 12.74942 | |
| 132 | Castela di San Gennaro | | 41.67904, 12.72272 |
| 132 | Unidentified Roman building (*Sublanuvium mansio?*) | | 41.68003, 12.71984 |
| 132 | Ancient buttressing | | 41.68257, 12.71702 |
| 133 | Ancient substructure | | 41.68539, 12.71393 |

# Appendix 4: GPS Coordinates for Places Mentioned

| | | | |
|---|---|---|---|
| 133 | Roman structure incorporated into a modern building | | 41.68854, 12.70975 |
| 133 | 325 m of ancient pavement (Genzano di Roma) | 41.69049, 12.70725<br>41.69257, 12.70450 | |
| 133 | MP 19 in situ | 41.69319, 12.70368 | |
| 135 | Aricia deviation (2500 m) | 41.70996, 12.68172<br>41.72405, 12.66380 | |
| 137 | Aricia viaduct (approx.) | 41.71490, 12.67577<br>41.71604, 12.67345 | |
| 138 | Sanctuary of Diana of Nemi | | 41.72447, 12.70924 |
| **Aricia** | | | |
| 139 | Southeast city gate/Porta Urbica | 41.71701, 12.67152 | |
| 140 | Southwest city gate/Porta Romana | 41.71911, 12.66597 | |
| 140 | Roman ruins built into a modern structure | 41.71799, 12.67008 | |
| 140 | Osteriaccia | 41.71716, 12.67075 | |
| 140 | Recently destroyed structure | 41.71846, 12.66681 | |
| 140 | MP 16 (approx.) | 41.71850, 12.66713 | |
| **Day 7** | | | |
| 143 | Tomb of Horatii and Curiatii (Aricia) | 41.72381, 12.66363 | |
| 144 | Sanctuary of Jupiter Latiaris | 41.75150, 12.70980 | |
| 145n7 | Main gate of castra of Legio II Parthica (Albano) | 41.72911, 12.65910 | |
| 145 | Tomb of Pompey the Great (Albano Laziale) | 41.73220, 12.65485 | |
| 146 | Large tomb at MP 14 | 41.73992, 12.64632 | |
| 146 | Sanctuary of Bona Dea (Castel Gandolfo) | 41.74322, 12.64261 | |
| 147 | MP 13 (approx.) | 41.75012 12.63487 | |
| 147 | Torraccio at MP 12 | 41.76030, 12.62346 | 41.76034, 12.62370 |
| 148 | Circus of Bovillae | | 41.75752, 12.62170 |
| 148 | Ancient road at McDonald's in Frattocchie | | 41.76775, 12.61629 |
| 150 | Torre Secchi | 41.77602, 12.60584 | 41.77610, 12.60608 |
| 150 | MP 11 (approx.) | 41.77055, 12.61200 | |

| | | | |
|---|---|---|---|
| 150 | Tabernaculo excavations | | 41.77473, 12.60740 |
| 151 | Paving and bath complex | 41.77530, 12.60666 | 41.77520, 12.60647 |
| 151 | La Mola tomb | 41.77600, 12.60588 | 41.77613, 12.60606 |
| 151 | Sepolcro di Giovannino | 41.77780, 12.60388 | 41.77773, 12.60378 |
| 151 | MP 10 (approx.) | 41.78082, 12.60048 | |
| 151 | Large tomb at beginning of paving | | 41.78120, 12.60023 |
| 151 | Greek cross tomb over bath complex | | 41.78445, 12.59625 |
| 151 | Circular tomb of imperial period | | 41.78518, 12.59546 |
| 151 | Monte di Terra tomb | | 41.78716, 12.59301 |
| 151 | MP 9 (approx.) and Tomb of Gallienus | 41.79106, 12.58902 | 41.79091, 12.58875 |
| 152 | Circular tomb by quarry | 41.79430, 12.58541 | 41.79426, 12.58533 |
| 152n24 | Berretta del Prete | 41.79694, 12.58246 | 41.79716, 12.58291 |
| 152 | Brick tomb on high podium | 41.79721, 12.58215 | 41.79728, 12.58222 |
| 152 | Republican temple | 41.80089, 12.57802 | 41.80078, 12.57781 |
| 152 | MP 8 (approx.) | 41.80126, 12.57761 | |
| 152 | Tumulus by MP 8 | 41.80147, 12.57739 | 41.80135, 12.57719 |
| 153n25 | Brick tomb with two columns | | 41.80301, 12.57523 |
| 153 | Tomb with exedra | | 41.80646, 12.57202 |
| 153n25 | Exedra tomb with three niches | | 41.80756, 12.57092 |
| 153 | First deviation | 41.81030, 12.56747<br>41.81373, 12.56366 | |
| 153 | Tomb of the Vase | | 41.81122, 12.56619 |
| 153 | MP 7 (approx.) | 41.81133, 12.56579 | |
| 154 | Bench with three funerary busts | 41.81408, 12.56326 | 41.81412, 12.56330 |
| 155 | Inscription of Euhodus | 41.81553, 12.56164 | 41.81556, 12.56169 |
| 155 | So-called tomb of Pompey/Torre Selce | 41.81656, 12.56047 | 41.81671, 12.56073 |
| 156 | Columbarium of the "6 Arcosolia" | 41.81763, 12.55926 | 41.81756, 12.55917 |
| 156 | Temple-shaped Tomb of the Griffins | 41.81804, 12.55881 | 41.81793, 12.55866 |
| 156 | Casal Rotondo | 41.82099, 12.55552 | 41.82110, 12.55574 |
| 156 | MP 6 (approx.) | 41.82166, 12.55475 | |

## Appendix 4: GPS Coordinates for Places Mentioned

| | | | |
|---|---|---|---|
| 157 | Pyramidal tomb relating to the Villa Quintilli | 41.82920, 12.54630 | 41.82931, 12.54646 |
| 157 | Two tumuli of the "Horatii" | 41.82863, 12.54695<br>41.82885, 12.54669 | 41.82854, 12.54676<br>41.82870, 12.54652 |
| 157 | Beginning of second deviation | 41.83048, 12.54486 | |
| 158 | Tumulus of Curiatii | 41.83065, 12.54472 | 41.83056, 12.54451 |
| 158 | Round tomb (nontumulus) | 41.83169, 12.54356 | 41.83161, 12.54345 |
| 158 | MP 5 (approx.), end of second deviation | 41.83187, 12.54331 | |
| 158 | Jewish freedmen inscription | 41.83233, 12.54280 | 41.83231, 12.54275 |
| 159 | Tomb of married couple and two children | 41.83505, 12.53975 | 41.83500, 12.53967 |
| 159 | Tomb with Gorgon and Erotes | 41.83508, 12.53971 | 41.83505, 12.53963 |
| 159 | Tomb of G. Rabirius Hermodorus | 41.83593 12.53875 | 41.83592 12.53871 |
| 160 | Tomb of Tib. Claud. Secundus | 41.83729, 12.53724 | 41.83724, 12.53719 |
| 160 | Hilarius Fuscus busts | 41.83804, 12.53638 | 41.83803, 12.53635 |
| 160 | Inscription of Sextus Pompeius Iustus | 41.83929, 12.53500 | 41.83934, 12.53507 |
| 160n39 | Early-Imperial circular tomb | 41.84066, 12.53345 | 41.84074, 12.53357 |
| 160n39 | Inscription of M. Servilius Quartus | 41.84172, 12.53226 | 41.84176, 12.53225 |
| 160 | MP 4 (approx.) | 41.84208, 12.53186 | |
| 160 | Relief of a Greek warrior | 41.84220, 12.53165 | |
| 161 | Capo di Bove | 41.84877, 12.52437 | 41.84848, 12.52396 |
| 161 | Tomb of Caecilia Metella | 41.85202, 12.52071 | 41.85215, 12.52095 |
| 161 | MP 3 (approx.) | 41.85229, 12.52041 | |
| 162 | Circus of Maxentius | | 41.85443, 12.51976 |
| 162 | Tomb of Romulus | | 41.85518, 12.51853 |
| 163 | Basilica of San Sebastiano | 41.85606, 12.51624 | 41.85583, 12.51576 |
| 164 | Monumentum Volusiorum columbarium | 41.86017, 12.51157 | 41.86025, 12.51171 |
| 164 | Columbarium of Livia's freedmen | 41.86196, 12.50953 | |
| 164 | MP 2 (approx.) | 41.86250, 12.50895 | |
| 164 | Columbarium of Augustus's freedmen | 41.86398, 12.50729 | 41.86412, 12.50751 |
| 166 | End of straightaway from Aricia | 41.86557, 12.50549 | |

| | | | |
|---|---|---|---|
| 166 | Church of Domine Quo Vadis | 41.86639, 12.50363 | 41.86651, 12.50371 |
| 166 | Junction with Via Ardeatina | 41.86641, 12.50356 | |
| 167n50 | Tomb of Priscilla | 41.86671, 12.50330 | 41.86661, 12.50301 |
| 167 | Temple of Mars Gradiva? | | 41.86730, 12.50336 |
| 168 | Bridge over the Almo River | 41.86855, 12.50246 | |
| 167 | First alternate location of Temple of Mars | 41.87096, 12.50194 | |
| 171 | Copy of MP 1 in wrong location | 41.87247, 12.50184 | |
| 167 | Second alternate location of Temple of Mars | 41.87273, 12.50178 | 41.87285, 12.50231 |
| 169 | Porto San Sebastiano/*Area carruces* | 41.87352, 12.50155 | |
| 170 | MP 1 (approx. proper location) | 41.87376, 12.50147 | |
| 172 | Columbarium 1 of Vigna Codini | 41.87422, 12.50128 | 41.87443, 12.50205 |
| 172 | Columbarium 2 of Vigna Codini | 41.87446, 12.50118 | 41.87462, 12.50173 |
| 172 | Columbarium 3 of Vigna Codini | 41.87500, 12.50089 | 41.87513, 12.50124 |
| 173 | Tomb of the Scipios | 41.87588, 12.50030 | 41.87595, 12.50058 |
| 175 | Approx. position of Arch of Drusus | 41.87926, 12.49652 | |
| 175 | *Mutatorium Caesaris* | 41.88014, 12.49535 | 41,88070, 12.49569 |
| 177 | Porta Capena | 41.88390, 12.49041 | 41.88390, 12.49041 |
| **Rome** | | | |
| 180 | Castra Peregrina (?) | | 41.88400, 12.49700 |
| 181 | Castra Praetoria | | 41.90640, 12.50765 |
| 184 | Santa Maria in Via Lata | | 41.89817, 12.48139 |
| 187 | S. Paulo in Regola | | 41.89300, 12.47350 |

# Bibliography

Adams, Colin. 2012. "Transport." Pages 218–40 in *The Cambridge Companion to the Roman Economy*. Edited by Walter Scheidel. Cambridge: Cambridge University Press. https://doi.org/10.1017/CCO9781139030199.015.

Addessi, Andrea, and Angela Baldanza. 2014. "La Via Appia 'Antica': Approccio geo-litologico per la valorizzazione del tracciato tra Fondi ed Itri (LT)." *Culture Territori Linguaggi* 4:169–83.

Aglietti, Silvia, Francesca Diosono, Consuelo Manetta, Alessia Palladino, and Birte Poulsen. 2022. "Villa or sanctuary? The So-called Villa of Clodius at the Via Appia." *Analecta Romana Instituti Danici* 45:77–120.

Aharoni, Yigael, and Michael Avi-Yonah. 1977. *The Macmillan Bible Atlas*. Rev. ed. New York: Macmillan.

Alföldi, Andrew. 1960. "Diana Nemorensis." *American Journal of Archaeology* 64:137–44. https://doi.org/10.2307/502539.

Amalfitano, Paolo, Giuseppe Camodeca, and Maura Medri. 1990. *I Campi Flegrei: un itinerario archeologico*. Venice: Marsilio.

Appian. 1912. *Roman History, Volume I*. Edited and translated by Brian McGing. Loeb Classical Library. Cambridge, MA: Harvard University Press.

Appian. 1913. *Roman History, Volume IV: The Civil Wars, Books 3.27–5*. Translated by Horace White. Loeb Classical Library. Cambridge, MA: Harvard University Press.

Aranegui, Carmen, and Ricardo Mar. 2009. "Lixus (Morocco): From a Mauretanian Sanctuary to an Augustan Palace." *Papers of the British School at Rome* 77:29–64. https://doi.org/10.1017/S0068246200000039.

Arata, Francesco Paolo. 2014. "La *navigabilis fossa* di Nerone: *Audacia, ingenium e utilitas*." *Mélanges de l'École française de Rome-Antiquité* 126: 277–94. https://doi.org/10.4000/mefra.2114.

Arthur, Paul. 1995. "Roman Exports to the North: Wine in the West; A View from Campania." Pages 241–51 in *Italy in Europe: Economic Relations 700 BC–AD 50*. Edited by Judith Swaddling, Susan Walker, and Paul Roberts. British Museum Occasional Paper 97. London: British Museum.

Ashby, Thomas. 1907. "The Classical Topography of the Roman Campagna, Part III, Section I." *Papers of the British School at Rome* 4: 3–157.

Ashby, Thomas. 1927. *The Roman Campagna in Classical Times*. London: Benn.

Athenaeus. 2007. *The Learned Banqueters, Volume I: Books 1–3.106e*. Edited and translated by S. Douglas Olson. Loeb Classical Library. Cambridge, MA: Harvard University Press.

Athenaeus. 2010. *The Learned Banqueters, Volume VI: Books 12–13.594b*. Edited and translated by S. Douglas Olson. Loeb Classical Library. Cambridge, MA: Harvard University Press.

Aubert, Jean-Jacques. 2005. "Corpse Disposal in the Roman Colony of Puteoli." Pages 141–57 in *Noctes Campanae: Studi di storia antica ed archeologia dell'Italia preromana e romana in memoria di Martin W. Frederiksen*. Edited by William V. Harris and Elio Lo Cascio. Naples: Luciano.

Baillie Reynolds, P.K., and T. Ashby. 1923. "Castra Peregrinorum." *Journal of Roman Studies* 13:152–67. https://doi.org/10.2307/295749.

Ballance, M. H. 1951. "The Roman Bridges of the Via Flaminia." *Papers of the British School at Rome* 19:78–117. https://doi.org/10.1017/S0068246200006279.

Barnes, Ian. 2010. *Historical Atlas of the Bible*. New York: Chartwell.

Barrett, C. K. 1998. *Acts 15–28*. International Critical Commentary. London: T&T Clark.

Beard, Mary. 2015. "Fannia falanghina." *Mary Beard: A don's life* (blog). October 9, 2015. https://www.the-tls.co.uk/articles/fannia-falanghina/.

Beck, John A. 2015. *Discovery House Bible Atlas*. Grand Rapids: Discovery House.

Beitzel, Barry J. 2009. *The New Moody Atlas of the Bible.* Chicago: Moody.

Bekker-Nielsen, Tønnes. 2013. "Roads, Roman Empire." Pages 5852–57 in *The Encyclopedia of Ancient History.* Edited by Roger Bagnall. 13 vols. Malden, MA: Wiley-Blackwell. https://doi.org/10.1002/9781444338386.wbeah18111.pub2.

Bellini, Giovanna Rita. 2007. "*Minturnae* Porto del Mediterraneo." *Romula* 6:7–28.

Bock, Darrell L. 2007. *Acts.* Baker Exegetical Commentary on the New Testament. Grand Rapids: Baker Academic.

Bodel, John. 2017. "Trimalchio's cargo (Petr. 76, 6)." Pages 75–87 in *Il Mediterraneo e la storia II: Naviganti, popoli e culture ad Ischia e in altri luoghi della costa tirrenica.* Edited by Laura Chioffi, Mika Kajava, and Simo Örmä. Rome: Institutum Romanum Finlandiae.

Boon, Marjolein Helena van der. 2017. "A Stroll Down Memory Lane: A Biography of the First Eleven Miles of the Via Appia Antica in Suburban Rome, Italy." MA thesis, Faculty of Archaeology, University of Leiden.

Brettman, Estelle Shohet, Amy Hirschfeld, Florence Wolsky, and Jessica Dello Russo. 2017. *Vaults of Memory: The Roman Jewish Catacombs and Their Context in the Ancient Mediterranean World.* Rome: International Catacomb Society. http://www.catacombsociety.org/international-catacomb-society-publications/vaults-of-memory-manuscript/vaults-of-memory-the-roman-jewish-catacombs-and-their-context-in-the-ancient-mediterranean-world/.

Brookes, Alan C. 1974. "Minturnae: The Via Appia Bridge." *American Journal of Archaeology* 78:41–48. https://doi.org/10.2307/503755.

Brouwer, H. H. J. 1989. *Bona Dea: The Sources and a Description of the Cult.* Leiden: Brill.

Bruce, F. F. 1990. *The Acts of the Apostles: The Greek Text with Introduction and Commentary.* 3rd ed. Grand Rapids: Eerdmans.

Bruno, Matthias, Donato Attanasio, and Walter Prochaska. 2015. "The Docimium Marble Sculptures of the Grotto of Tiberius at

Sperlonga." *American Journal of Archaeology* 119:375–94. https://doi.org/10.3764/aja.119.3.0375.

Bunbury, Edward Herbert. 1857. "Via Appia." Pages 1288–95 in vol. 2 of *Dictionary of Greek and Roman Geography*. Edited by William Smith. 2 vols. Boston: Little, Brown.

Buonopane, Alfredo. 2011. "Il più antico di tutti ora esistenti: Mommsen, Barnabei e le vicende del miliario arcaico di Mesa (Latina)." Pages 35–46 in *I miliari lungo le strade dell'impero: Atti del Convegno, Isola della Scala, 28 Novembre 2009*. Edited by Patrizia Basso. Verona: Cierre.

Camodeca, Giuseppe. 1994. "Puteoli porto annonario e il commercio del grano in età imperial." Pages 103–28 in *Le ravitaillement en blé de Rome et des centres urbains des débuts de la République jusqu'au Haut-Empire: Actes du Colloque international, Naples, 14–16 février 1991*. Naples: Centre Jean Bérard.

Camodeca, Giuseppe. 2018. *Puteoli Romana: Istituzioni e Società, Saggi*. Naples: Unior.

Cancellieri, Margherita. 1990. "Il Territorio Pontino e La Via Appia." Pages 61–71 in *La Via Appia: Decimo incontro di studio del Comitato per l'archeologia laziale*. Edited by Stefania Quilici Gigli. Archeologia laziale 10.1. Rome: Consiglio Nazionale delle Richerche.

Canina, Luigi. 1853. *La prima parte della Via Appia dalla Porta Capena a Boville*. Vol. 1: *Descrizione*. Rome: Bertinelli.

Carbonara, Andrea, and Gaetano Messineo. 1998. *Via Appia, III: Da Cisterna a Minturno*. Antiche Strade, Lazio. Rome: Istituto Poligrafico e Zecca dello Stato.

Cascella, Sergio. 2016. *Suessa: Storia e Monumenti di una Città della Campania Romana*. Naples: Università degli studi di Napoli "l'Orientale."

Cascella, Sergio. 2017. "Scavi lungo il tracciato dell'Appia e i suoi diverticoli a sud di Sinuessa: Dati preliminari." *Oebalus: Studi sulla Campania nell'Antichita* 12:7–77.

Cassieri, Nicoletta. 1990. "Edificio funerario lungo la via Appia presso Cisterna di Latina." Pages 179–81 in *La Via Appia: Decimo incontro di studio del Comitato per l'archeologia laziale*. Edited by Stefania Quilici Gigli. Archeologia laziale 10.1. Rome: Consiglio Nazionale della Ricerche.

Casson, Lionel. 1951. "Speed under Sail of Ancient Ships." *Transactions and Proceedings of the American Philological Association* 82:136–48. https://doi.org/10.2307/283426.

Casson, Lionel. 1980. "The Role of the State in Rome's Grain Trade." *Memoirs of the American Academy in Rome* 36:21–33. https://doi.org/10.2307/4238693.

Casson, Lionel. 1995. *Ships and Seamanship in the Ancient World*. Baltimore: Johns Hopkins University Press.

Cavacchioli, Marco. 2021. *Via Appia Antica IX–XIII miglio, Ciampino-Marino, Itinerario Storico–Archeologico*. Marino: Genzano di Roma.

Cevoli, Tsao, and Nicola Meluziis. 2015. "La Via Consolare Campana Puteolis Capuam." *Archeomafie* 7:27–52.

Chadwick, Henry. 1957. *St. Peter and St. Paul in Rome: The Problem of the Memoria Apostolorum ad Catacumbas*. Oxford: Clarendon.

Cicero. 1923. *Pro Archia. Post Reditum in Senatu. Post Reditum ad Quirites. De Domo Sua. De Haruspicum Responsis. Pro Plancio.* Translated by N. H. Watts. Loeb Classical Library. Cambridge, MA: Harvard University Press.

Cicero. 1930. *Pro Quinctio. Pro Roscio Amerino. Pro Roscio Comoedo. On the Agrarian Law.* Translated by J. H. Freese. Loeb Classical Library. Cambridge, MA: Harvard University Press.

Cicero. 1999. *Letters to Atticus, Volume I*. Edited and translated by D. R. Shackleton Bailey. Loeb Classical Library. Cambridge, MA: Harvard University Press.

Cicero. 2002. *Letters to Quintus and Brutus. Letter Fragments. Letter to Octavian. Invectives. Handbook of Electioneering*. Edited and translated by D. R. Shackleton Bailey. Loeb Classical Library. Cambridge, MA: Harvard University Press.

Cicero. 2010. *Philippics 1–6*. Edited and translated by D. R. Shackleton Bailey. Revised by John T. Ramsey and Gesine Manuwald. Loeb Classical Library. Cambridge, MA: Harvard University Press.

Cioffi, Robert L. 2016. "Travel in the Roman World." Pages 1–41 in *Oxford Handbook Topics in Classical Studies*. https://doi.org/10.1093/oxfordhb/9780199935390.013.110.

Cirillo, Clelia, Giovanna Acampora, Luigi Scarpa, and Ugo Zannini. 2012. "Exploring the Landscape of Northern Campania in Roman Times and the Route of the Appian Way from Sinuessa to Capua." *Rendiconti online Società Geologica Italiana* 21:741–42.

Cirillo, Clelia, Luigi Scarpa, Ugo Zannini, Giovanna Acampora, and Marina Russo. 2014. "The Appian Way: Enhancement of the Landscape between Nature and Culture from Rome to Capua." Pages 269–75 in *Best Practices in Heritage Conservation and Management: From the World to Pompeii*. Edited by Carmine Gambardella. Naples: La scuola di Pitagora.

Cisterna di Latina. n.d. "Tres Tabernae." Comune di Cisterna di Latina (website). Accessed October 30, 2022.

Claridge, Amanda. 1998. *Rome*. Oxford Archaeological Guides. Oxford: Oxford University Press.

Coarelli. Filippo. 1988. *Il Sepolcro degli Scipioni a Roma*. Rome: Palombi.

Coarelli, Filippo. 2014. *Rome and Environs: An Archaeological Guide*. Updated ed. Berkeley: University of California Press.

Collins, J. J. 1983. "Sibylline Oracles." Pages 317–472 in vol. 1 of *The Old Testament Pseudepigrapha*. Edited by James H. Charlesworth. 2 vols. New York: Doubleday.

Cook, John Granger. 2012. "Crucifixion as Spectacle in Roman Campania." *Novum Testamentum* 54:68–100.

Cooley, Alison E. 2009. *Res Gestae Divi Augusti: Text, Translation, and Commentary*. Cambridge: Cambridge University Press.

Cooley, Alison E. 2012. *The Cambridge Manual to Latin Epigraphy*. Cambridge: Cambridge University Press.

Cooley, Alison E., and M. G. L. Cooley. 2014. *Pompeii and Herculaneum: A Sourcebook*. 2nd ed. London: Routledge.

Coppola, Maria Rosaria. 1984. "Il foro emiliano di Terracina: Rilievo, analisi tecnica, vicende storiche del monumento." *Mélanges de l'école française de Rome: Antiquité* 961:325–77. https://doi.org/10.3406/mefr.1984.1410.

Coulston, Jon. n.d. "What Was Trajan's Column For?" Trajan's Column, A School of Classics Research Project, University of St Andrews. Accessed October 30, 2022. https://arts.st-andrews.ac.uk/trajans-column/the-project/what-was-trajans-column-for/.

Coulston, Jon. 2001. "Travel and Transport on the Column of Trajan." Pages 106–37 in *Travel and Geography in the Roman Empire*. Edited by Colin Adams and Ray Laurence. London: Routledge.

Crogiez, Sylvie. 1990. "Les stations du cursus publicus de Rome à Terracine." Pages 95–103 in *La Via Appia: Decimo incontro di studio del Comitato per l'archeologia laziale*. Edited by Stefania Quilici Gigli. Archeologia laziale 10.1. Rome: Consiglio Nazionale delle Richerche.

Cuntz, Otto. 1929. *Itineraria Romana I: Itineraria Antonini Augusti et Burgdigalense*. Leipzig: Teubner.

Cupello, Katherine E., and Lisa A. Hughes. 2010. "Reuse, the Roman Funerary Monument and the Rabirii: Violation of Memory or Commemoration of Past and Present?" *Annali della Scuola Normale Superiore di Pisa: Classe di Lettere e Filosofia* 2.1:3–23.

Currid, John D., and David P. Barrett. 2010. *Crossway ESV Bible Atlas*. Wheaton, IL: Crossway.

Curtis, Adrian. 2009. *The Oxford Bible Atlas*. 4th ed. New York: Oxford University Press.

Dalby, Andrew. 2000. *Empire of Pleasure: Luxury and Indulgence in the Roman World*. London: Routledge.

D'Arms, John H. 1970. *Romans on the Bay of Naples: A Social and Cultural Study of the Villas and Their Owners from 150 B.C. to A.D. 400*. Cambridge: Harvard University Press.

Davis, Danny Lee. 2009. "Commercial Navigation in the Greek and Roman World." PhD diss., University of Texas. https://repositories.lib.utexas.edu/handle/2152/18420.

De Carlo, Nicola. 2009. "Per una carta archeologica *dell'Ager Campanus* (Comuni di Giugliano in Campania, Qualiano, Villaricca: I.G.M. F. 184)." MA thesis, University of Milan.

De Caro, Stefano. 2012. *La terra nera degli antichi campani: Guida archeologica della provincia di caserta*. Naples: Arte'm.

De Gaetano, Elizabeth. 2013. "Reconstructing Pozzuoli: Textual and Visual Reconstructions of a Roman Port Town." 2 vols. PhD diss., University of Southampton.

De Haas, Tymon, Gijs Tol, Kayt Armstrong, and Peter Attema. 2017. "Craft Production and Trade in the Central Italian Countryside: Approaches and First Results of the Minor Centers Project." Pages 501–12 in *Emptor et mercator: Spazi e rappresentazioni del commercio romano*. Edited by Sara Santoro. Bari: Edipuglia.

Della Portella, Ivana, ed. 2004. *The Appian Way: From Its Foundation to the Middle Ages*. Los Angeles: Getty Museum.

Della Valle, Chiara. 2010. "Testimonianze storico-archeologiche della Via Appia a Capua antica." Pages 23–26 in *Guida del Gruppo archeologico "Francesco Saverio Gualtieri" di Caserta*. Caserta: Società Editrice L'Aperia.

Dessau, H. 1882. "Intorno la colonna milliaria del Campidoglio." *Bullettino dell'Instituto di corrispondenza archeologica* 5:121–27.

Di Fazio, Clara. 2012. "Il circuito murario romano di Fondi e i resti nel palazzo Caetani." Pages 15–41 in *Il palazzo Caetani di Fondi: Cantiere di studi*. Edited by Giovanni Pesiri and Pio Francesco Pistilli. Fondi: Creia.

Di Fazio, Massimiliano. 2012. "Feronia: The Role of an Italic Goddess in the Process of Cultural Integration in Republican Italy." Pages 337–54 in *Processes of Integration and Identity Formation in the Roman Republic*. Edited by Saskia T. Roselaar. Mnemosyne Supplements 342. Leiden: Brill. https://doi.org/10.1163/9789004229600_021.

Di Rosa, Andrea. 2018. "Strutture rupestri di età romana nel territorio di Terracina (Lazio meridionale)." *BABESCH* 93:165–208. http://doi.org/10.2143/BAB.93.0.3284851.

Dilke, O. A. W., and Margaret S. Dilke. 1961. "Terracina and the Pomptine Marshes." *Greece & Rome* 8:172–78. https://doi.org/10.1017/S0017383500014406.

Dorcey, Peter F. 1992. *The Cult of Silvanus: A Study in Roman Folk Religion*. Columbia Studies in the Classical Tradition 20. Leiden: Brill.

Dowley, Tim, ed. 2004. *The Kregel Bible Atlas*. Grand Rapids: Kregel.
Dubbini, Rachele. 2016. "A New Republican Temple on the Via Appia, at the Borders of Rome's Urban Space." *Journal of Roman Archaeology* 29:327–47. https://doi.org/10.1017/S1047759400072160.
Duinker, Heleen Ellen. 2015. "Buried in Collectivity: The Social Context of the Early Imperial Roman Columbaria." MA thesis, University of Groningen.
Dummett, Jeremy. 2010. *Syracuse, City of Legends: A Glory of Sicily*. London: Tauris.
Dunn, James D. G. 1996. *The Acts of the Apostles*. Peterborough, UK: Epworth.
Eastman, David L. 2011. *Paul the Martyr: The Cult of the Apostle in the Latin West*. Writings from the Greco-Roman World Supplements. Atlanta: Society of Biblical Literature.
Emmerson, Allison L. C. 2013. "Memoria et Monumenta: Local Identities and the Tombs of Roman Campania." PhD diss., University of Cincinnati. https://etd.ohiolink.edu/apexprod/rws_olink/r/1501/10?p10_etd_subid=90493&clear=10.
Emmerson, Allison L. C. 2020. *Life and Death in the Roman Suburb*. Oxford: Oxford University Press.
Fee, Gordon D. 1995. *Paul's Letter to the Philippians*. Grand Rapids: Eerdmans.
Ferrante, Cristina, and Daria Mastrorilli. 2016. "Minturno (Minturnae), Introduzione." Pages 87–98 in *Fana, templa, delubra: Corpus dei luoghi di culto dell'Italia antica (FTD) – 4; Regio I; Fondi, Formia, Minturno, Ponza*. Edited by Cristina Ferrante, Jean-Claude Lacam, and Daniela Quadrino. New ed. Paris: Collège de France. https://books.openedition.org/cdf/4272.
Fiocchi Nicolai, Vincenzo. 2015. "Memorie paleocristiane della mansio di Tres Tabernae al XXXIII della via Appia." Pages 125–35 in *Humanitas: Studi per Patrizia Serafin*. Edited by Alessandra Serra. Rome: UniversItalia.
Florescu, G. 1925. "Aricia: Studio storico-topografico." *Ephemeris Dacoromana* 3:1–57.

Forbes, S. Russell. 1897. *The Footsteps of St. Paul in Rome*. 4th ed. New York: Nelson.

Freier, Bruce W. 1969. "Points on the Topography of Minturnae." *Historia* 18:510–12.

Freier, Bruce W. 1980. *Landlords and Tenants in Ancient Rome*. Princeton: Princeton University Press.

Gambash, Gil. 2015. "Between Mobility and Connectivity in the Ancient Mediterranean: Coast-Skirting Travellers in the Southern Levant." Pages 155–72 in *The Impact of Mobility and Migration in the Roman Empire*. Edited by Elio Lo Cascio and Laurens Ernst Tacoma. Impact of Empire 22. Leiden: Brill. https://doi.org/10.1163/9789004334809_010.

Garland, David E. 1999. *Second Corinthians*. New American Commentary. Nashville: Broadman & Holman.

Gentile, Franceso. 2011. *Pozzuli Percorsi*. Naples: Intra Moenia.

Gialanella, Costanza, Francesco Garcea, Lucia Manuela Proietti, Gianluca Soricelli, and Celestino Grifa. 2022. "Contesti di età augustea dal Rione Terra di Pozzuoli." Pages 77–92 in *The Production and Distribution Network of the Bay of Naples: From a Regional to a Mediterranean Perspective*. Edited by Marco Giglio and Luana Toniolo. Heidelberg: Propylaeum. https://doi.org/10.11588/propylaeum.851.c10947.

Gowers, Emily. 1993. "Horace, 'Satires' 1.5: An Inconsequential Journey." *Proceedings of the Cambridge Philological Society* 39:48–66. https://doi.org/10.1017/S0068673500001723.

Haenchen, Ernst. 1971. *The Acts of the Apostles: A Commentary*. Philadelphia: Westminster.

Hamblin, Dora Jane, and Mary Jane Grunsfeld. 1974. *The Appian Way, A Journey*. New York: Random House.

Haverfield, F., and G. Owen. 1900. "The 'Bridge' at Aricia." *Classical Review* 14.1:86–88.

Hawthorne, Gerald F. 1983. *Philippians*. Waco, TX: Word.

Hemer, Colin J. 1985. "First Person Narrative in Acts 27–28." *Tyndale Bulletin* 36:79–109.

Hewson, Dave. 2020. *The Appian Way, the People, the Places and the Road That Led to Europe*. Self-published, Kindle.

Hohlfelder, Robert L. 2000. "Beyond Coincidence? Marcus Agrippa and King Herod's Harbor." *Journal of Near Eastern Studies* 59:241–53. https://doi.org/10.1086/468859.

Holden, Peregrine, and Nicholas Purcell. 2000. *The Corrupting Sea: A Study of Mediterranean History*. Oxford: Blackwell.

Horace. 1881. *The Works of Horace*. Translated by Theodore Martin. Edinburgh: Blackwood.

Horace. 1926. *Satires. Epistles. The Art of Poetry*. Translated by H. Rushton Fairclough. Loeb Classical Library. Cambridge, MA: Harvard University Press.

Horace. 2005. *The Epistles*. Translated by A. S. Kline. Poetry in Translation. Last modified March 15, 2005. https://www.poetryintranslation.com/PITBR/Latin/Horacehome.php.

Houston, George W. 1987. "Lucian's *Navigium* and the Dimensions of the Isis." *American Journal of Philology* 108:444–50.

Huissen, Gerard. 2020. "Tarracina, The Fourth Harbour of Trajan." Roman Ports. June 22, 2020. https://www.romanports.org/en/articles/ports-in-focus/677-tarracina-the-fourth-harbour-of-trajan.html.

Humm, Michel. 1996. "Appius Claudius Caecus et la construction de la via Appia." *Mélanges de l'Ecole française de Rome: Antiquité* 108:693–746. https://doi.org/10.3406/mefr.1996.1958.

Ihm, Maximilianus. 1899. "Additamenta ad corporis vol. IX et X." Pages 1–221 in vol. 8 of *Ephemeris epigraphica: Corporis inscriptionum Latinarum supplementum*. Edited by W. Henzen. 9 vols. Berlin: Remarus.

Ilan, Tal. 2008. *Lexicon of Jewish Names in Late Antiquity, Part III: The Western Diaspora 330 BCE–650 CE*. Texte und Studien zum antiken Judentum 126. Tübingen: Mohr Siebeck.

Irving, Washington. 1824. *Tales of a Traveller*. 2 vols. London: Murray.

Jacobson, David M. 2019. "Coins of the First Century Roman Governors of Judaea and Their Motifs." *Electrum* 26:73–96.

Jerome. 1933. *Select Letters*. Translated by F. A. Wright. Loeb Classical Library. Cambridge, MA: Harvard University Press.

Jerome. 2005. *The Chronicle of St. Jerome* [or *Chronicon*]. Edited by Roger Pearse. Tertullian.org. https://www.tertullian.org/fathers/index.htm#jeromechronicle.

Johannowsky, Werner. 1975. "Problemi Archeologici Campani." *Rendiconti dell'Accademia di Archeologia, Lettere e Belle Arti* 50:3–38.

Johannowsky, Werner. 1989. *Capua Antica*. Naples: Banco di Napoli.

Johnson, Luke Timothy. 1992. *The Acts of the Apostles*. Sacra Pagina. Collegeville, MN: Liturgical Press.

Josephus. 1987. *The Works of Josephus: New Updated Version*. Translated by William A. M. Whiston. Peabody, MA: Hendrickson.

Juvenal. 2004. "The Satires of Juvenal." In *Juvenal and Persius*. Edited and translated by Susanna Morton Braund. Loeb Classical Library. Cambridge, MA: Harvard University Press.

Kaster, Robert. A. 2012. *The Appian Way: Ghost Road, Queen of Roads*. Chicago: University of Chicago Press.

Keener, Craig S. 2015. *Acts: An Exegetical Commentary*. Vol. 4, 24:1–28:31. Grand Rapids: Baker Academic.

Keppie, Lawrence. 1991. *Understanding Roman Inscriptions*. Baltimore: Johns Hopkins University Press.

Keppie, Lawrence. 2009. *The Romans on the Bay of Naples: An Archaeological Guide*. Stroud: History Press.

Kilgallen, John J. 2007. "Luke Wrote to Rome—a Suggestion." *Biblica* 88:251–55.

de Kleijn, Maurice, Rens de Hond, and Oscar Martinez-Rubi. 2016. "A 3D Spatial Data Infrastructure for Mapping the Via Appia." *Digital Applications in Archaeology and Cultural Heritage* 3:23–32. https://doi.org/10.1016/j.daach.2016.03.001.

Knowling, Richard John. 1903. "The Acts of the Apostles." Pages 3–554 in vol. 2 of *Expositor's Greek Testament*. Edited by W. Robertson Nicoll. New York: Doran.

Knox, Wilfred L. 1948. *The Acts of the Apostles*. Cambridge: Cambridge University Press.

Kolb, Anne. 2015. "Communication and Mobility in the Roman Empire." Pages 649–70 in *The Oxford Handbook of Roman Epigraphy*. Edited by Christopher Bruun and Jonathan Edmondson. Oxford: Oxford University Press.

Kolb, Anne. 2016. "*Mansiones* and *Cursus Publicus* in the Roman Empire." Pages 3–8 in *Statio amoena: Sostare e vivere lungo le strade romane*. Edited by Patrizia Basso and Enrico Zanini. Oxford: Archaeopress.

Kolb, Anne. 2019. "Via ducta–Roman Road Building: An Introduction to Its Significance, the Sources and the State of Research." Pages 3–21 in *Roman Roads: New Evidence–New Perspectives*. Edited by Anne Kolb. Berlin: de Gruyter. https://doi.org/10.1515/9783110638332-002.

La Blanchère, René de. 1888. "La poste sur la voie Appienne de Rome à Capoue." *Mélanges de l'école française de Rome* 8:54–68. https://doi.org/10.3406/mefr.1888.6536.

Lacam, Jean-Claude. 2016. "Fundi (Fondi): Introduction." Pages 7–17 in *Fana, templa, delubra: Corpus dei luoghi di culto dell'Italia antica (FTD) – 4; Regio I; Fondi, Formia, Minturno, Ponza*. Edited by Cristina Ferrante, Jean-Claude Lacam, and Daniela Quadrino. New ed. Paris: Collège de France. https://books.openedition.org/cdf/4230.

Lacam, Jean-Claude, and Daniela Quadrino. 2016. "Itri: Gola di S. Andrea; *Apollinis (?) templum/oratorium*." Pages 30–34 in *Fana, templa, delubra: Corpus dei luoghi di culto dell'Italia antica (FTD) – 4; Regio I; Fondi, Formia, Minturno, Ponza*. Edited by Cristina Ferrante, Jean-Claude Lacam, and Daniela Quadrino. New ed. Paris: Collège de France. https://books.openedition.org/cdf/4241.

Lacam, Jean-Claude, and Alessandro Vella. 2016. "Formiae (Formia): Introduction." Pages 47–57 in *Fana, templa, delubra: Corpus dei luoghi di culto dell'Italia antica (FTD) – 4; Regio I; Fondi, Formia, Minturno, Ponza*. Edited by Cristina Ferrante, Jean-Claude Lacam, and Daniela Quadrino. New ed. Paris: Collège de France. https://books.openedition.org/cdf/4248.

Laing, Gordon J. 1908. "Roman Milestones and the Capita Viarum." *Transactions and Proceedings of the American Philological Association* 39:15–34. https://doi.org/10.2307/282673.

Lake, Kirsopp, and Henry J. Cadbury. 1933. *Commentary*. Vol. 4 of *The Beginnings of Christianity, Part I: The Acts of the Apostles*. Edited by F. J. Foakes Jackson and Kirsopp Lake. London: T&T Clark.

Lampe, Peter. 2003. *From Paul to Valentinus: Christians at Rome in the First Two Centuries*. Minneapolis: Fortress.

Lanciani, Rodolfo. 1907. *Storia degli Scavi di Roma e notizie intorno le collezioni romane di antichità*. Vol. 3. Rome: Loescher.

Laney, J. Carl. 2019. "Paul's Journey to Rome." Pages 411–29 in *Lexham Geographic Commentary on Acts through Revelation*. Edited by Barry J. Beitzel. Bellingham, WA: Lexham Press.

Laurence, Ray. 1999. *The Roads of Roman Italy: Mobility and Cultural Change*. London: Routledge.

Laurence, Ray. 2020. "Ostia between Rome and the World." Pages 57–63 in *Life and Death in a Multicultural Harbour City: Ostia Antica from the Republic through Late Antiquity*. Edited by Arja Karavieri. Rome: Institutum Romanum Finlandiae.

Lawrence, Paul. 2006. *IVP Atlas of Bible History*. Downers Grove, IL: IVP Academic.

Le Pera Buranelli, Susanna, and Rita Turchetti. 2003. *Sulla Via Appia da Roma a Brindisi: Le fotografie di Thomas Ashby 1891–1925*. Rome: Bretschneider.

Lendering, Jona. 2018. "Praetorian prefect." https://www.livius.org/articles/concept/praetorian-prefect/.

Leonard, W. 1961. "From Malta to the Seven Hills: St. Paul's Arrival in Rome." *Australian Catholic Record* 38:23–32.

Leoni, Umberto, and Giovanni Staderini. 1907. *On the Appian Way: A Walk from Rome to Albano*. Rome: Bemporad.

Libertini, Giacinto, ed. 2019. *Liber Colonarium (The Book of Colonies)*. Frattamaggiore: Institute of Atellan Studies.

Lightfoot, J. B. 1873. *Saint Paul's Epistle to the Philippians: A Revised Text and Introduction Notes, and Dissertations*. London: Macmillan.

Ling, Roger. 1970. "The San Vito Tomb at Pozzuoli." *Papers of the British School at Rome* 38:153–82. https://doi.org/10.1017/S0068246200011235.

Lipsius, Richard A. 1891. *Acta apostolorum apocrypha*. Vol. 1. Leipzig: Mendelssohn.

Liverani, Paolo, and Jan Stubbe Østergaard. 2013. "Caligula: Notes and an Hypothesis on the Context." http://www.digitalsculpture.org/papers/liverani/liverani_paper.html.

Livy, 1919. *History of Rome, Volume I: Books 1–2*. Translated by B. O. Foster. Loeb Classical Library. Cambridge, MA: Harvard University Press.

Livy. 1924. *History of Rome, Volume III: Books 5–7*. Translated by B. O. Foster. Loeb Classical Library. Cambridge, MA: Harvard University Press.

Livy. 1926. *History of Rome, Volume IV: Books 8–10*. Translated by B. O. Foster. Loeb Classical Library. Cambridge, MA: Harvard University Press.

Livy. 1938. *History of Rome, Volume XII: Books 40–42*. Translated by Evan T. Sage, Alfred C. Schlesinger. Loeb Classical Library. Cambridge, MA: Harvard University Press.

Livy. 2017. *History of Rome, Volume IX: Books 31–34*. Edited and translated by J. C. Yardley. Introduction by Dexter Hoyos. Loeb Classical Library. Cambridge, MA: Harvard University Press.

Livy. 2020a. *History of Rome, Volume VI: Books 23–25*. Edited and translated by J. C. Yardley. Loeb Classical Library. Cambridge, MA: Harvard University Press.

Livy. 2020b. *History of Rome, Volume VII: Books 26–27*. Edited and translated by J. C. Yardley. Loeb Classical Library. Cambridge, MA: Harvard University Press.

Lookadoo, Jonathon. 2021. *The Shepherd of Hermas: A Literary, Historical, and Theological Handbook*. London: T&T Clark.

Lucian. 1905. *Works of Lucian of Samosta*. Translated by H. W. Fowler and F. G. Fowler. Oxford: Clarendon.

Maglio, Emma. 2016. "Il 'luogo detto Acquataccio sopra la Via Appia': Usi e riusi dei luoghi dell'accoglienza nel suburbio romano (XVII–XIX secolo)." *Citta e Storia* 11:339–61. https://doi.org/10.17426/84834.

Malizia, Rosario. 1988. "Il percorso urbano dell'Appia traianea." Pages 73–86 in *La via Appia a Terracina: La strada romana e i suoi monumenti*. Edited by Anna Rita Mari, Rosario Malizia, Pietro Longa, and M. Iride Pasquali. Terracina: Comune di Terracina; Archaeoclub d'Italia.

Malizia, Rosario. 2017. *Lungo L'Appia a Terracina nel 1789: Sulle tracce del viaggio di Orazio*. Terracina: Bookart.

Malizia, Rosario. 2020. "L'identificazione del tetrastilo di Tiberio e Livia nel Foro Emiliano di Terracina." Pages 15–32 in *Vitam Inpendere Iusto: Studi in onore di Antonio Di Fazio per il suo 80esimo compleanno*. Edited by Massimiliano Di Fazio and Pier Giacomo Sottoriva. Rome: n.p.

Martial. 1897. *The Epigrams of Martial*. Translated by Henry G. Bohn. London: Bell & Sons.

Marucchi, Orazio. 1903. *Le Memorie degli Apostoli Pietro e Paolo in Roma*. Rome: Federico Pustet.

McKay, Alexander G. 1962. *Naples and Campania: Texts and Illustrations, with Introductions, Bibliography, and Index*. Exeter, NH: Vergilian Society of America.

Mecham, F. A. 1973. "And So We Came to Rome." *Australian Catholic Record* 50:170–73.

Meiggs, Russell. 1973. *Roman Ostia*. 2nd ed. Oxford: Clarendon.

Meijer, Fik. 2000. *Paulus' zeereis naar Rome: Een reconstructive*. Amsterdam: Athenaeum-Polak & Van Gennep.

Melillo Faenza, Luigia, Danila Jacazzi, and Pasquale Argenziano. 2009. "Il sito di San Lorenzo ad Septimum sulla Via Campana: Permanenze sincroniche e modificazioni diacroniche." Pages 211–52 in *Le Vie dei Mercanti: Cielo dal Mediterraneo all'Oriente; Atti del Sesto Forum Internazionale di Studi, Caserta, Capri 5–7 Giugno 2008*. Edited by Carmine Gambardella. Naples: Edizioni Scientifiche Italiane.

Metzger, Bruce M. 1975. *A Textual Commentary on the Greek New Testament*. 2nd ed. New York: United Bible Societies.

Meyer, Eduard. 1915. "Die Götter Rediculus und Tutanus." *Hermes* 50.1:151–54.

Millar, Fergus. 2004. *Government, Society and Culture in the Roman Empire*. Vol. 2 of *Rome, the Greek World, and the East*. Edited by Hannah M. Cotton and Guy M. Rogers. Chapel Hill: University of North Carolina Press.

Miniero, Paola. 2006. *Baia: The Castle, Museum, and Archaeological Sites*. Naples: Electra.

Mitchell, Stephen. 1976. "Requisitioned Transport in the Roman Empire: A New Inscription from Pisidia." *Journal of Roman Studies* 66:106–31. https://doi.org/10.2307/299783.

Mommsen, Theodore, and Adolf von Harnack. 1895. "Zu Apostelgesch. 28,16 (Στρατοπεδάρχης = Princeps peregrinorum)." *Sitzungsberichte der Königlich Preußischen Akademie der Wissenschaften zu Berlin* 1:491–503.

Morton, H. V. 1936. *In the Steps of St. Paul*. New York: Dodd, Mead & Co.

Mounce, William D. 2000. *Pastoral Epistles*. Word Biblical Commentary 46. Dallas: Word.

Mueller, K. O. 1880. *Sexti Pompei Festi de verborum, significatione*. Leipzig: Weidmann.

Netzer, Ehud. 2008. *The Architecture of Herod, the Great Builder*. Grand Rapids: Baker Academic.

Nicolai, Nicola Maria. 1800. *De'bonificamenti delle Terre Pontine libri IV: Opera storica, critica, legale, economica, idrostatica*. Rome: Pagliarini.

Nixey, Catherine. 2020. "Pliny the Younger's Journey to Asia Minor." *BBC World Histories Magazine* 24. https://www.scribd.com/article/477458309/Pliny-The-Younger-s-Journey-To-Asia-Minor.

O'Connor, Colin. 1993. *Roman Bridges*. Cambridge: Cambridge University Press.

Ostrow, Steven E. 1976. "The Topography of Puteoli and Baiae on the Eight Glass Flasks." *Puteoli, studi di storia antica* 3:77–140.

Owens, E. J. 2012. "Roads, Roman Republic." Pages 5857–60 in *The Encyclopedia of Ancient History*. Edited by Roger S. Bagnall et al. 13 vols. Chichester: Wiley-Blackwell. https://doi.org/10.1002/9781444338386.wbeah20116.

Pagano, Mario. 1978. "Note su una località della Via Appia fra Sinuessa e Capua: Il 'Pons Campanus.'" *Rendiconti della Accademia di Archeologia, Lettere e Belle Arti* 53:227–34.

Pagano, Mario. 1991–1992. "La Via Appia fra Sinuessa e Capua alla luce di un nuovo miliario." *Rendiconti della Accademia di Archeologia: Lettere e Belle Arti* 63:109–24.

Pagano, Mario. 1995. "Nuove osservazioni sulle colonie romane di Minturnae e Sinuessa." *Rendiconti della Accademia di Archeologia: Lettere e Belle Arti* 65:51–71.

Pancotti, Andrea. 2019. "Castrimoenium Ritrovata." Pages 77–89 in *Alle pendici dei colli Albani: Dinamiche insediative e cultura materiale ai confini con Roma*. Edited by Agnese Livia Fischetti and Peter Attema. Groningen: Groningen Institute of Archaeology.

Parisi, Giovanni. 1959. *La prima dimora di San Paolo a Roma*. Torino: Carteggio.

Pennetta, Micla, Corrado Stanislao, Veronica D'Ambrosio, Fabio Marchese, Carmine Minopoli, Alfredo Trocciola, Renata Valente, and Carlo Donadio. 2016. "Geomorphological Features of the Archaeological Marine Area of Sinuessa in Campania, Southern Italy." *Quaternary International* 425:198–213. https://doi.org/10.1016/j.quaint.2016.04.019.

Pennetta, Micla, and Alfredo Trocciola, eds. 2017. *Sinuessa, un approdo sommerso di epoca Romana: Archeologia, geomorfologia costiera, strategie sostenibili di valorizzazione*. Rome: ENEA.

Peterson, John. 2015. "Modelling Roman Surveying in the Pontine Plain." Pages 445–49 in *1st International Conference on Metrology for Archaeology Benevento, Italy, 22–23 October 2015*. Benevento: n.p.

Petrucci, Francesco. 2007. "Il *Clivus Aricinum* o 'Sostruzione' dell'Appia Antica." *Annali Aricino-Nemorense* 1:52–57.

Petrucci, Francesco. 2019. "Il Mausoleo di Marco Azio Balbo più noto come 'Sepolcro degli Orazi e Curiazi.'" *Lazio ieri e oggi* 55.625:161–77.

Petrucci, Francesco. 2021. "Ariccia: Riemergono resti del Forum Aricinum sull'Appia Antica." *Palazzo Chigi Ariccia News,* January 22, 2021. https://www.palazzochigiariccia.it/ariccia-riemergono-resti-del-forum-aricinum-sullappia-antica/.

Piranesi, Giovanni Battista. 1757. *Le antichità Romane.* Vol. 2. Rome: Rotilj.

Pliny the Elder. 1855. *The Natural History.* Translated by John Bostock and H. T. Riley. London: Bohn.

Pliny the Younger. 1969. *Letters, Volume I: Books 1–7.* Translated by Betty Radice. Loeb Classical Library. Cambridge, MA: Harvard University Press.

Plutarch. 1917. *Lives, Volume V: Agesilaus and Pompey. Pelopidas and Marcellus.* Translated by Bernadotte Perrin. Loeb Classical Library. Cambridge, MA: Harvard University Press.

Plutarch. 1918. *Lives, Volume VI: Dion and Brutus. Timoleon and Aemilius Paulus.* Translated by Bernadotte Perrin. Loeb Classical Library. Cambridge, MA: Harvard University Press.

Plutarch. 1919. *Lives, Volume VII: Demosthenes and Cicero. Alexander and Caesar.* Translated by Bernadotte Perrin. Loeb Classical Library. Cambridge, MA: Harvard University Press.

Pobjoy, Mark. 1997. "A New Reading of the Mosaic Inscription in the Temple of Diana Tifatina." *Papers of the British School at Rome* 65:59–88. https://doi.org/10.1017/S0068246200010588.

Polybius. 2010. *The Histories, Volume II: Books 3–4.* Translated by W. R. Paton. Revised by F. W. Walbank and Christian Habicht. Loeb Classical Library. Cambridge, MA: Harvard University Press.

Popkin, Maggie L. 2018. "Urban Images in Glass from the Late Roman Empire: The Souvenir Flasks of Puteoli and Baiae." *American Journal of Archaeology* 122.3:427–61. https://doi.org/10.3764/aja.122.3.0427.

Pritchard, James B. 2010. *HarperCollins Atlas of Bible History.* New York: HarperCollins.

Quilici, Lorenzo. 1989a. *Via Appia: Da Porta Capena ai Colli Albani.* Rome: Palombi.

Quilici, Lorenzo. 1989b. *Via Appia: Dalla Pianura Pontina a Brindisi.* Rome: Palombi.

Quilici, Lorenzo. 1991. "Il Ponte di Mele sulla Via Appia." *Archeologia Classica* 43:317–27.

Quilici, Lorenzo. 2003. "Il tempio di Apollo ad clivum Fundanum sulla via Appia al valico di Itri." Pages 127–76 in *Santuari e luoghi di culto nell'Italia antica.* By Lorenzo Quilici and Stefania Quilici Gigli. Atlante Tematico di Topografia Antica 12. Rome: Bretschneider.

Quilici, Lorenzo. 2009. "Land Transport, Part 1: Roads and Bridges." Pages 551–79 in *The Oxford Handbook of Engineering and Technology in the Classical World.* Edited by John Peter Oleson. Oxford: Oxford University. https://doi.org/10.1093/oxfordhb/9780199734856.013.0023.

Quilici, Lorenzo, and Stefania Quilici Gigli. 2013. "Fondi: La romanizzazione della città e del territorio." *Orizzonti: Rassegna di Archeologia* 14:51–60.

Quilici Gigli, Stefania. 2020a. "La Blanchère e il tema del 'drainage profond des campagnes latines.'" Pages 115–30 in *Marie-René de La Blanchère: Dalle terre pontine all'Africa Romana.* Edited by Stéphane Bourdin and Alessandro Pagliara. Rome: Publications de l'École française de Rome. http://books.openedition.org/efr/5971.

Quilici Gigli, Stefania. 2020b. "La via Appia nella Campania. settentrionale Apporti dalle immagini aeree e satellitari." *Archeologia Aerea* 14:83–92.

Quilici Gigli, Stefania. 2022. "La Via Appia nella Campania settentrionale, suoi principali allacciamenti e diramazioni." *Orizzonti: Rassegna Di Archeologia* 23:193–205.

Rackham, R. B. 1919. *The Acts of the Apostles: An Exposition.* London: Methuen.

Rainey, Anson F., and R. Steven Notley. 2006. *The Sacred Bridge: Carta's Atlas of the Biblical World.* Jerusalem: Carta.

Ramsay, William M. 1895. *St. Paul the Traveller and Roman Citizen*. London: Hodder & Stoughton.
Ramsay, William M. 1910. *Pictures of the Apostolic Church: Studies in the Book of Acts*. London: Hodder & Stoughton.
Rapske, Brian. 1994. *The Book of Acts and Paul in Roman Custody*. Vol. 3 of *The Book of Acts in Its First Century Setting*. Edited by Bruce W. Winter. Grand Rapids: Eerdmans.
Rasmussen, Carl. 2010. *Zondervan Atlas of the Bible*. Rev. ed. Grand Rapids: Zondervan.
Rendall, Frederic. 1897. *The Acts of the Apostles in Greek and English*. London: Macmillan.
Richardson, John. 1976. *Roman Provincial Administration, 227 BC to AD 117*. London: Bristol Classical Press.
Richardson, Lawrence, Jr. 1976. "Formiae." Page 334 in *The Princeton Encyclopedia of Classical Sites*. Edited by Richard Stillwell. Princeton: Princeton University Press.
Richardson, Lawrence, Jr. 1992. *A New Topographical Dictionary of Ancient Rome*. Baltimore: Johns Hopkins University Press.
Richmond, I. A. 1927. "The Relation of the Praetorian Camp to Aurelian's Wall of Rome." *Papers of the British School at Rome* 10:12–22. https://doi.org/10.1017/S0068246200005742.
Richmond, I. A. 1933. "Commemorative Arches and City Gates in the Augustan Age." *Journal of Roman Studies* 23:149–74. https://doi.org/10.2307/297243.
Rizzi-Zannoni, Giovanni. 1793. *Topografia dell'Agro Napoletano con le sue adjacenze*. Naples: Rizzi-Zannoni. https://davidrumsey.georeferencer.com/maps/0dca96ab-cbd7-4569-bbcd-d96f9556d44c/view.
Ruebel, James S. 1979. "The Trial of Milo in 52 B.C.: A Chronological Study." *Transactions of the American Philological Association* 109:231–49. https://doi.org/10.2307/284060.
Ruegg, Bro. S. Dominic. 1983. "The Underwater Excavation in the Garigliano River: Final Report 1982; The Roman Port and

Bridge at Minturnae, Italy." *International Journal of Nautical Archaeology and Underwater Excavation* 12:203–18. https://doi.org/10.1111/j.1095-9270.1983.tb00136.x.

Ruggi D'Aragona, Maria Grazia, and Sergio Cascella. 2017. "L'area archeologica urbana." Pages 29–32 in *Sinuessa, un approdo sommerso di epoca Romana: Archeologia, geomorfologia costiera, strategie sostenibili di valorizzazione*. Edited by Micla Pennetta and Alfredo Trocciola. Rome: ENEA.

Ruggi D'Aragona, Maria Grazia, and Maria Ester Castaldo. 2007. "Mondragone, località Triglione: Indagini lungo la via Appia." Pages 35–44, 324 in *In itinere: Ricerche di archeologia in Campania; Atti del I e del II ciclo di conferenze di ricerca archeologica nell'Alto Casertano*. Edited by Francesco Sirano. Caserta: Lavieri.

Rumiz, Paolo. 2017. *Appia*. Rome: Feltrinelli.

Saylor, Steven. 1996. *A Murder on the Appian Way*. New York: St. Martin's Press.

Scagnetti, Franciscus, and Joseph Grande. 1986. *Roma Urbs Imperatorum Aetate*. 2nd ed. Rome: ME di Maggiore Cristina.

Schellenberg, Ryan S. 2011. "'Danger in the Wilderness, Danger at Sea': Paul and the Perils of Travel." Pages 141–61 in *Travel and Religion in Antiquity*. Edited by Philip A. Harland. Waterloo, ON: Wilfrid Laurier University Press.

Schmisek, Brian. 2017. *The Rome of Peter and Paul: A Pilgrim's Handbook to New Testament Sites in the Eternal City*. Eugene, OR: Pickwick.

Schnabel, Eckhard J. 2012. *Acts*. Zondervan Exegetical Commentary on the New Testament. Grand Rapids: Zondervan.

Schnabel, Eckhard J. 2019. "Paul as a Prisoner in Judea and Rome." Pages 398–410 in *Lexham Geographic Commentary on Acts through Revelation*. Edited by Barry J. Beitzel. Bellingham, WA: Lexham.

Seneca. 1917. *Epistles, Volume I: Epistles 1–65*. Translated by Richard M. Gummere. Loeb Classical Library. Cambridge, MA: Harvard University Press.

Severini, Francesca. 2001. *Via Appia–II: Da Bovillae a Cisterna di Latina*. Antiche Strade, Lazio. Rome: Libreria dello Stato.

Shackleton Bailey, D. R., ed. and trans. 1993. *Martial, Epigrams*. Vol. 1. Loeb Classical Library. Cambridge, MA: Harvard University Press.

Sherwin-White, A. N. 1963. *Roman Law and Roman Society in the New Testament*. Oxford: Clarendon.

Sherwood, Andrew N., Milorad Nikolic, John W. Humphrey, and John P. Oleson. 2020. *Greek and Roman Technology: A Sourcebook of Translated Greek and Roman Texts*. 2nd ed. London: Routledge.

Short, William. 1789. "To Thomas Jefferson from William Short, 11 February 1789." Founders Online, National Archives. Accessed October 30, 2022. https://founders.archives.gov/documents/Jefferson/01-14-02-0303.

Smith, Christopher. 2020. "Urban Networks in Latium." *Journal of Urban Archaeology* 1:85–97. https://doi.org/10.1484/J.JUA.5.120911.

Speidel, Michael P. 1982/1983. "The Roman Army in Judaea under the Procurators: The Italian and the Augustan Cohort in the Acts of the Apostles." *Ancient Society* 13/14:233–40.

Spera, Lucrezia, and Sergio Mineo. 2004. *Via Appia–I: Da Romam a Bovillae*. Antiche Strade. Rome: Libreria dello Stato.

Staccioli, Romolo Augusto. 2003. *The Roads of the Romans*. Los Angeles: Getty Museum.

Statius. 2015. *Silvae*. Edited and translated by D. R. Shackleton Bailey. Revised by Christopher A. Parrott. Loeb Classical Library. Cambridge, MA: Harvard University Press.

Stefanile, Michele. 2015. "The Project PILAE, for an Inventory of the Submerged Roman Piers: A Preliminary Overview." *International Journal of Environment and Geoinformatics* 2.3:34–39. https://doi.org/10.30897/ijegeo.303559.

Stothard, Peter. 2012. *Spartacus Road: A Personal Journey through Ancient Italy*. New York: Overlook.

Strabo. 1923. *Geography, Volume II: Books 3–5*. Translated by Horace Leonard Jones. Loeb Classical Library. Cambridge, MA: Harvard University Press.

Suetonius. 1914a. *Lives of the Caesars, Volume I: Julius. Augustus. Tiberius. Gaius. Caligula*. Translated by J. C. Rolfe. Introduction by K.

R. Bradley. Loeb Classical Library. Cambridge, MA: Harvard University Press.

Suetonius. 1914b. *Lives of the Caesars, Volume II: Claudius. Nero. Galba, Otho, and Vitellius. Vespasian. Titus, Domitian. Lives of Illustrious Men: Grammarians and Rhetoricians. Poets (Terence. Virgil. Horace. Tibullus. Persius. Lucan). Lives of Pliny the Elder and Passienus Crispus*. Translated by J. C. Rolfe. Loeb Classical Library. Cambridge, MA: Harvard University Press.

Sumner, G. V. 1966. "Cicero, Pompeius, and Rullus." *Transactions and Proceedings of the American Philological Association* 97:569–82. https://doi.org/10.2307/2936030.

Swanson, Reuben. 1998. *New Testament Greek Manuscript: Variant Readings Arranged in Horizontal Lines against Codex Vaticanus; The Acts of the Apostles*. Sheffield: Sheffield Academic Press; Pasadena, CA: William Carey International University Press.

Talbert, Richard J. A., ed. 2000. *Barrington Atlas of the Greek and Roman World*. Princeton: Princeton University Press.

Talbert, Richard J. A. 2010. *Rome's World: The Peutinger Map Reconsidered*. Cambridge: Cambridge University Press.

Tallini, Marco, A. Di Leo, C. Rossetti, and F. Berardi. 2013. "The Sacred Almone River of the Appian Way Regional Park in Rome: Ancient Myths, a Ritual Link between Rome and Asia Minor and Water Uses in the Modern Age." *Water Supply* 13.3:727–34. https://doi.org/10.2166/ws.2013.098.

Tannehill, Robert C. 1990. *The Narrative Unity of Luke-Acts*. 2 vols. Minneapolis: Fortress.

Thompson, Glen L. 2005. "Constantius II and the First Removal of the Altar of Victory." Pages 85–106 in *A Tall Order: Writing the Social History of the Ancient World; Essays in Honor of William V. Harris*. Edited by Jean-Jacques Aubert and Zsuzsanna Várhelyi. Munich: Saur.

Thompson, Glen L., and Mark Wilson. 2016. "Paul's Walk to Assos: A Hodological Inquiry into Its Geography, Archaeology, and Purpose." Pages 269–313 in *Stones, Bones and the Sacred: Essays on Material Culture and Ancient Religion in Honor of Dennis E.*

Smith. Edited by Alan Cadwallader. Early Christianity and Its Literature. Atlanta: SBL Press.

van Tilburg, Cornelius. 2007. *Traffic and Congestion in the Roman Empire*. London: Routledge.

Tol, Gijs, and Barbara Borgers. 2016. "An Integrated Approach to the Study of Local Production and Exchange in the Lower Pontine Plain." *Journal of Roman Archaeology* 29:349–70. https://doi.org/10.1017/S1047759400072172.

Tol, Gijs, Tymon de Haas, and Carmela Anastasia. 2019. "Il ruolo dei centri minori nell'economia romana: Una panoramica dei risultati delle indagini archeologiche nei diti di Forum Appii ed Ad Medias." Pages 29–42 in *Alle pendici dei Colli Albani: Dinamiche insediative e cultura materiale ai confini con Roma*. Edited by Agnes Livia Fischetti and Peter Attema. Groningen Archaeological Studies 35. Eelde: Barkhuis. https://doi.org/10.2307/j.ctv13nb6j7.7.

Treggiari, Susan. 1975. "Family Life among the Staff of the Volusii." *Transactions of the American Philological Association* 105: 393–401. https://doi.org/10.2307/283951.

Uggeri, Giovanni. 1990. "La via Appia nella politica espansionistica di Roma." Pages 21–28 in *La Via Appia: Atti del X Incontro di studio del Comitato per l'archeologia laziale*. Edited by Stefania Quilici Gigli. Archeologia laziale 10.1. Rome: Consiglio Nazionale delle Richerche.

UNESCO World Heritage Convention. 2006a. "Bradyseism in the Flegrea Area." Tentative Lists. UNESCO World Heritage Convention. Submitted June 1, 2006. Accessed October 30, 2022. https://whc.unesco.org/en/tentativelists/2030/.

UNESCO World Heritage Convention. 2006b. "Via Appia 'Regina Viarum.'" Tentative Lists. UNESCO World Heritage Convention. Submitted June 1, 2006. Accessed November 3, 2022. https://whc.unesco.org/en/tentativelists/349/.

Urbini, Stefano, Bottari Carla, Marco Marchetti, and Lili Cafarella. 2010. "The Tres Tabernae Archeological Site (Cisterna Di Latina, Italy): New Evidence Revealed through an Integrated

Geophysical Investigation." *Annals of Geophysics* 53.5–6:43–49. https://doi.org/10.4401/ag-4775.

Velestino, Daniela. 2015. *La Galleria Lapidaria dei Musei Capitolini.* Rome: De Luca.

Ventre, Francesca. 2004. "From the Pontine Plain to Benevento." Pages 106–45 in *The Appian Way: From Its Foundation to the Middle Ages.* Edited by Ivana Della Portella. Los Angeles: Getty Museum.

Vincenti, Maria Cristina. 2007. "Il XVI miliario della Via Appia." *Annali Aricino-Nemorense* 1:93–94.

Vincenti, Maria Cristina. 2017. "L'Appia Antica ad Ariccia: Contesti e rinvenimenti," *Gazzetta Ambiente: Appia Antica, l'ambiente e il paesaggio attraverso la storia dei luoghi* 23:143–58.

Virgil. 1916. *Eclogues. Georgics. Aeneid: Books 1–6.* Translated by H. Rushton Fairclough. Revised by G. P. Goold. Loeb Classical Library. Cambridge, MA: Harvard University Press.

Virgil. 1918. *Aeneid: Books 7–12. Appendix Vergiliana.* Translated by H. Rushton Fairclough. Revised by G. P. Goold. Loeb Classical Library. Cambridge, MA: Harvard University Press.

Vistoli, Fabrizio. 2013. *Saggio bibliografico sull'antica via Appia.* Rome: Società Magna Grecia.

Vitruvius. 1914. *The Ten Books on Architecture.* Translated by Morris H. Morgan. Cambridge, MA: Harvard University Press.

Volpe, Rita. 2014. "Sepolcro degli Scipioni." *Bullettino della Commissione Arceologica Comunale di Roma* 115:175–91.

Walker, Peter. 2008. *In the Steps of Paul.* Grand Rapids: Zondervan.

Wallace-Hadrill, Andrew. 1994. *Houses and Society in Pompeii and Herculaneum.* Princeton: Princeton University Press.

Wansink, Craig. 1996. *Chained in Christ: The Experience and Rhetoric of Paul's Imprisonments.* Journal for the Study of the New Testament Supplements 130. Sheffield: Sheffield Academic.

Wieseler, Karl Georg. 1848. *Chronologie des apostolischen Zeitalters bis zum Tode der Apostel Paulus und Petrus.* Göttingen: Vandenhoeck &Ruprecht.

Wilson, Mark. 2016. "The Lukan Periplus of Saint Paul's Third Journey with a Textual Conundrum in Acts 20:15." *Acta Theologica* 36:229–54.

Wilson, Mark. 2018a. "The Denouement of Claudian Pamphylia-Lycia and its Implications for the Audience of Galatians." *Novum Testamentum* 60.4, 337–60.

Wilson, Mark. 2018b. "Paul's Journeys in 3D: The Apostle as Ideal Ancient Traveller." *Journal of Early Christian History* 8:16–34. https://doi.org/10.1080/2222582X.2017.1411204.

Wilson, Mark. 2019a. "The Geography of Galatia." Pages 483–93 in *Lexham Geographic Commentary: Acts through Revelation*. Edited by Barry J. Beitzel. Bellingham, WA: Lexham Press.

Wilson, Mark. 2019b. "The Roman Road System around the Mediterranean." Pages 175–94 in *Lexham Geographic Commentary: Acts through Revelation*. Edited by Barry J. Beitzel. Bellingham, WA: Lexham Press.

Wilson, Mark. 2020a. "Eutychus in Troas: The Architecture and Archaeology of His Fall." *Biblica* 101:231–47. https://doi.org/10.2143/BIB.101.2.3288264.

Wilson, Mark. 2020b. *The Spirit Said Go: Lessons in Guidance from Paul's Journeys*. Rev. ed. Eugene, OR: Wipf & Stock.

Wilson, Mark. 2021. "Hindrance as a Motivation in Divine Guidance: The Example of Paul." *HTS Theological Studies* 77.4:a6097. https://doi.org/10.4102/hts.v77i4.6097.

Wilson, Mark. 2022a. "Luke's Use of a Departure-Arrival Formula in the Book of Acts." *Scriptura* 121.1:1–11. http://doi.org/10.7833/121-1-1999.

Wilson, Mark. 2022b. "Luke for Landlubbers: The Translation and Interpretation of ὑποπλέω in Acts 27." *Acta Theologica* 42.2:343–66.

Wiseman, T. P. 1970. "Republican Road Building." *Papers of the British School at Rome* 38:122–52. https://doi.org/10.1017/S0068246200011223.

Witherington, Ben, III. 1998. *The Acts of the Apostles: A Social-Rhetorical Commentary*. Grand Rapids: Eerdmans.

Zahn, Theodor. 1897. *Einleitung in das Neue Testament*. Vol. 1. Leipzig: Deichert.

Zannini, Ugo. 2007. "Miliaria, itineraria, archaeologia: La via Appia da Formiae a Sinuessa." Pages 55–84 in *La via Appia racconta … Risorse, Strategie, Proposte*. Edited by Anna Clara Valletrisco. Minturno: Caramanica.

Zannini, Ugo. 2014a. "Costruzione e lastricatura, gli itineraria picta et adnotata e le varianti della Via Appia nell'altomediocvo." *Civiltà aurunca* 30–31.95–98:119–34.

Zannini, Ugo. 2014b. "La Via Appia da Formiae al Pons Aufidi." *Civiltà aurunca* 30–31.95–98:39–102.

Zannini, Ugo, Luigi Scarpa, Clelia Cirillo, and Giovanna Acampora. 2012. "Changes to Route of the Appian Way in Northern Campania: Subsidence and Swamping of Coastal Areas." Poster presented at the 86th Congresso Nazionale della Società Geologica Italiana. Rome, 28–30 September 2012.

# Index of Bible Passages

## Matthew
24:1–28 ............................. 145

## Luke
20:17 ................................ 169

## Acts
1:8 ..................................... 175
10:9 .................................. 9n26
10:23 ..................... 3n8, 9n26
10:24 ............................... 9n26
11:12 .................................. 3n8
13:14 ................................... 23
14:1 ..................................... 23
17:4 ..................................... 23
18:1 ..................................... 23
19:1 ................................... 3n8
19:7 ................................... 3n8
19:8 .................................... 23
19:29 ..................................... 6
20:4 ............................... 3n9, 6
20:6 ............................... 5, 25
21:4 ............................... 5, 25
21:8–10 ................................ 5
21:33 .................................... 4
22:29–30 ............................. 4
22:29–24:21 ....................... 4
23:11 ........................... 26, 122
23:35 .................................... 1
24:23–24 ............................. 1
24:27 ................................. 1n3
25:6 .................................. 9n26
25:13 ................................... 2
25:23 ........................... 2, 9n26
25:26–27 ............................. 2
26:29 ................................ 4n11
26:32 ................................... 2
27–28 ...................... xvi–xvii
27:1 ..................................... 2
27:2 ................................... 3n9
27:3 ................................. 2, 5
27:5 .................................. 5n19
27:5–6 .................................. 5
27:8 ...................................... 6
27:9 ...................................... 6
27:10–11 .............................. 6
27:12–13 .............................. 6
27:13–44 .............................. 7
27:21–26 .............................. 7
27:24 .................................... 4
27:31–32 ............................. 4
27:33–37 .............................. 7
27:35 ............................. 122n21
27:42–43 ............................. 4
27:42–44 .............................. 7
27:44 .................................. 26
28:1–10 ................................ 7
28:11 .................................... 7
28:11–31 ............................ xx
28:12 .................................... 8
28:13 .................................... 9
28:13–14 ........................ 21n45
28:14 .................................... 5
28:15 .............. 25–26, 29, 121
28:16 .... 1n1, 179, 180–81, 186
28:23 ........................... 183–84
28:30 ................................ 184
28:30–31 ........................... 187
28:31 ................................. 188

## Romans
1:8 ............................... 122n21
1:11–15 ............................. 121
7:24 ................................... 153
8:39 ................................... 154
15:23 ................................. 121
15:24 ................................. 188
15:28 ................................. 188

## 1 Corinthians
6:9–10 ................................. 19

## 2 Corinthians
2:14 ................................... 145

## Philippians
1:7 ..................................... 4n11
1:12 ................................... 183
1:13 ...................... 183, 185, 187
2:25 ...................................... 6
4:15–19 ......................... 184n13
4:18 ...................................... 6
4:22 ................................... 187

## Colossians

4:10 ............................... 6n20

## 1 Thessalonians

4:3–5 ................................. 13

## 1 Timothy

6:9 ..................................... 13
6:17 ................................... 13

## 2 Timothy

1:15 ................................. 188

4:13–14 ........................... 188
4:16–17 ........................... 188
4:20 ................................. 188

## Philemon

24 .................................. 6n20

# Index of Ancient Sources

Acta Pauli .................................................. 186

Acts of Peter and Paul ....................... 19n41

Apocryphal Acts of Peter ....................... 19

Appian, *Civil Wars*
    1.14.120 ...................................................... 51
    3.41 ................................................... 167n51
    5.8.72 ........................................................ 16
    5.8.74 ........................................................ 16

Appian, *Punic Wars*
    9.66 ...................................................... 145n5

Apuleius, *Metamorphoses*
    11.16–17 ................................................... 7–8

Asconius, *Commentary on Cicero's For Milo* ................................................ 147n10

Athenaeus *Deipnosophists*
    1.27a ..................................................... 94n6
    12.36 ........................................................ 51

Aurelius Victor, *On the Caesars*
    1.6 ....................................................... 17–18

Caesar, *Gallic Wars*
    5.1 ............................................................ 80

Catullus, *Poems*
    34.9–13 .............................................. 139n21

Cicero, *Agrarian Law*
    2.76, 78, 85, 96 ........................................ 58
    2.86 ..................................................... 48–49
    3.16 ........................................................... 58

Cicero, *For Milo* ........................................ 147
    31 ............................................................ 146

Cicero, *For Plancius*
    10 .............................................................. 78

Cicero, *For Rabirius Postumus* ......... 159n38

Cicero, *Letters to Atticus* ............................ 18
    1.3.2 .......................................................... 84
    7.9.1 ........................................................ 163
    9.15.6–16.1 .............................................. 72
    16.10 ..................................................... 75n2
    16.13.1 ..................................................... 75

Cicero, *Letters to Quintus*
    3.7.1 ....................................................... 168

Cicero, *Philippics* ....................................... 84
    12.7 ........................................................... 49
    2.102 ........................................................ 57
    3.15–17 .................................................. 139

Cicero, *Tusculan Disputations*
    1.7 ........................................................... 173

*Corpus Inscriptionum Latinarum*
    12.21 .................................................... 49n32
    12.1004 .............................................. 117n14

| 12.1212 | 155 |
| 12.1719 | 97n13 |
| 4.1679 | 66 |
| 4.9983a | 21 |
| 6.830 | 164 |
| 6.975 | 175n68 |
| 6.1859 | 160 |
| 6.2246 | 159 |
| 6.4414 | 172n61 |
| 6.4416 | 172n61 |
| 6.4458 | 172n61 |
| 6.19483 | 160 |
| 6.24520 | 160 |
| 6.27959 | 158 |
| 10.3832 | 51 |
| 10.4727 | 67nn16–17 |
| 10.6305 | 107 |
| 10.6306 | 107 |
| 10.6812–13 | 170n57 |
| 10.6819 | 125 |
| 10.6820 | 125n1 |
| 10.6824 | 32n11 |
| 10.6825 | 121n16 |
| 10.6833 | 114n11 |
| 10.6835 | 114n11 |
| 10.6838 | 53 |
| 10.6846 | 111n5 |
| 10.6849 | 102 |
| 10.6854 | 98 |
| 10.6859 | 87n22 |
| 10.6861 | 87n22 |
| 10.6870 | 69n19 |
| 10.6941 | 53 |
| 10.6944 | 53 |
| 15.7239b–c | 179n2 |

Digest (of Justinian)

| 2.11.1 | 27 |
| 19.2.13 | 169 |

Dio Cassius, *History*

| 38.7.3 | 51 |
| 40.48–54 | 147n10 |
| 54.8.4 | 177n73 |
| 63.3.1 | 21 |
| 67.14.1 | 31 |

Diodorus Siculus, *Library*

| 14.16.5 | 104 |

Festus, *On the Meaning of Words*

| 3 | 67n17 |

Forma Urbis Romae ......................... 175

Gregory the Great, *Dialogues*

| 7.3 | 92 |

Herodotus, *Histories*

| 5.53 | 27n56 |

Homer, *Odyssey*

| 12.73–125 | 9 |

Horace, *Epistles*

| 1.1.83 | 13 |
| 1.11 | 196 |

Horace, *Odes*

| 4.2.50–52 | 145n5 |

Horace, *Satires*

| 1.5 | 66, 80, 110–11, 113, 118, 140, 195–96 |

Hyginus Gromaticus, *Agrimensores* ......................... 102n22

Inscriptiones Latinae Selectae

| 1.280 | 32n11 |
| 21.5819 | 170n57 |
| 21.6073 | 175n68 |
| 22.7213 | 167n51 |

Jerome, *Against Jovian*

| 1.26 | 174n65 |

# Index of Ancient Sources

Jerome, *Chronicon*
  B530 .................................................. 14n31

Jerome, *Commentary on Philemon* ...184n12

John Chrysostom, *Homilies on the Acts of the Apostles*
  53.1 ............................................................ 6

Josephus, *Antiquities of the Jews*
  17.330 ....................................................... 23
  332–338 ........................................ 23, 24n49
  18.6.4 ........................................................ 10
  18.6.5 .................................................. 183n11
  19.205 ......................................................... 9
  20.7.2 ....................................................... 1n2

Josephus, *Jewish War*
  2.101–104 ................................................. 23
  2.383, 386 ................................................. 18
  7.5.3–6 .................................................. 145n6

Juvenal, *Saturnalia*
  4.117–118 ............................................ 138n20

Liber colonarium ................................. 97n11

Livy, *History of Rome*
  1.24–26 ................................................... 143
  1.25.14 .................................................... 157
  1.44.3 ...................................................... 177
  4.59.4 ...................................................... 111
  6.5.7 ................................................... 167n51
  7.31.1 ....................................................... 48
  8.14.10 ............................................... 80, 95
  8.19 ........................................................... 95
  10.21.7–8 .................................................. 71
  10.23.12 .................................................. 167
  10.47.4 .................................................... 129
  19.15 ................................................... 168n53
  22.13–14 ................................................... 72
  22.15 ....................................................... 104
  25.12 ....................................................... 144
  25.40.1–3 ................................................ 177
  26.21.7 .................................................... 144
  33.23.3 ................................................ 144n4
  34.45 ......................................................... 15
  36.35 ................................................... 168n53
  38.28.3 .................................................... 167
  38.36.7–9 ........................................... 80, 95
  38.56.2–4 ................................................ 174
  39.44.6 ..................................................... 94
  40.51.2 .................................................... 101
  42.1 ........................................................... 50
  42.21.7 ................................................ 144n4

Lucan, *Civil War*
  6.73–75 ........................................... 138–39n21

Lucian, *Navigium*
  5 ................................................................ 17
  9 .................................................................. 7

Martial, *Epigrams*
  2.19 ..................................................... 138n20
  3.47 ......................................................... 177
  9.64 ......................................................... 152
  10.30.1, 11–15 .......................................... 81
  11.82 ......................................................... 69
  12.32.10 ............................................. 138n20
  13.19 ................................................... 139n21
  13.23 ....................................................... 119
  13.111 ....................................................... 66
  13.112 ..................................................... 119
  13.115 .................................................. 94n6

Optatus of Milevis, *Against the Donatists*
  1.24 .................................................... 127n4

Orosius, *History against the Pagans*
  5.9.4 ......................................................... 72

Ovid, *Fasti*
  4.259 ................................................. 168n53
  4.335–342 .......................................... 168n54
  6.59 ................................................ 138–39n21

Pausanias, *Description of Greece*
- 2.27.4–5 ................................. 138

Petronius, *Satyricon*
- 6–8 ........................................ 19

Philo, *On the Embassy to Gaius*
- 155–157 ................................ 186

Pliny the Elder, *Natural History*
- 2.47 .......................................... 7
- 3.6 .......................................... 26
- 3.9.5 ................................... 71–72
- 8.3 .......................................... 18
- 10.60.122 ........................ 164n45
- 14.8 ..................................... 31n7
- 14.8.2 ..................................... 66
- 14.8.61 ........................... 94, 119
- 16.76.3 ............................. 19–20
- 19.1.3 ...................................... 17
- 31.4.1 ..................................... 69
- 36.14.2 .................................... 17

Pliny the Younger, *Epistles*
- 10.15 .................................. 4n13
- 10.57 ................................ 180n4
- 10.64 ..................................... 24
- 10.120 .................................. 3n7

Plutarch, *Aemilius Paulus*
- 32.1–34.8 .......................... 145n5

Plutarch, *Caesar*
- 10 ........................................ 146
- 58.8–10 ................................. 30
- 58.10 ................................ 19–20

Plutarch, *Cicero*
- 28–29 .................................. 146
- 47.4–48.4 .............................. 84

Plutarch, *Marcellus*
- 22.1 ..................................... 144

Plutarch, *Marius*
- 37–40 ................................ 78n7

Polybius, *Histories*
- 3.91.2 .................................... 15

Procopius, *Wars*
- 5.14.6 .................................... 27

Res Gestae Divi Augusti
- 11 .................................... 177n72

Seneca the Elder, *Suasoriae*
- 6.18–20 ................................. 84

Seneca the Younger, *Letters*
- 5.7 .................................. 183n10
- 51.1–3 ................................... 13
- 57.1–2 .............................. 36–37
- 77.1–2 ................................... 19

Shepherd of Hermas
- 1.3 ..................................... 30n3
- 5.1 ..................................... 30n3

Sibylline Oracles ................. 157n32

Statius, *Silvae*
- 2.2.12 ............................... xviin8
- 3.1.55–60 ........................ 139n21
- 3.2.21–24 .............................. 18
- 4.3 ........................................ 32
- 5.1 ................................... 167n50

Strabo, *Geography*
- 5.3.5 ..................................... 75
- 5.3.6 ............... 76, 81, 94, 104, 112, 115
- 5.3.12 .................................. 138
- 5.4.3 ..................................... 58
- 5.4.6 ............................. 11–12, 15
- 5.4.7 ................................ 36–37
- 5.4.9 ..................................... 10

# Index of Ancient Sources

Suetonius, *Augustus*

| 1 | 104n26 |
| 4 | 139 |
| 37 | 53 |
| 98.2 | 10 |
| 100 | 147 |

Suetonius, *Claudius*

| 3 | 175 |
| 20.1–3 | 20 |
| 25.2 | 18, 107 |

Suetonius, *Gaius*

| 19 | 13 |
| 32 | 13 |

Suetonius, *Galba*

| 8 | 98 |

Suetonius, *Julius Caesar*

| 44.3 | 30 |

Suetonius, *Nero*

| 31.3–4 | 31 |

Suetonius, *Tiberius*

| 5.1 | 97 |
| 39 | 94n5 |
| 72 | 153 |

Suetonius, *Titus*

| 5 | 9 |

Suetonius, *Life of Terence*

| 5 | 168 |

Tacitus, *Annales*

| 2.41 | 147 |
| 3.2 | 105, 121n19 |
| 4.59 | 94 |
| 4.67.5 | 10 |
| 12.66 | 69 |
| 15.18.3 | 20 |
| 15.23 | 147 |
| 15.41 | 94 |

Tacitus, *Histories*

| 4.1–2 | 181 |
| 4.3 | 105 |
| 4.46 | 148n12 |

Varro, *On the Latin Language*

| 6.15 | 168n53 |

Vegetius, *On Military Matters*

| 4.39 | 6n21, 7 |

Velleius Paterculus, *Roman History*

| 1.14.2 | 76 |

Vergil, *Aeneid*

| 3.679–681 | 139n21 |
| 7.761–782 | 138 |
| 7.799–800 | 111 |
| 11.532–567 | 115 |

Vitruvius, *On Architecture* ........ 83

| 1.6.6–8 | 96n9 |
| 2.6.1 | 12 |

# Index of Modern Authors

Adams, Colin, xixn13
Addessi, Andrea, 88n24
Aglietti, Silvia, 146n9
Aharoni, Yigael, 189n1
Alföldi, Andrew, 138n21
Amalfitano, Paolo, 36n18
Anastasia, Carmela, 119–20
Aranegui, Carmen, 145n8
Arata, Francesco Paolo, 30n6, 31
Argenziano, Pasquale, xviii, 46
Armstrong, Kayt, 117, 118n15
Arthur, Paul, 66
Ashby, Thomas, xv, 33n13, 33n15, 138n19, 174n66, 180
Attanasio, Donato, 94n5
Attema, Peter, 117, 118n15
Aubert, Jean-Jacques, 23
Avi-Yonah, Michael, 189n1
Baillie Reynolds, P.K., 180
Baldanza, Angela, 88n24
Baldi, Lazzaro, 174n65
Ballance, M.H., 111n5
Barnes, Ian, 189
Barrett, C.K., 8, 24, 26n52, 27n55
Barret, David P., 189
Beard, Mary, 196n1
Beck, John A., 189n1
Beitzel, Barry J., 189
Bekker-Nielsen, Tønnes, 32n9
Bellini, Giovanna Rita, 77
Berardi, F., 168n54
Bodel, John, 19n40
Bock, Darrell L., 27n55
Bohn, Henry G., 66

Boon, Marjolein Helena van der, 150n17
Borgers, Barbara, 118n15
Brettman, Estelle Shohet, 163n43
Brookes, Alan C., 77
Bruce, F.F., 24, 121
Bruno, Matthias, 94n5
Bunbury, Edward Herbert, 128
Buonopane, Alfredo, 53n37
Cadbury, Henry J., 26
Cafarella, Lili, 128n8
Camodeca, Giuseppe, xviii, 18, 36n18
Cancellieri, Margherita, 110n3
Canina, Luigi, 156
Carbonara, Andrea, 98n15, 104n25, 117n14
Carla, Bottari, 128n8
Cascella, Sergio, xviii, 30n4, 72nn24–25, 76
Cassieri, Nicoletta, 129
Casson, Lionel, 5, 9, 17–18
Castaldo, Maria Ester, 67, 68n18
Cavacchioli, Marco, 150n16
Cevoli, Tsao, 35, 39
Chadwick, Henry, 163n42
Cioffi, Robert, xvin3
Cirillo, Clelia, 57, 62n7
Claridge, Amanda, 176, 177n75
Coarelli, Filippo, 158, 174n64, 177
Collins, J.J., 157n32
Cook, John Granger, 21, 22n47
Cooley, Alison E., 66n12, 117n13, 177n72
Cooley, M.G.L., 66n12
Coppola, Maria Rosaria, 104n25, 105n27
Coulston, Jon, 13, 102n18
Crogiez, Sylvie, 131n13
Cuntz, Otto, 62n5

Cupello, Katherine E., 159n38
Currid, John D., 189
Curtis, Adrian, 189n1
Dalby, Andrew, 121n18
D'Ambrosio, Veronica, 72
D'Arms, John H., 17, 20
Davis, Danny Lee, 6, 8, 17
De Carlo, Nicola, 41n23
De Caro, Stefano, 50–51, 55n1, 64n8, 67n17, 68, 71, 75n1
De Gaetano, Elizabeth, 20n44
de Haas, Tymon, 117, 118n15, 119–20
de Hond, Rens, 157n33,
de Kleijn, Maurice, 157n33
Della Portella, Ivana, xvn2
Della Valle, Chiara, 55n1
Dello Russo, Jessica, 163n43
Dessau, H., 171n58
Di Fazio, Clara, 96, 97n11
Di Fazio, Massimiliano, 111n4
Di Leo, A., 168n54
Di Rosa, Andrea, xviii–xix, 110n3
Dilke, O.A.W., 112
Dilke, Margaret S., 112
Diosono, Francesca, 146n9
Donadio, Carlo, 72
Dorcey, Peter F., 152
Dowley, Tim., 189n1
Dubbini, Rachele, 167
Duinker, Heleen Ellen, 164, 172n59
Dummett, Jeremy, 8
Dunn, James D., 24
Eastman, David L., 163n42, 188n29
Emmerson, Allison L.C., 35, 36n18, 52n34
Fee, Gordon D., 184n13, 187n25
Ferrante, Cristina, 79n10
Fiocchi Nicolai, Vincenzo, 128n7
Florescu, G., 137n18
Forbes, S. Russell, 187n22
Freier, Bruce W., 76n3, 76n5, 183n11, 184,
Gambash, Gil, xixn14
Garcea, Francesco, 20

Garland, David E., 117, 145n5
Gentile, Francesco, 21n45
Gialanella, Costanza, 20
Gowers, Emily, 140n23
Grande, Joseph, 175n68, 176n69
Grifa, Celestino, 20
Grunsfeld, Mary Jane, 53n39
Haenchen, Ernst, 122n20
Hamblin, Dora Jane, 53n39, 191
Harnack, Adolf von, 180n4
Haverfield, F., 137n18
Hawthorne, Gerald F., 6n20
Hemer, Colin J., 3n10
Hewson, Dave, 174n65
Hirschfeld, Amy, 163n43
Hohlfelder, Robert L., 5n16
Holden, Peregrine, 26n53
Houston, George W., 17n36
Hughes, Lisa A., 159n38
Huissen, Gerard, 102n21
Humm, Michel, 64n8, 88n24, 114n11
Humphrey, John W., 37n19
Ihm, Maximilianus, 79n11
Ilan, Tal, 158n37
Irving, Washington, 107n32
Jacazzi, Danila, 46
Jacobson, David M., 2n4
Johannowsky, Werner, 55n1, 62n7, 64n8, 67n17, 76,
Johnson, Luke Timothy, 5n18
Kaster, Robert, 83n16
Keener, Craig, 25n51
Keppie, Lawrence, 15, 177n73
Kilgallen, John J., 188n27
Knowling, Richard John, 180n4
Knox, Wilfred L., 187n24
Kolb, Anne, 24–25, 32n11, 35n17, 53n36, 195
La Blanchère, Marie-René de, 131n13
Lacam, Jean-Claude, 81n15, 92n4, 96n7
Laing, Gordon J., 53n38
Lake, Kirsopp, 26

# Index of Modern Authors

Lampe, Peter, 186
Lanciani, Rodolfo, 171n58, 185n15
Laney, Carl J., 190
Laurence, Ray, 17, 26, 101, 106n31, 107, 113n9
Lawrence, Paul, 189
Lendering, Jona, 182n7
Leonard, W., 18n39, 113n9
Leoni, Umberto, 158n35
Le Pera Buranelli, Susanna, 138n19
Libertini, Giacinto, xviii, 64n11, 80n12, 97n11, 110
Lightfoot, J.B., 179n1, 182
Ling, Roger, 38n20
Lipsius, Richard A., 186
Liverani, Paolo, 148n12
Lookadoo, Jonathon, 30n3
McKay, Alexander G., 20
Maglio, Emma, 167n50
Malizia, Rosario, 102n22, 105, 106n31, 111n4
Manetta, Consuelo, 146n9
Mar, Ricardo, 145n8
Marchese, Fabio, 72
Marchetti, Marco, 128n8
Martinez-Rubi, Oscar, 157n33
Marucchi, Orazio, 185
Mastrorilli, Daria, 79n10
Mecham, F.A., 26
Medri, Maura, 36n18
Meiggs, Russell, 20
Meijer, Fik, 29n1
Melillo Faenza, Luigia, 46
Melluziis, Nicola, 35, 39,
Messineo, Gaetano, 98n15, 104n25, 117
Metzger, Bruce, 3n9, 5n19, 24n50, 179n1, 186n21
Meyer, Eduard, 166n48
Millar, Fergus, 4, 25
Mineo, Sergio, 164
Miniero, Paola, 13n30
Minopoli, Carmine, 72
Mitchell, Stephen, 2, 25, 60
Mommsen, Theodore, 180n4, 181n5, 185
Morton, H.V., 15n33
Mounce, William D., 188n28
Mueller, K.O., 67n17
Netzer, Ehud, 1n1
Nicolai, Nicola Maria, 92n4, 115n12
Nikolic, Milorad, 37n19
Notley, Steven, 189
O'Connor, Colin, 57, 76n4, 111
Oleson, John P., 37n19
Østergaard, Jan Stubbe, 148n12
Ostrow, Steven E., 21
Owen, G., 137n18
Owens, E.J., 33nn14
Pagano, Mario, xviii, 63n8, 64, 69n19, 72n23, 75n1, 79, 106n30
Palladino, Alessia, 146n9
Pancotti, Andrea, 148n13
Parisi, Giovanni, 183n8, 184n12, 185, 186nn20–21
Pennetta, Micla, 72, 75n1
Peterson, John, 112n6
Petrucci, Francesco, xviii–xix, 137n18, 140n25, 143n2
Piranesi, Giovanni Battista, 138, 169
Pobjoy, Mark, 51
Popkin, Maggie L., 15, 16n35, 21n46
Poulsen, Birte, 146n9
Pritchard, James B., 189
Prochaska, Walter, 94n5
Proietti, Lucia Manuela, 20
Purcell, Nicholas, 26n53
Quadrino, Daniela, 92n4
Quilici, Lorenzo, 49n32, 57nn2–3, 72, 92n4, 96n8, 98n14, 111, 131–33, 137, 140, 150n16, 156nn29–30, 163n44, 164, 166n48, 177n74
Quilici Gigli, Stefania, 52n35, 53, 57, 62n7, 96n8, 98n14, 131n10
Rackham, R.B., 122
Rainey, Anson F., 189

Ramsay, William M., 24, 26, 180n4
Rapske, Brian, 4n12, 7
Rasmussen, Carl, 189
Rendall, Frederic, 180n4
Richardson, John, 3
Richardson, Lawrence, 81, 83, 167, 168n54, 174n64, 174n66, 175n68, 176n69, 176n71, 177n74, 179n2, 180, 185
Richmond, I.A., 79n9, 179
Rizzi-Zannoni, Giovanni, 33n16, 43
Rossetti, C., 168n54
Ruebel, James S., 147n10
Ruegg, Bro. S. Dominic, 77
Ruggi d'Aragona, Maria Grazia, 67, 68n18, 72nn24–25
Rumiz, Paolo, 96, 98
Saylor, Steven, 147n10
Scagnetti, Franciscus, 175n68, 176n69
Schellenberg, Ryan S., 187
Schmisek, Brian, 128n6
Schnabel, Eckhard J., 6n21, 27n55, 182
Severini, Francesca, 133n16, 140n24
Shackleton Bailey, D.R., 177n74
Sherwin-White, A.N., 181n5
Sherwood, Andrew N., 37n19
Short, William, xv
Smith, Christopher, 114
Soricelli, Gianluca, 20
Speidel, Michael P., 2
Spera, Lucrezia, 164
Staccioli, Romolo Augusto, xixn13, 102n20
Staderini, Giovanni, 158n35
Stanislao, Corrado, 71
Stefanile, Michele, 15n34

Stothard, Peter, 51
Sumner, G.V., 58
Swanson, Reuben, 186n21
Talbert, Richard J.A., 33n12, 62n5, 62n7
Tallini, Marco, 168n54
Tannehill, Robert C., 5
Thompson, Glen, xviii, 25, 27, 121n19, 191
Tol, Gijs, 118–20
Treggiari, Susan, 164
Trocciola, Alfredo, 72
Turchetti, Rita, 138n19
Uggeri, 49
Urbini, Stefano, 128n8
Valente, Renata, 71
van Tilburg, Cornelius, xvi
Velestino, Daniela, 165n46
Vella, Alessandro, 81n15
Ventre, Francesca, 53n38
Vincenti, Maria Cristina, 137n19, 139n22, 140n26
Vistoli, Fabrizio, xvin4
Volpe, Rita, 174nn63–64
Walker, Peter, 67n14, 183
Wallace-Hadrill, Andrew, 184
Wansink, Craig, 4n12
Wieseler, Karl Georg, 185
Wilson, Mark, xixn13–14, 5n15, 5n17, 7n22, 25, 26n54, 27, 168n55, 183n7, 184, 188n26, 191
Wiseman, T.P., 33n14, 76
Witherington, Ben, III, 26n52
Witmer, Evelien, 119–20
Wolsky, Florence, 163n43
Zahn, Theodor, 180n4
Zannini, Ugo, xviii, 62n7, 64n9, 67n15, 69n21, 87n2

# About the Authors

**Glen L. Thompson** was academic dean and professor of New Testament and historical theology at Asia Lutheran Seminary in Hong Kong until his retirement. Besides authoring numerous books and articles, he continues to expand his website on early Christianity at fourthcentury.com. With Mark Wilson, he developed *The Anatolian Roads Project*, which combines GPS technology, aerial photography, and on-the-ground examination to more accurately map the Roman road system of Anatolia and the routes of Paul in particular.

**Mark Wilson** is the founder and director of the Asia Minor Research Center in Antalya, Turkey, the country in which he has lived since 2004. He is research fellow in biblical studies at the University of South Africa and Professor Extraordinary of New Testament at Stellenbosch University, South Africa. Mark regularly leads study trips to Turkey, Greece, Malta, and Italy. He is the author and editor of numerous books and articles, including *Biblical Turkey: A Guide to the Jewish and Christian Sites of Asia Minor*.

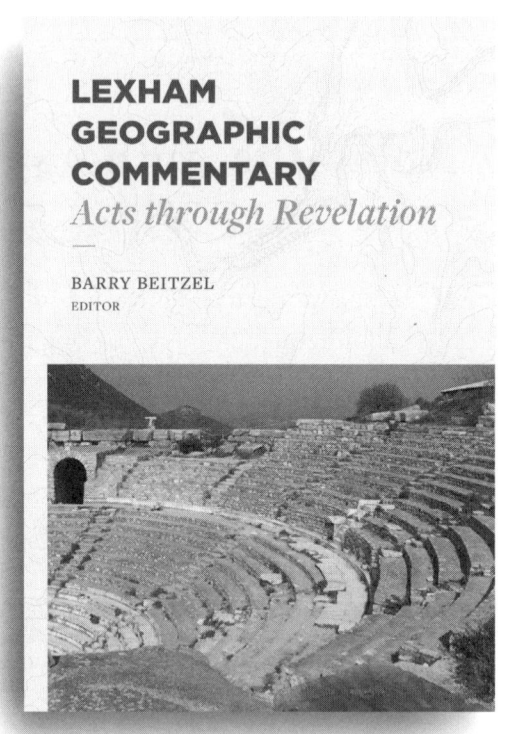

## LEXHAM GEOGRAPHIC COMMENTARY ON ACTS THROUGH REVELATION

A new kind of commentary. Lead editor Barry J. Beitzel puts first-century Christianity in context by focusing on the landscape, history, and character of the places where Acts and the writings of Paul and the apostles took place.

### Learn more at LexhamPress.com/Geographic-Commentary